Assessing Children's Well-Being
A Handbook of Measures

Assessing Children's Well-Being

A Handbook of Measures

Sylvie Naar-King, PhD
Deborah A. Ellis, PhD
Wayne State University
School of Medicine

Maureen A. Frey, PhD, RN
Children's Hospital of Michigan

LAWRENCE ERLBAUM ASSOCIATES, PUBLISHERS
2004   Mahwah, New Jersey   London

Lawrence Erlbaum Associates, Inc., Publishers
10 Industrial Avenue
Mahwah, NJ 07430

Cover design by Sean Sciarrone

Library of Congress Cataloging-in-Publication Data

Child assessment in pediatric settings : handbook of measures for health care
professionals / [edited by] Sylvie Naar-King, Deborah A. Ellis, Maureen Frey.
    p.   cm.
   Includes bibliographical references and index.
   ISBN 0–8058–3173–8 (hbk. : alk. paper)
    1. Children—Medical examinations—Handbooks, manuals, etc.
2. Children—Diseases—Diagnosis—Handbooks, manuals, etc. 3. Child
development—Testing—Handbooks, manuals, etc. 4. Medical screening—
Methodology—Handbooks, manuals, etc. I. Naar-King, Sylvie. II. Ellis,
Deborah A. III. Frey, Maureen A.
   RJ50.C479 2003
   618.92'0075—dc21   2002041680

Books published by Lawrence Erlbaum Associates are printed on acid-free paper,
and their bindings are chosen for strength and durability.

Printed in the United States of America
10 9 8 7 6 5 4 3 2 1

To our families and our mentor, Patricia T. Siegel
S.N.K. and D.A.E.

To Jennifer, Andy, Shannon, and Sam
M.A.F.

Primary Authors

Sylvie Naar-King, Department of Psychiatry and Behavioral Neurosciences, Wayne State University School of Medicine, Detroit, Michigan

Deborah A. Ellis, Department of Psychiatry and Behavioral Neurosciences, Wayne State University School of Medicine, Detroit, Michigan

Maureen A. Frey, PhD, Department of Nursing Administration, Children's Hospital of Michigan, Detroit, Michigan

Contributing Authors

Ronald T. Brown, PhD, College of Health Professions, Medical University of South Carolina, Charleston, South Carolina

Dennis Drotar, PhD, Department of Pediatrics, Rainbow Babies and Children's Hospital and Case Western Reserve University School of Medicine, Cleveland, Ohio

Sheila M. Eyberg, PhD, ABPP, Department of Clinical and Health Psychology, University of Florida, Gainesville, Florida

Michelle Macias, MD, Department of Pediatrics, Medical University of South Carolina, Charleston, South Carolina

Jocelyn McCrae, PhD, Department of Hematology/Oncology, Children's Hospital of Michigan, Detroit, Michigan

Lilless McPherson Shilling, PhD, College of Health Professions, Medical University of South Carolina, Charleston, South Carolina

Arthur Robin, PhD, Department of Psychiatry and Behavioral Neurosciences, Wayne State University School of Medicine, Detroit, Michigan

Conway F. Saylor, PhD, Department of Psychology, The Citadel, Charleston, South Carolina

Patricia T. Siegel, PhD, Department of Psychiatry and Behavioral Neurosciences, Wayne State University School of Medicine, Detroit, Michigan

Anthony Spirito, PhD, Department of Psychiatry and Human Behavior, Brown Medical School, Providence, Rhode Island

Branlyn E. Werba, PhD, Department of Psychology, Children's Hospital of Philadelphia, Pennsylvania

Contents

Contributors   vii

Preface   xiii

Chapter 1   **Health Status and Quality of Life**   1

Introduction by Dennis Drotar   1
Child Health and Illness Profile   4
Child Health Questionnaire   7
Functional Disability Inventory   9
Functional Status II (R)   11
Functional Status Questionnaire   13
Health And Daily Living—Youth Form   15
Pediatric Evaluation of Disability Inventory   17
Pediatric Quality of Life Inventory   19
WeeFIM   21

Chapter 2   **Adherence**   27

Introduction by Maureen A. Frey   27
Daily Phone Diary   29
Family Responsibility Questionnaire   31
Medication Electronic Monitoring System   33
Medical Compliance Incomplete Stories Test   35
Twenty-Four-Hour Recall Interview   37

Chapter 3   **Pain Management**   41

Introduction by Jocelyn McCrae   41
Bieri Faces Scale   43
Child-Adult Medical Procedure Interaction Scale–Revised   45
Children's Hospital of Eastern Ontario Pain Scale   46

Neonatal Facial Coding System   48
Neonatal Infant Pain Scale   49
Observational Scale of Behavioral Distress   51
Oucher   53
Pediatric Pain Questionnaire   55
Waldron-Varni Pediatric Pain Coping Inventory   56

Chapter 4   **Child Behavior**   **61**

Introduction by Arthur Robin   61
Hemophilia Clinic   62
Seizure Consult   63
Alternative Medicine Research Project   64
Behavioral Assessment System for Children   65
Child Behavior Checklist   68
Conners' Parent Rating Scale–Revised   72
Pediatric Behavior Scale   74
Pediatric Inpatient Behavior Scale   77
Pediatric Symptom Checklist   79
Piers-Harris 2   82
Self-Perception Profile for Children   84

Chapter 5   **Child Development**   **89**

Introduction by Michelle Macias
    and Conway F. Saylor   89
Levels of Developmental Evaluation   90
Domains of Development   91
Selection of Instruments for Developmental Screening   91
Ages and Stages Questionnaires   94
Autism Behavior Checklist   96
Bayley Infant Neurodevelopmental Screener   98
Child Development Inventory   100
Denver II   103
Developmental Indicators for the Assessment of Learning–3   107
Early Screening Profiles   109
Gilliam Autism Rating Scale   111

Chapter 6   **Child Coping**   **115**

Introduction by Anthony Spirito   115
Adolescent Coping Orientation for Problem Experiences   118
The Children's Coping Strategies Checklist and the
    How I Coped Under Pressure Scale   121

Coping Health Inventory for Children   124
Impact on Family Scale   126
KIDCOPE   128
Schoolagers' Coping Strategies Inventory   129

Chapter 7   Cognitions, Attributions, and Attitudes   **133**

Introduction by Lilless McPherson Shilling
    and Ronald T. Brown   133
Child Attitude Toward Illness Scale   136
Children's Health Care Attitudes Questionnaire   138
Children's Health Locus of Control Scale   140
The Health Self-Determinism Index for Children   142

Chapter 8   Environment   **147**

Introduction by Branlyn E. Werba and Sheila M. Eyberg   147
Family Adaptability and Cohesion Evaluation Scale   150
Family Environment Scale   153
Family Inventory of Life Events   156
Parents of Children with Disabilities Inventory   158
Parent-Child Relationship Inventory   160
Parenting Stress Index   162
Symptom Checklist–90-R and Brief Symptom Inventory   165

Chapter 9   Consumer Satisfaction   **169**

Introduction by Patricia T. Siegel   169
Assessment of Parent Satisfaction   172
Child Perceptions of Specialty Care   173
Child Satisfaction Questionnaire and the Physician
    Attribute Checklist   174
Client Satisfaction Questionnaire and the Service
    Satisfaction Scale   177
Measure of Processes of Care   179
Metro Assessment of Child Satisfaction   181
Parent Perceptions of Specialty Care   183
Patient Satisfaction Questionnaire   185

Appendix   **189**

Functional Disability Inventory   191
Functional Status Questionnaire   195
PedsQL   199

WeeFIM   205
Family Responsibility Questionnaire   209
Medical Compliance Incomplete Stories Test   213
Oucher   217
Pediatric Behavior Scale   221
Pediatric Symptom Checklist   227
Coping Health Inventory for Children   233
Children's Coping Strategies Checklist and How I Coped
    Under Pressure Scale   239
KIDCOPE   247
Schoolagers' Coping Strategies Inventory   251
Child Attitude Toward Illness Scale   259
Children's Health Care Attitudes Questionnaire   265
Children's Health Locus of Control Scale   273
Health Self-Determinism Index for Children   277
Assessment of Parent Satisfaction   285
Child Perceptions of Specialty Care   289
Parent Perceptions of Specialty Care   293

Author Index   **299**

Preface

The emphasis on collaborative management of children's health has led to the involvement of multiple disciplines in pediatric health care. This shift has resulted in an increasing focus on the assessment of children's functioning across multiple domains. The Task Force on Pediatric Education (1978) noted several decades ago that the types of children's health problems that are reported in pediatric settings include developmental, behavioral, psychological, and educational difficulties, as well as those related to their physical health. While attention to assessment issues in behavioral pediatrics has historically lagged behind that given to intervention and treatment, the field has reached a point in its maturity where numerous measures are available for the assessment of infants, children, and adolescents.

The goal of this volume is to provide a single source reference to key screening instruments for clinicians and researchers who work with pediatric populations. Practitioners with a variety of backgrounds, including physicians, social workers, nurses, and psychologists, are increasingly using standardized measures and should find this book useful in selecting an appropriate screening tool. The volume is also intended to serve as a comprehensive guide for study instrumentation for researchers. Although other overviews of assessment measures are available, they tend to be more circumscribed in nature (i.e., overviews of family assessment measures) and do not cover the full range of areas that child health care professionals may need to assess.

The areas targeted by this volume were chosen to cover the range of assessment issues faced by child health clinicians and researchers, including health status and quality of life, adherence to medical regimen, pain, development, behavior, children's coping and cognitions, family functioning, and consumer satisfaction. Each chapter begins with an expert overview of the theoretical construct being measured, and any special concerns. Following the overview, key measures are reviewed.

It should be noted that only quantitative measures with some evidence of adequate psychometric properties were considered for inclusion in the volume; qualitative measures and those with minimal data regarding psychometrics were not presented. In general, Mash and Terdal's (1990) criteria for judging the utility of behavioral pediatric measures guided the selection of measures for inclusion. They recommend that measures should be appropriate for use in health care settings, have both a health and a systems orientation, have a developmental perspective, and be effective, time efficient, and economical. Finally, assessment tools were required to be general enough to be appropriate for both the general pediatric and chronically ill populations. Although disease-specific measures are not reviewed in detail, a reference table of available disease-specific measures is included at the end of applicable chapters.

The review of each measure is organized in the following format. First, the key reference and information on how to obtain the measure are provided. Second, a general statement about the purpose of the measure and a more detailed description of the measure are presented. A discussion of any standardization procedures, normative data, or at a minimum a description of the sample used during instrument development follows.

Reliability and validity are then evaluated. Reliability includes both internal consistency and test-retest reliability. There are numerous terms used interchangeably to describe validity. For consistency, three general categories of validity that subsume all proposed forms of validity are considered (Kaplan, Bush, & Berry, 1976): *content validity, criterion validity,* and *construct validity.* Content validity indicates whether the items that make up the measure adequately represent the domain they are supposed to sample. Face validity, a term that refers to whether the item appears to relate to the domain measured, is only one component of content validity. Specific procedures, such as expert review and interviews with target subjects, are necessary to fully ensure content validity.

Criterion validity refers to the extent to which scores on the measure are related to scores on other relevant instruments that are thought to accurately reflect the domain of interest. The scores may relate either concurrently (measured at the same time) or predictively (measured at a later time). Empirical or statistical validity are other terms that have been used interchangeably with criterion validity.

Finally, construct validity refers to the extent to which a measure truly assesses the theoretical construct it is designed to measure. Instrument developers often use factor analytic techniques to demonstrate construct validity. Convergent and divergent validity assess statistical relationships between the measure and other measures assumed to be similar to or different from the construct and are additional forms of construct validity.

The presentation of each measure ends with a summary of strengths and weaknesses that synthesizes the previous information, and emphasizes applicability to pediatric settings. Additional relevant references are also included. Finally, each author of a measure was sent a copy of the report and offered an opportunity to respond. Their comments, if any, are included at the end of the review.

Measures that were not copyrighted or those that the authors gave permission to reproduce are included in an appendix.

We would like to thank the contributors to this volume for their patience and coopoeration in the process of putting together this reference guide in a timely manner, and for providing the necessary theoretical framework. We give special thanks to Dr. Michele Ondersma for her assistance with the initial groundwork for this volume. We would also like to thank our editor, Susan Milmoe for her patience and guidance. Finally, we would like to thank the staff of the Children's Hospital Medical Library as well as several assistants (Eboni Black, Jolene Daniel, and Eileen Mitchell) for their assistance with the extensive research necessary for this type of work.

REFERENCES

Kaplan, R. M., Bush, J. W., & Berry, C. C. (1976). Health status: Types of validity and the index of well-being. *Health Services Research, 11,* 478–507.

Mash, E. J., & Terdal, L. G. (1990). Assessment strategies in clinical behavioral pediatrics. In A. M. Gross & R. S. Drabman (Eds.), *Handbook of clinical behavioral pediatrics* (49–79). New York: Plenum Press.

Task Force on Pediatric Education. (1978). *The Future of Pediatric Education.* Evanston, IL: American Academy of Pediatrics.

Health Status and Quality of Life

Dennis Drotar

Case Western Reserve University School of Medicine

INTRODUCTION

Chronic health conditions that affect children represent an important and prevalent public health problem (Newacheck & Taylor, 1992) that can disrupt children's functioning and activities (Newacheck & Halfon, 1998) and increase family burden (Drotar, 1997). In recent years, advances in medical treatment have prolonged the lives of children with conditions such as cancer and very low birth weight and have necessitated increased attention to the assessment of their functioning and adaptation. Studies of the long-term outcomes of children with chronic health conditions place a primary emphasis on assessment of functioning (Thompson & Gustafson, 1996). As interventions are developed to enhance the functioning and adaptation of children with chronic illness, reliable and valid measures of functional outcome become increasingly important (Bauman, Drotar, Perrin, Pless, & Leventhal, 1997). For all the aforementioned reasons, the measurement of children's health status and quality of life has assumed increased importance (Spieth & Harris, 1996).

Health status refers to a description of the child's overall level of health that includes the severity of the illness. Quality of life (QOL) refers to functional effect of an illness as perceived by the child or others who are knowledgeable about the child, such as caretakers (Spilker, 1990). One advantage of the construct of QOL is the fact that it is comprehensive and measures well-being in multiple domains such as physical, mental, and social (WHO, 1948).

Health status and QOL assessments have several important applications. One of these is the ability to provide a comprehensive description
of children's health status, which can have multiple purposes. For example, assessments can provide descriptive information on current health
status, comparison of patients at different disease stages, evaluation of
the efficacy of different treatment protocols, and assessment of the child's
progress over time in response to medical treatment.

A second application is the identification of acute dysfunctions,
chronic dysfunctions, or both following an illness or treatment. This is an
emerging problem among long-term survivors of illnesses such as cancer,
and individuals who are at risk for the development of psychological difficulties (Eiser, 1995; Mulhern et al., 1989). QOL assessment can be used to
identify children with a chronic illness who may be at risk for developing
future psychological, physical difficulties, chronic symptoms, or all of
the aforementioned.

A third application of measures of health status and QOL is the evaluation of treatment efficacy and clinical decision making. Traditionally,
health outcome indicators have included information on mortality, morbidity, hospital re-admission, re-treatment rates, the results of laboratory
and other diagnostic tests, complications, or all of the above (Bowling,
1995). Furthermore, assessments of QOL that are potentially sensitive to
morbidity associated with alternative treatments are necessary to document the costs versus benefits of available treatments (Eiser, 1995). By
providing information about patients' subjective experience and morbidity associated with different treatments, QOL measures can also facilitate
the clinical decision making in deciding between alternative treatments.
Finally, measures of health status and QOL describe the substantial variations in response to treatment and long-term prognosis within populations of children with chronic illnesses.

Research is needed to develop and support the various applications of
health status and QOL assessments in children and adolescents. In particular, research is needed to document the utility and validity of measures
of health status and QOL in clinical decision making, that is, to answer
questions such as: How can practitioners utilize assessments of health status and QOL in making treatment-related decisions and assessments?
How do health status and QOL measures improve efficiency of assessment and clinical decision making?

Another area of needed research concerning clinical application
involves the use of health status and QOL measures to evaluate the
impact of managed care and health services on children's health and well-
being. Measures of health status and QOL have the potential to provide
valuable data that can be utilized to evaluate the impact of comprehensive health care for children with chronic health conditions.

Over and beyond research related to clinical applications of measures of health status and QOL, more basic research questions need to be addressed (Drotar, 1998). Developmental research has underscored significant differences in how children of different ages appraise their health (Tinsley, 1992). Research is needed to document the impact of developmental differences in children's perceptions of their health status and QOL across various ages. Research is also needed to document changes in perceptions of health status and QOL that occur in response to specific developmental stages (e.g., adolescence). Studies that describe differences in the perceptions of health status and QOL among children, adolescents, and parents from different cultural groups and families from different economic levels and structure would be highly desirable. Because it is not always possible to obtain reports from parent and child, research is needed to identify domains of health status and QOL for which a parent's proxy report is sufficient versus those for which a child's report supplies unique information. Other unanswered questions concerning informants' reports that should be addressed in future research concern the differential validity of child versus parent reports of health status of QOL for various research questions and outcomes. Finally, the clinical significance and validity of discrepancies in parents' versus children's perceptions of health status and QOL should be described (Drotar, 1998).

In order to address these potential clinical applications and research questions, researchers and practitioners who are interested in measurement of health status and QOL require access to these constructs. Such access is especially important because many of the measures of health status and QOL are relatively new. The authors of this volume provided an important service to potential users of these instruments by summarizing information concerning available measures of health status and QOL in a succinct, user-friendly format.

REFERENCES

Bauman, L. J., Drotar, D., Perrin, E., Pless, F. B., & Leventhal, J. (1997). A review of the effects of psychosocial interventions for children with chronic health conditions. *Pediatrics, 100,* 244–251.

Bowling, A. (1995). *Measuring disease: A review of disease-specific quality of life measurement scales.* Philadelphia: Open University Press.

Drotar, D. (1997). Intervention research: Pushing back the frontiers of pediatric psychology. *Journal of Pediatric Psychology, 22,* 593–606.

Drotar, D. (Ed.). (1998). *Measuring health related quality of life in children and adolescents: Implications for research and practice.* Mahwah, NJ: Lawrence Erlbaum Associates.

Eiser, C. (1995). Choices in measuring quality of life in children with cancer: A comment. *Psychooncology, 4,* 121–131.

Mulhern, R. K., Horowitz, M. E., Ochs, J., Friedman, A. G., Armstrong, F. D., Copeland, D.,

& Kun, L. E. (1989). Assessment of quality of life among pediatric patients with cancer. *Psychological Assessment, 1,* 130–138.

Newacheck, P. W., & Halfon, N. (1998). Prevalence and impact of disabling chronic conditions in childhood. *American Journal of Public Health, 88,* 610–617.

Newacheck, P. W., & Taylor, W. R. (1992). Childhood chronic illness: Prevalence, severity, and impact. *American Journal of Public Health, 82,* 364–371.

Spieth, L. E., & Harris, C. V. (1996). Assessment of health related quality of life in children and adolescents: An integrative review. *Journal of Pediatric Psychology, 21,* 175–193.

Spilker, B. (1990). *Quality of life assessments in clinical trials.* New York: Raven Press.

Thompson, R. J., & Gustafson, K. E. (1996). *Adaptation to chronic childhood illness.* Washington, DC: American Psychological Association.

Tinsley, B. J. (1992). Multiple influences on the acquisition and socialization of children's health attitudes and behavior: An integrative review. *Child Development, 63,* 1043–1069.

World Health Organization. (1948). *Constitution of the World Health Organization.* Geneva, Switzerland: Author.

CHILD HEALTH AND ILLNESS PROFILE

Source

Starfield, B., Riley, A. W., Green, B. F., Ensminger, M. E., Ryan, S. A., Kelleher, K., Kim-Harris, S., Johnston, D., & Vogel, K. (1995). The adolescent & child health and illness profile: A population-based measure. *Medical Care, 33,* 553–556.

Availability

From the assistant to the first author. The Johns Hopkins University School of Hygiene and Public Health, Department of Health Policy and Management, 624 N. Broadway, Baltimore, MD 21205. The measure is copyrighted.

Purpose. The Child Health and Illness Profile (CHIP) was designed to measure self-reported health status beyond biological and physiological measures. There is an adolescent version for youth ages 11 to 17 (CHIP-AE™), and there are parent and child versions for children ages 6 to 11 (CHIP-CE™). The population-based instrument assesses person-focused general health status, functional status, and overall well-being for groups of adolescents. Person-focused general health status includes concepts of satisfaction with health, quality of life and characteristics of development that influence health, such as self-esteem and resilience factors. The applications for which the CHIP has been validated are needs assessments and evaluations of health services and policy interventions. The authors note that the measure is intended to describe the health of groups of adolescents and not of individuals.

Description. The CHIP-AE consists of 123 items of varying formats in five domains: Satisfaction, Discomfort, Risks, Resilience, and Achievement. The domains include 20 subdomains that function as scales. The sixth domain of Disorders has 45 items. This domain does not have to be administered. Items can be completed by analyzing medical records. There are 16 items in the optional Demographics section. The instrument requires a fifth-grade reading level and takes approximately 30 minutes to complete. The CHIP-CE includes 45 items for the same five domains, and all items use a 5-point response format. Parents can complete an additional 30 items that allows the scoring of 20 subdomains, and an additional 44 items for the domain of Disorders. A technical manual is available from the authors. No training is required for administration.

Standardization and Norms. The CHIP-AE was developed in several phases of testing with more than 2,000 adolescents in middle and high schools. Testing also included 70 children from an adolescent primary care clinic servicing low-income families, and 74 children from chronic illness specialty clinics (cystic fibrosis, juvenile rheumatoid arthritis, and gastroenterology). Though the measure has not been normed on a national sample, standard scores have been established based on a school sample of 877 adolescents. The school sample was 54% female and 88% African American. The CHIP-CE was piloted on a sample of 247 mothers and children, and 55 fathers from medical centers and physician offices in an urban setting. The revised measure was then tested in two urban medical settings, one on the east coast and one on the west coast. After additional revisions, the measure was administered to 900 children in school and to their parents by mail. Results of this study are in press (see additional readings, mentioned later).

Reliability and Validity. The authors took great care to establish content validity. First, they conducted focus groups with parents and adolescents to determine families' conceptions of health. Second, a multidisciplinary sample of experts analyzed the resulting domains and sample items to determine missing or poorly defined domains and subdomains. Third, seven experts categorized the items into the hypothesized domains and subdomains for confirmation. Finally, these experts along with nine adolescents analyzed the items for clarity and ease of comprehension.

The authors did extensive studies of reliability and validity of the CHIP-AE. The most comprehensive results were reported from a sample of 3,451 respondents from urban and rural schools in four geographic locations (Starfield et al., 1995). All subdomains except academic achievement achieved an internal consistency alpha of .70 or higher in two or more of the four samples. The subdomains also demonstrated adequate test–retest reliability over a 1-week period. As evidence of construct validity of the CHIP-AE, the measure discriminated between males and females, between older and younger adolescents, and between ill and well adolescents (Starfield et al., 1993, 1995, 1996). Factor analyses confirmed the structure of the subdomains, and led to slight modifications in domain structure. As evidence of criterion validity, the authors point to correlations between adolescents' reports and those of their parents and schools (e.g., grades compared to academic achievement).

The authors report that all domains of the CHIP-CE demonstrate internal consistency reliabilities in excess of .80 for both the parent and child versions. The subdomains of the parent version have alphas in excess of .65. Factor analyses confirm the structure of the domains and subdomains. Data demonstrating test-retest reliability, construct validity, and criterion validity of the CHIP-CE is forthcoming.

Summary of Strengths and Limitations. The CHIP measures provide a comprehensive, psychometrically sound, and easy to administer assessment of child and adolescent health. The authors thoroughly demonstrated reliability and validity of the CHIP-AE with the exception of the Academic Performance subdomain. The authors attribute the marginal internal consistency of this subdomain to the dichotomous format of four of the six items and the low base rate of several items (e.g., failing a grade). Data demonstrating the validity of the CHIP-CE is forthcoming. A limitation in pediatric settings is that the measure is designed to assess groups, and has not been tested for describing the health of individuals. The authors plan to determine the usefulness of the measure for this purpose and the instrument's ability to detect changes in response to clinical systems and policy interventions.

Additional Readings

Rebok, G., Riley, A., Forrest, C., Starfield, B., Green, B., Robertson, J., & Tambor, E. (in press). Development of a child health status questionnaire using cognitive interviewing methods. Quality of Life Research.

Riley, A. W., Green, B. F., Starfield, B., Forrest, C. B., Kang, M., & Ensminger, M. (1998) A taxonomy of adolescent health need: Development of the adolescent health and illness profiles. *Medical Care, 36,* 1228.

Riley, A. W., Forrest, C. B., Starfield, B., Green, B., Kang, M., & Ensminger, M. (1998). A taxonomy of adolescent health need: Reliability and validity of the adolescent health and illness profiles. *Medical Care, 36,* 1237–1248.

Starfield, B., Bergner, M., Ensminger, M., Riley, A., Ryan, S., & Green, B. (1993). Adolescent health status measurement: Development of the child health and illness profile. *Pediatrics, 91,* 430–435.

Starfield, B., Riley, A. W., Green, B., Ensminger, M. E., Ryan, S. A., & Kelleher, K. (1995). The adolescent child health and illness profile: A population based measure of health. *Medical Care, 33,* 553–566.

Starfield, B., Forrest, C. B., Riley, A. W., Ensminger, M. E., & Green, B. F. (1996). Health status of well versus ill adolescents. *Archives of Pediatric Adolescent Medicine, 150,* 1249–1256.

Developers' Comments

The description of the CHIP-AE provides an accurate summary of the six domain model of health underlying the adolescent and child versions of the CHIP, the applications of this population-based health assessment, and the psychometric testing and development of this adolescent self-report health status measure. The authors are currently validating companion instruments for assessing the health of children 6–11 years old that can be completed by the children and their parents. A longitudinal study of children and adolescents is planned for evaluating the predictive validity of the instruments.

CHILD HEALTH QUESTIONNAIRE

Source

Landgraf, J. M., Abetz, L., & Ware, J. E. (1996). *The CHQ User's Manual.* Boston, MA: The Health Institute, New England Medical Center.

Availability

From the first author. Jeanne Landgraf, M.A., Healthact, 205 Newbury Street, 4th Floor, Boston, MA 02116. *www.healthact.com, JML@healthact.com.* The measure is copyrighted.

Purpose. The Child Health Questinnaire (CHQ) was designed to measure physical, emotional, behavioral, and social well-being, building on the core concepts of available generic child health instruments. The measure was developed using a tripartite model that advocates measuring each dimension along the parameters of status, disability, and personal evaluation. The instrument is the result of the Child Health Assessment Project, a research program emphasizing the development of generic, practical, yet comprehensive tools for measuring functional status and well-being.

Description. The CHQ includes three versions of a parent-completed measure (98, 50, and 28 items) and a single child-completed version (87 items). Due to the fact that most of the reliability and validity data were reported for the 50 and 28 item parent versions, discussion will be limited to these two formats. The parent versions can be used for children ages 5 and older, and the children ages 10 years and older can independently complete the child version. Younger children may be able to complete the child version if items are read to them. All three versions of the instrument include the following 12 concepts: Physical Functioning, Role/social-physical, Bodily Pain, General Behavior, Mental Health, Self-Esteem, General Health Perceptions, Change in Health, Family Activities, and Family Cohesion. The parent versions include two additional scales: Parental Impact–emotional and Parental Impact–Time. The child version includes two additional scales: Role/social-emotional and Role/social-behavioral. In the parent versions, these two scales are combined into a single scale. The number of items for each concept varies from one to six for the parent form, and from 1 to 16 for the child form. Response sets vary across each concept. Subjects are asked to recall the previous 4 weeks when answering most items. A comprehensive user's manual describes the scoring procedure. Raw scores are calculated using the mean response for each scale. The manual also provides algorithms to compute transformed raw scores from 0 to 100. Factor analytic studies of the 10 scales administered in all the field trials suggested a two-factor solution corresponding to physical and psychosocial well-being. These two summary scales are scored using a norm-based method. Z-scores for the 10 scales are calculated based on the normative data presented in the manual. Each aggregate summary score is then calculated by multiplying the scale scores by their factor coefficient and summing the 10 products. Formulas for these calculations are provided in the manual. Finally each summary score may be transformed into a norm-based ($M = 50, SD = 10$) score with a simple calculation.

Standardization and Norms. The parent versions were standardized using a general U.S. population sample ($N = 391$). The authors report that the sociodemographic characteristics of this sample were comparable to those of the general U.S. population. The parent versions were also standardized using five clinical condition benchmarks: asthma, attention-deficit hyperactivity disorder, juvenile rheumatoid arthritis, and psychiatric disorder. The manual includes norms for the population sample by age, gender, parent ethnicity, parent gender, parent education, and parent work status. The manual also provides benchmark data for the clinical samples. Preliminary benchmark data for the child version are forthcoming. The CHQ is currently being used across a variety of other conditions in addition to the benchmarks described in the manual. These include behavior disorders, burns, cancer, cardiology, cerebral palsy, chronic pain, cystic fibrosis, diabetes, epilepsy, head injury, HIV, Kawasaki disease, muscular dystrophy, and renal failure.

Reliability and Validity. Extensive studies of the psychometric properties of the CHQ are described in the manual. These data suggest strong internal consistency, content validity, and construct validity. Numerous tests of criterion validity are underway as the CHQ is being used in a large number of studies in the United States, Europe, and Australia. Currently, there are more than 25 translations of the CHQ, using stringent international criteria. A short-form of the child self-report version is currently underway using data from the Unites States, United Kingdom, Australia, and the Netherlands.

Summary of Strengths and Limitations. The CHQ is one of the most comprehensive and psychometrically sound generic measures currently available. The developers have thoroughly demonstrated reliability and validity, though further research is necessary to confirm criterion validity. Additional normative and validity studies of the child version of the measure are necessary. The measures are generally brief and easy to administer, though the child version may be too long for some pediatric settings. The small number of items in some of the scales limits their utility for research purposes, but the summary scales may be used for statistical analyses.

Developers' Comments

The developers forwarded several editorial suggestions to the aforementioned description, but did not provide additional comments.

FUNCTIONAL DISABILITY INVENTORY

Source

Walker, L. S., & Greene, J. W. (1991). The functional disability inventory: Measuring a neglected dimension of child health status. *Journal of Pediatric Psychology, 16,* 39–58.

Availability

From the first author. Lynn S. Walker, Division of Adolescent Medicine, 436 Medical Center South, Vanderbilt University, Nashville, Tennessee 37232.

Purpose. The Functional Disability Inventory (FDI) was designed to be a global measure of functional disability, defined as impairments in physical and psychosocial functioning due to physical illness. The measure can be used across a wide range of illnesses and disabilities. The dimensions of functioning were drawn from an adult measure, the Sickness Impact Profile (Bergner et al., 1981; cited in Walker and Greene, 1991).

Description. Children ages 8 years and above and their parents rate the amount of difficulty the child has with 15 tasks on a 5 point scale from "No Trouble" to "Impossible." They are reminded that they are being asked about difficulty related to physical health. The measure yields a single total score with higher scores indicating greater disability.

Standardization and Norms. No norms are reported. The initial sample included 47 children ages 9 to 17 years, and their mothers who were recruited from an adolescent outpatient clinic in a university medical setting. Demographic data were not reported. A second validation study included 110 children ages 8 to 16 years, and their mothers who were recruited from a pediatric outpatient clinic. Children were classified into three groups: abdominal pain with organic etiology, recurrent abdominal pain, and well children. The authors report mean scores for each group; however, demographic data were not reported for the second sample.

Reliability and Validity. In both studies, the FDI demonstrated good internal consistency with Cronbach's alphas ranging from .85 to .94 for the child version and from .94 to .95 for the parent version. Test-retest correlations were also significant for 3- and 6-month follow-ups in the recurrent abdominal pain group. As evidence of construct validity, the authors report significant correlations between the FDI and other measures of physical and emotional health. Also, the FDI significantly discriminated between the three groups in the second study. As evidence of criterion validity (both concurrent and predictive), the authors point to the high correlations between parent and child versions, a significant association between the FDI and school absences, and significant correlations between the FDI and school absences 3 months later. The manual includes data on internal consistency of the seven-item short version, .78 for ill children and .73 for well children all ages combined. Reliability was not as strong for well children less than 1 year and well children 2 and 3 years. Relationships between the seven-item version and the longer versions of the scale were not reported.

Summary of Strengths and Limitations. The FDI provides a relatively short, easy to administer assessment of functioning. Although the FDI was designed to address physical and psychosocial functioning, the emphasis of the items is on physical functioning. Few items address social or emotional well-being. The authors report strong evidence of its psychometric properties, and a unique strength of the measure is the availability of psychometrically sound parent and child versions. A limitation is the lack of data about the development sample. Thus, the generalizability of the FDI's psychometric properties across different populations is unclear. The lack of established norms also hinders ease of interpretation for clinical purposes. Further research is needed to determine the validity of the seven-item short version of the measure.

FUNCTIONAL STATUS II(R)

Source

Stein, R.E.K., & Jessop, D. J. (1990). Functional Status II(R): A measure of child health status. *Medical Care, 28,* 1041–1055.

Stein, R.E.K., & Jessop, D. J. (1991). *Manual for the Functional Status II(R).* PACTS Papers. Bronx, New York: Albert Einstein College of Medicine.

Availability

From the first author. Ruth E. K. Stein, M.D., Department of Pediatrics, Albert Einstein College of Medicine/Montefiore Medical Center; Centennial 1, 111 East 210th Street; Bronx, NY 10467. The measure is copyrighted.

Purpose. The Functional Status II(R) [FS II(R)] was designed as a structured research tool to measure behavioral manifestations of illness that interfere with performance of developmentally appropriate activities across disease categories. The original instrument, FS I, was developed to measure behavior reflected in disturbances observable by a parent in multiple areas of social role performance. Conceptually, the instrument is based on Starfield's (1976; cited in Stein & Jessop, 1990) activity continuum: communication, mobility, mood, energy, play, sleep eating, and toileting. As conceptualized, it is useful for health services research, program evaluation, and studies of children with chronic disorders.

Description. The measure has been validated to assess functional status of children from birth to 16 years based on parent report and was designed to be administered by a trained interviewer. In Part I of the FS II(R), parents rate the frequency of behaviors on a 3-point scale from "never or rarely" to "some of the time" to "all the time." Part II probes whether ratings of poor functioning on the Part I items were due "fully," "partly," or "not at all" to the child's health problem. When the parent reports "not at all" on Part II the original behavior rating in Part I is receded to reflect no dysfunction (i.e., no health-related dysfunction). For example, if the parent rates "act moody" as "all the time" in Part I but then in Part II states this is "not at all due to illness," the original response is recoded to "never or rarely." The authors strongly recommend completing all the Part I questions before initiating the follow-up probes on the Part I items indicating dysfunction. This is to avoid a respondent response set. Reverse-scored items are recoded so that higher scores indicate better function. Missing values are assigned the mode of the item before recoding reverse scored items. Standard scores are computed as the percent of the total possible score for that scale.

There are several versions of the FS II(R) scale. In the original full version of the FS II(R) scale, separate groups of items exist for infants less than 1 year, children 1 to 2 years, children 2 to 4 years, and children greater than or equal to 4 years. Factor analyses suggested that subscales in the long version vary by age group. For all ages, there is a General Health Factor and a second factor that is age-specific: Responsiveness, for children less than 2 years; Activity, for children 2 to 3 years; Interpersonal Functioning, for children 4 years and older.

Fourteen items, common to all age groups, can be used as a short version that yields a total functional status score. There is also a shorter version of the FS II(R) that consists of seven items. Data and author recommendations favor the use of the 14-item version over that of the 7-item version.

Administration time, depending on the version of the instrument and age of child, takes 5–15 minutes to complete. English and Spanish versions are available.

Standardization and Norms. The authors administered 53 items, including 35 items taken directly from the original FS I (Stein & Jessop, 1990, 1991) to parents of 732 children ages 2 weeks to 16 years. The sample included children with significant chronic conditions seen in a tertiary care setting, children with ongoing health conditions seen for regularly scheduled appointments in a subspecialty clinic, and children seen for routine health care screened to rule out ongoing health conditions. The children with and without chronic disorders did not differ in ethnicity or parents' level of education and represented urban families, both poor and middle class.

On the 14-item version, the mean score for children with chronic disorders was 87% (SD = 15.7), and the mean score for well children was 96% (SD = 8.2). The authors recommend that the optimal cutoff point depends on the purpose of the study. They suggest three standard deviations below the mean for well children as a cutoff. Further research is necessary to confirm the utility of this cutoff.

Reliability and Validity. The measure shows satisfactory internal consistency for the 14-item version (alpha = .86–.87 for the two groups of children). Cronbach's alpha by age and in longer versions, for all subscales were above .80. Criterion validity, evaluated by correlating the functional status scores with traditional health indicators (e.g., days in bed, hospitalizations, and days absent from school), produced correlations in the expected direction for most indicators across ages. Test-retest reliability was not evaluated.

Additional Readings

Lewis, C. C., Pantell, R. H., & Kieckhefer, G. M. (1989). Assessment of children's health status. *Medical Care, 27,* S54–S65.

Stein, R.E.K., & Jessop, D. J. (1990). Functional Status II(R): A measure of child health status. *Medical Care, 28,* 1041–1055.

Stein, R.E.K., & Jessop, D. J. (1991). *Manual for the Functional Status II(R) Measure. PACTS Papers.* Bronx, NY: Albert Einstein College of Medicine.

Developers' Comments

The developers forwarded several editorial suggestions to the aforementioned description, but did not provide additional comments.

FUNCTIONAL STATUS QUESTIONNAIRE

Source

Lewis, C. C., Pantell, R. H., & Kieckhefer, G. M. (1989). Assessment of children's health status: Field test of new approaches. *Medical Care, 27,* S54–S65.

Availability

From the first author. Catherine C. Lewis, Ph.D., Department of Pediatrics and Psychiatry, University of California at San Francisco, 400 Parnassus Avenue, Room A 206, San Francisco, CA 94143–0314.

Purpose. The Functional Status Questionnaire (FSQ) is a modification of the FSII(R) in an attempt to improve the ease of information gathering. The resulting measure is shorter and self-administered.

Description. The measure includes the 14 items from the FSII(R) that apply to all children ages 0 to 16. Parents rate 14 statements about their children's behavior during the last 2 weeks as "Never or rarely," "Some of the time," or "Almost always." The responses indicating poorer health are marked with an asterisk. The administrator then asks parents to return to those responses marked by an asterisk and determine whether the behavior (or lack thereof) was due to the illness—"Yes," "Sometimes," or "No." Responses are coded as affecting functional status only if the problem was specifically related to the illness, and the items are summed into a single summary score (FSQ-S). In addition, the authors calculated a general FSQ score (FSQ-G) by summing the original responses to statements whether or not the problem was due to a chronic medical condition. The 14-item measure takes less than 10 minutes to complete.

Standardization and Norms. The FSQ was administered to parents of 113 chronically ill children ages 4 to 16 (mean age = 8.7 years). Of the 113 children, 100 were asthmatics and 13 had other chronic conditions. Children were seen in community and university general pediatric practices in an urban center. Of the 113 parents, 45% were Caucasian, 21% were African American, 19% were Hispanic, 12% were Asian, and 4% were of other ethnicity. The socioeconomic level of the sample was not described, and normative data (means and standard deviations) were not reported. The FSQ was administered to a subsample (N = 47) of parents at 6 weeks and at 3, 6, and 12 months following the original administration. At the time of publication, 24 families completed the last follow-up. Demographic data for the subsample were not reported.

Reliability and Validity. The FSQ-S showed adequate reliability. The Cronbach's alpha of .78 was comparable to that from the original FSII (R). Cronbach's alphas for the FSQ-G ranged from .73 to .89 across the five data points. Both the FSQ-G and the FSQ-S showed good test-retest reliability at all data points with one exception. The FSQ-S at the original administration was significant lower than at 6 months of follow-up. As evidence of criterion and construct validity, the authors' report significant correlations between the FSQ-S and FSQ-G and another health status measure, the 7-item RAND scale, and between the FSQ scales and indices of functioning (e.g., number of medical visits, school absences). Neither of the FSQ scales correlated with an asthma severity scale.

Summary of Strengths and Limitations. The FSQ may be used with adolescents, but further research is necessary to demonstrate their utility with populations other than well children. Further information about validity is necessary to fully evaluate the measure. Reliability for the social functioning indices was low, most likely due to the dichotomous scoring. Adaptation of these indices to a Likert scale format may improve reliability. The measure does not yield a summary score combining two or more indices. Thus, a limitation for research purposes is the need for separate analyses for each index.

HEALTH AND DAILY LIVING — YOUTH FORM

Source

Moos, R. H., Cronkite, R. C., & Finney, J. W. (1990). *Health and daily living form manual.* Redwood City, CA: Mind Garden.

Availability

Mind Garden, 1690 Woodside Road, Suite 202, Redwood City, CA 94061. Phone: 650–261–3500. Fax: 650–261–3505. The measure is copyrighted.

Purpose. The Health and Daily Living (HDL) was developed to provide information about the psychological and physical functioning of adolescents. The HDL also includes questions about academic and peer functioning. The measure has been utilized with parents about their younger children (see following).

Description. The HDL assesses adaptation of adolescent children ages 12 to 18. The adult HDL should be used for youth (ages 16–18) who are no longer in school. Adolescents complete 38 items rated on a 4-point Likert scale, and 23 yes/no items. Indices of health related function include Self-Confidence (six items), Positive Mood (six items), Distressed Mood (six items), Physical Symptoms (eight items), Medical Conditions (six items), and Health Risk Behaviors (four items). Adolescents rate the frequency or self-descriptive accuracy of these items from 0 to 3. Thus, the six-item scale indices range from 0 to 18, the four-item index ranges from 0 to 12, and the eight-item index ranges from 0 to 24. The exception is the Medical Conditions index, which is scored by tallying the "yes" responses. The item "acne or pimples" is dichotomized as "yes" for "seldom" to "fairly often" and "no" for never." The indices of social functioning include Family Activities (10 items), Activities with Friends (10 items), and Social Integration in School (seven items). These indices are also calculated by tallying the "yes" responses. The authors do not discuss the use of a total score or sum of the indices. A manual describing coding, scoring, and handling of missing data is available.

Standardization and Norms. The HDL was administered to 70 children of depressed patients and 77 children of community adults. Socioeconomic level of the sample was not described in the manual. Normative data (means and standard deviations) are presented in the manual, but no clinical cutoff scores are offered.

Reliability and Validity. For the health-related indices, Cronbach's alphas ranged from .61 to .83 for all adolescents, with the exception of the distressed mood scale alpha, which was .43 for the children of community adults. Internal consistency for the social functioning indices ranged from .58 to .65. Validity data are not reported in the manual, but Billings and Moos (1983) reported that most dimensions of the measure significantly distinguished between children of depressed parents and controls. In this study, parents completed the HDL for younger children, thus their responses may reflect their own cognitions rather than solely their children's health.

Summary of Strengths and Limitations. The health-related indices show promise for use with adolescents, but further research is necessary to demonstrate their utility with populations other than well children. Further information about validity is necessary to fully evaluate the measure. Reliability for the social functioning indices was less than satisfactory, most likely due to the dichotomous scoring. Adaptation of these indices to a Likert scale format may improve reliability. The measure does not yield a summary score combining two or more indices. Thus, a limitation for research purposes is the need for separate analyses for each index.

Additional Readings

Billings, A. G., & Moos, R. H. (1983). Comparisons of children of depressed and nondepressed parents: Social-environmental perspective. *Journal of Abnormal Child Psychology, 11,* 463–486.

Developers' Comments

The developers forwarded several editorial suggestions to the above description, but did not provide additional comments.

PEDIATRIC EVALUATION OF DISABILITY INVENTORY

Source

Feldman, A. B., Haley, S. M., & Coryell, J. (1990). Concurrent and construct validity of the Pediatric Evaluation of Disability Inventory. *Physical Therapy, 70,* 602–610.

Haley, S. M., Coster, W., Ludlow, L. H., Haltiwanger, J. T., & Andrellos, P. J. (1992). *Pediatric Evaluation of Disability Inventory (PEDI): Development, standardization and administration manual.* Boston, MA: Trustees of Boston University.

Availability

PEDI Research Group, Department of Rehabilitation Medicine, New England Center Hospital, 750 Washington Street, Boston, MA 02111–1901. The measure is copyrighted.

Purpose. The Pediatric Evaluation of Disability Inventory (PEDI) is a standardized pediatric functional assessment instrument for young children with physical or combined physical and cognitive disabilities. It can be used across a wide range of conditions and can be completed by professionals familiar with the child or by parents. The instrument was designed to assess down to the lower end of the functional skills continuum.

Description. The PEDI was designed to assess functional status and change based on functional skill level, caregiver assistance, and modifications or adaptive equipment used. The measure is appropriate for children ages 6 months to 7.5 years. Professionals and parents can complete the measure independently, or the measure can be administered as a structured interview. The PEDI consists of 197 functional skill items, and 20 items assessing caregiver assistance and environmental modifications. The functional skill items are rated dichotomously, with a score of 0 when the child is capable of performing the skill in most situations and a score of 1 when the child is unable or limited in capability. Thus, when items are summed, higher scores equal greater disability. The assistance items are scored on a 6-point scale from independent (score = 5) to total assistance (score = 0), with higher scores indicating more independence. The modification scale is a frequency count of four possible types of modifications: no modifications, child-oriented (non-specialized) modifications, rehabilitation equipment, and extensive modifications. All items are grouped into three domains of self-care, mobility, and social functioning. For each domain, three separate scale scores are computed by summing items related to skill level, caregiver assistance, and modifications. A total score is also computed for each scale by summing across the three domains. The measure requires 45 to 60 minutes to complete. The administrator should have a background in pediatrics, experience with children with disabilities, and strong training in child development.

Standardization and Norms. The instrument was standardized on a normative sample of 421 children in the North East region of the United States, a region that closely approximated the demographic characteristics of the country based on 1980 U.S. census data. Compared to the census data, African-American families, and parents with college level and above education were oversampled. However, the authors noted that these demographic characteristics were poorly correlated with the total raw score of the Functional Skills Scale. Based on these normative data, raw scores can be transformed into standard scores with a mean of 50 and a standard deviation of 10. The manual also provides benchmark data (standard score ranges, mean and standard deviation of scale scores) for three clinical samples. The first sample included 46 children hospitalized at a pediatric trauma center. The second sample consisted of 32 children with severe disabilities enrolled in hospital-based school program. The third sample included 24 children with cerebral palsy, developmental delay, and traumatic brain injury also enrolled in a day school program.

Reliability and Validity. The authors report excellent internal consistency and inter-rater reliability. Strong content validity was established by a panel of 31 experts who provided quantitative ratings of appropriateness of items (Haley, Coster, & Faas, 1991). Construct validity was demonstrated in two ways. First, normative data suggested that raw scores increase with age reflecting the expected increase functional ability with age in a normal population. In addition, the pattern of change of the scales by age group was consistent with expected patterns of normal developmental change. Second, the authors suggest that the discrepancy between the age of attainment of a functional skill and the age of attainment of independence (based on level of caregiver assistance) demonstrates the uniqueness of the two scales. As evidence of criterion validity, the authors report significant correlations between PEDI functional skill level and caregiver assistance summary scores with the Battelle Developmental Inventory Screening Test (BDIST; Newborg, Strock, & Wnek, 1984) and with the WeeFim (see the following). The BDIST is a much longer measure of adaptive functioning, which does not take into account the need for assistance. Due to its length, the BDIST is not included in this text. Discriminant analyses suggested that the PEDI was able to discriminate between the normative and clinical samples, and the authors report data demonstrating the ability of the PEDI to detect change in capabilities and performance.

Summary of Strengths and Limitations. The PEDI is a comprehensive measure of functional performance with excellent psychometric properties. It is concise and easy to administer, and it allows a comparison of professional and parent ratings. Its ability to discriminate and to detect change has been demonstrated. A possible limitation is the extent of education and training required of the administrator. The measure is admittedly biased towards the lower end of functional skills, and seems to be most appropriate for younger children with significant physical disabilities. The measure is not appropriate for use with the more general population of children with chronic illness, and may not sufficiently discriminate in children with mild disabilities. The authors do not report the reading level required to independently complete the assessment and note that highly educated families were over-represented in the standardization sample. The structured interview format can address this concern, but further reliability and validity data with a lower socioeconomic status sample may enhance the psychometric properties of the measure.

Additional Readings

Haley, S. M., Coster, W. J., & Fass, R. M. (1991). A content validity study of the Pediatric Evaluation of Disability Inventory. *Pediatric Physical Therapy, 3,* 177–184.

Newborg, J., Strock. J., & Wnek, L. (1984). *Batelle Developmental Inventory.* Allen, TX: DLM Teaching Resources.

PEDIATRIC QUALITY OF LIFE INVENTORY

Source

Varni, J. W., Seid, M., & Kurtin, P.S. (2001). PedsQl 4.0: Reliability and validity of the Pediatric Quality of Life Inventory version 4.0 generic core scales in healthy and patient populations. *Medical Care, 39*(8), 800–812.

Availability

From the first author. James W. Varni, Ph.D., Professor and Senior Scientist, Center for Child Health Outcomes, Children's Hospital and Health Center, 3020 Children's Way, MC 5053, San Diego, CA 92123. *www.pedsql.org* The measure is copyrighted.

Purpose. The Pediatric Quality of LIfe Inventory (PedsQL™ 4.0) takes a modular approach to the measurement of health-related quality of life. The Generic Core Scales are designed to be used non-categorically, and there specific modules have been developed for a number of conditions to increase measurement sensitivity. Consistent with the focus of the chapter, this summary describes the non-categorical scales.

Description. There are a number of versions of the Generic Core Scales of the PedsQL, and each includes 23 items. There are four parent report versions based on the age of the child (2–4, 5–7, 8–12, and 13–18). There are three child report versions for children age 5 and older. The 23 items are categorized into 4 subscales: Physical Functioning (eight items), Emotional Functioning (five items), Social Functioning (five items) and School Functioning (five items). The latter three scales can be summed into a psychosocial health summary score, and all 23 items can be summed for a total scale score. Patents and children are asked about the frequency of problems in the last month, and all items are rated on a 5-point Likert scale from "never" to "almost always."

Standardization and Norms. Norms for the PedsQL were developed from a sample of 963 children aged 7 to 18 years and 1,629 parents of children age 2 to 18. Subjects were from multiple sources: children seen outpatient or inpatient in the last 3 months (78%), children seen for a well-child visit (10%), and children seen for orthopedics (7.6%), cardiology (0.3%), rheumatology (5.7%) or diabetes (2.8%). Overall, 41% of children had a chronic medical condition, 12.3% had an acute medical condition, and 34% were healthy. The authors provide detailed demographic data suggesting a diverse sample with regard to both SES and [...]. Norms for a number of chronic conditions are available as part [...] collected during the development of the disease-specific [...] date, these conditions include, asthma, cancer, cardiac [...] betes, and rheumatology, and additional modules are forth[...]

Reliability and Validity. In the initial field study, [...] test-retest reliability for the summary scale approached .90 [...] and the child versions. In the most recent study dev[...] alphas exceeded .70 for most of the subscales. As evi[...] validity, the authors report the ability of the Peds[...]

between children with chronic or acute conditions and healthy children, and to factor analyses confirming the scale structure. As evidence of criterion validity, the summary scale score has correlated significantly with the number of days the child was ill, needed a caretaker, or missed school, and the number of days the parent missed from work, had problems following the work routine, and difficulty concentrating at work.

Summary of Strengths and Limitations. The PedsQL appears to be the most promising measure for assessing quality of life in pediatric settings, particularly when dealing with multiple illnesses and conditions. The measure is also to be commended for accounting for developmental concerns with its four age-related versions. While the generic measure may not be as comprehensive as some of the instruments described in this chapter, its brevity makes it very appealing for pediatric settings. Normative data are readily available, and the normative sample was diverse. The measure shows good reliability and validity for the summary scale, and the subscales appear to have adequate reliability. Criterion validity of the subscales has not yet been published. The disease-specific modules enhance its clinical and research utility for specific population, and studies are underway to develop modules for additional chronic conditions.

Additional Readings

Varni, J. W., Seid, M., & Kurtin, P. S. (1999). Pediatric health-related quality of life measurement technology: A guide for health care decision technology. *Journal of Clinical Outcomes Management, 6,* 33–40.
Varni, J. W., Seid, M., & Rode, C. A. (1999). The PedsQL™: Measurement model for the Pediatric Quality of Life Inventory, *Medical Care, 37,* 126–139.

WEEFIM

Source

Uniform Data System for Medical Rehabilitation. (1998). *WeeFIM System Clinical Guide: Version 5.* Buffalo, NY: University of Buffalo.

Availability

Uniform Data System for Medical Rehabilitation, 232 Parker Hall, 3435 Main Street, Buffalo, NY, 14214–3007. Phone: 716–829–2076, Fax: 716–829–2080, EMAIL: *info@weefim.org,* Website: *www.weefim.org.* The WeeFIM is copyrighted.

Purpose. The WeeFIM measures the functional performance of children with congenital, developmental, and acquired disabilities by building on the organization of the Functional Independence Measure for Adults (Granger & Hamilton, 1992). It was designed to measure the performance of individuals or groups of individuals, and intended to be used in conjunction with other assessments of cognitive, communication, and motor skills. The measure is intended to describe the child's typical behavior not the child's potential capabilities.

Description. The WeeFIM consists of 18 items rated on a 7-point scale from requiring total assistance (score = 1) to performing independently (score = 7). The manual provides specific criteria for each level on the scale. Eight items assess self-care, five items assess mobility, and three items assess cognition. A trained administrator completes the items based on observation or interview with the parents. For children with developmental or functional delay, the measure may be used with children between 6 months and 21 years. The measure may be used with children ages 6 months to 7 years who do not have known delays. Administration time is approximately 15 to 30 minutes. A software program is available to assist in scoring and interpretation.

Standardization and Norms. The manual indicates that the WeeFIM norms are based on a "stratified sample of 424 children with no developmental delay or disability." No other sample information is provided. Msall et al. (1994a) reported normative data for a community sample of 417 children (possibly the same sample described in the manual). The sample was 50% male and 82% Caucasian. Forty-four percent of families were of low SES status. Msall et al. (1994b) also reported mean total WeeFim scores and standard deviations for children with limb deficiencies, Down's syndrome, spina bifida, cerebral palsy, and extreme prematurity.

Reliability and Validity. The WeeFIM has good interrater reliability (Kappa values from .44 to .82) and test-retest reliabilities (greater than .95; Ottenbacher et al., 1997). Internal consistency reliability has not been published to date. Criterion validity has been established with correlations in excess of .85 between the WeeFim and the Battelle Developmental Screening Inventory and between the WeeFim and the Vineland Adaptive Behavior Scales. Also, camp counselor observations of children were significantly correlated with WeeFIM scores (Msall et al., 1994b). Construct validity may be evidenced by the increase of total WeeFIM scores with age in the normative sample, but construct validity of the subscales remains to be demonstrated.

Summary of Strengths and Limitations. The WeeFim provides a brief, easy to administer, discipline-free measure of disability in children with a variety of conditions. Test-retest and inter-rater reliability is excellent, but internal consistency has not been reported. Construct and criterion validity for the total WeeFim score has been adequately demonstrated, but validity of subscales is suspect. As a result, interpretation of motor, communication, and cognition items separate from the total score is not recommended without further research. Although the WeeFim appears to detect changes based on age, Ketellar, Vermeer, and Helders (1998) suggested that its evaluative capability, the ability to detect change based on programming, has not been demonstrated to date.

Additional Readings

Granger, C. V., & Hamilton, B. B. (1992). The Uniform Data System for medical rehabilitation report of first admissions for 1990. *American Journal of Physical Medicine and Rehabilitation, 71,* 108–113.

Ketelaar, M., Vermeer, A., & Helders, P.J.M. (1998). Functional motor abilities of children with cerebral palsy: A systematic literature review of assessment measures. *Clinical Rehabilitation, 12,* 369–380.

Msall, M. E., Digaudio, K., Duffy, L. C., LaForest, S., Braun, S., & Granger, C. V. (1994a). Normative sample of an instrument for tracking functional independence in children. *Clinical Pediatrics, 33,* 431–438.

Msall, M. E., Digaudio, K., Rogers, B. T., LaForest, S., Catanzaro, N.L., Wilczenski, F., & Duffy, L. C. (1994). The Functional Independence Measure for Children (WeeFIM). *Clinical Pediatrics, 33,* 421–430.

Ottenbacher, K. H., Msall, M. E., Lyon, N. R., Duffy, L. C., Granger, C. V., & Braun, S. (1997). Interrater agreement and stability of the Functional Independence Measure for Children (WeeFIM): Use in children with developmental disabilities. *Archives of Physical Medicine and Rehabilitation, 78,* 1309–1315.

TABLE 1.1
Disease-Specific Measures

Disease	Measure	Reference
Asthma	About My Asthma	Mishoe et al. (1998)
	Childhood Asthma Questionnaire–B	Christie, French, Sowden, & West (1993)
	Childhood Asthma Symptom Checklist	Fitz & Overholser (1989)
	Children's Health Survey for Asthma (CHSA)	Asmussen et al. (1999)

(Continued)

TABLE 1.1 (Continued)

Disease	Measure	Reference
Asthma (continued)	Pediatric Asthma Quality of Life Questionnaire	Juniper, Guyatt, Feeny, Griffith, & Townsend (1995)
	Usherwood Questionnaire	Usherwood, Scrimgeour, & Barber (1990)
Cystic Fibrosis	Cystic Fibrosis Questionnaire	Quittner (1998)
Diabetes	Diabetes Quality of Life Measure	DCCT Research Group (1998)
	Diabetes Quality of Life for Youth	Ingersoll & Marero (1991)
HIV/AIDS	ACTG Quality of Life Questionnaire	Testa & Lendering (1995)
	General Health Assessment for Children	Gortmaker et al. (1998)
Juvenile Rheumatoid Arthritis	Child Health Assessment Questionnaire	Billings, Moos, Miller, & Gottlieb (1987)
	Juvenile Arthritis Quality of Life Questionnaire	Duffy, Arsenault, Duffy, Paquin, & Stawczynski (1997)
Dermatology	Children's Dermatology Life Quality Index	Lewis-Jones & Finlay (1995)
Oncology	Behavioral Affective and Somatic Experiences Scale	Phipps, Hinds, Channell, & Bell (1994)
	Play Performance Scale for Children	Lansky, List, Lansky, Cohen, & Sinks (1985)
	The Pediatric Cancer Quality of Life Inventory	Varni et al. (1998)
	Pediatric Oncology Quality of Life Scale	Goodwin, Boggs, & Graham-Pole (1994)
	Quality of Well-Being Scale	Bradlyn, Harris, Warner, Ritchey, & Zaboy (1993)
Epilepsy	Impact of Childhood Illness Scale	Hoare & Russell (1995)
	Quality of Life in Epilepsy	Keene, Higgins, & Ventureyra, 1997; Wildrick, Parker-Fisher, & Morales (1996)
Spina Bifida	Quality of Life and Spina Bifida Questionnaire	Parkin et al. (1997)
Crohn's Disease	Quality of Life in Children with Crohn's Disease	Rabbett et al. (1996)

(Continued)

TABLE 1.1 *(Continued)*

Disease	Measure	Reference
Neuromuscular Disorders	Life Satisfaction Index for Adolescents	Reid & Renwick (1994)
Short Stature	Attitude to Growth Scale	Boulton, Dunn, Quigley, Taylor, & Thompson (1991)
	Self-Assessment Questionnaire Well-being in Children with Short Stature	Parkin et al. (1997)
	Visual Analogue Scales for Children	Wiklund, Wiren, Erling, Karlberg, & Albertsson-Wikland (1994)

References

Asmussen, L., Olson, L. M., Grant, E. N., Fagan, J., & Weiss, K. B. (1999). Reliability and validity of the Children's Health Survey for Asthma. *Pediatrics, 104*(6), e71.

Billings, A., Moos, R., Miller, J., & Gottlieb, J. (1987). Psychosocial adaptation in juvenile rheumatic disease: A controlled evaluation. *Health Psychology, 6*(4), 343–359.

Boulton, T. J., Dunn, S. M., Quigley, C. A., Taylor, J. J., & Thompson, L. (1991). Perceptions of self and short stature: Effects of two years of growth hormone treatment. *Acta Paediatrica Scandinavica, 377,* 20–27.

Bradlyn, A. S., Harris, C. V., Warner, J. E., Ritchey, A. K., & Zaboy, K. (1993). An investigation of the validity of the Quality of Well-Being Scale with pediatric oncology patients. *Health Psychology, 12,* 246–250.

Christie M. J., French, D., Sowden, A., & West, A. (1993). Development of child-centered disease-specific questionnaires for living with asthma. *Psychosomatic Medicine, 55,* 541–548.

DCCT Research Group. (1998). Reliability and validity of a diabetes quality-of-life measure for the diabetes control and complications trial (DCCT). *Diabetes Care, 11,* 725–32.

Duffy, C. M., Arsenault, L., Duffy, K. N., Paquin, J. D., & Stawczynski, H. (1997). The Juvenile Arthritis Quality of Life Questionnaire—development of a new responsive index for juvenile rheumatoid arthritis and juvenile spondyloarthritides. *Journal of Rheumatology, 24,* 738–746.

Fitz, G. K., & Overholser, J. C. (1989). Patterns of response to childhood asthma. *Psychosomatic Medicine, 51,* 347–355.

Goodwin, D.A.J., Boggs, S. R., & Graham-Pole, J. (1994). Development and validation of the Pediatric Oncology Quality of Life Scale. *Psychological Assessment, 6,* 321–328.

Gortmaker, S. L., Lendering, W. R., Clark, C., Lee, S., Fowler, M. G., Oleske, J. M., & ACTG 219 Team. (1998). Development and use of a pediatric quality of life questionnaire in AIDS Clinical Trials: Reliability and validity of the General Health Assessment for Children. In D. Drotar (Ed.), *Measuring health related quality of life in children and adolescents* (pp. 219–235). Mahwah, NJ: Lawrence Erlbaum Associates.

Hoare, P., & Russell, M. (1995). The quality of life of children with chronic epilepsy and their families: Preliminary findings with a new assessment measure. *Developmental Medicine & Child Neurology, 37,* 689–696.

Ingersoll, G. M., & Marero, D. G. (1991). A modified quality of life measure for youths: Psychometric properties. *Diabetes Education, 17,* 114–118.

Juniper, E. F., Guyatt, G. H., Feeny, D. H., Griffith, L. E., & Townsend, M. (1995). Measuring quality of life in children with asthma. *Journal of Allergy and Clinical Immunology, 95,* 226.

Keene, D. L., Higgins, M. J., & Ventureyra, E. C. (1997). Outcome and life prospects after surgical management of medically intractable epilepsy in patients under 18 years of age. *Children's Nervous System, 13,* 530–535.

Lansky, L. L., List, M. A., Lansky, S. B., Cohen, M. E., & Sinks, L. F. (1985). Toward the development of a play performance scale for children (PPSC). *Cancer, 56*(7), 1837–1840.

Lewis-Jones, M. S., & Finlay, A. Y. (1995). The Children's Dermatology Life Quality Index (CDLQI): Initial validation and practical use. *British Journal of Dermatology, 132,* 942–949.

Mishoe, S. C., Baker, R. R., Poole, S., Harrell, L. M., Arant, C. B., & Rupp, N. T. (1998). Development of an instrument to assess stress levels and quality of life in children with asthma. *Journal of Asthma, 35,* 553–563.

Parkin, P. C., Kirpalani, H. M., Rosenbaum, P. L., Fehlings, D. L., Van Nie, A., Willan, A. R., & King, D. (1997). Development of a health-related quality of life instrument for use in children with spina bifida. *Quality of Life Research, 6,* 123–132.

Phipps, S., Hinds, P. S., Channell, S., & Bell, G. L. (1994). Measurement of behavioral, affective, and somatic responses to pediatric bone marrow transplantation: Development of the BASES Scale. *Journal of Pediatrc Oncology Nursing, 11,* 109–17; discussion 118–119.

Quittner, A. L. (1998). Measurement of quality of life in cystic fibrosis. *Current Opinions in Pulmonary Medicine, 4,* 326–331.

Rabbett, H., Elbadri, A., Thwaites, R., Northover, H., Dady, I., Firth, D., Hillier, V. F., Miller, V., & Thomas, A. G. (1996). Quality of life in children with Crohn's disease. *Journal of Pediatric Gastroenterology Nutrition, 23,* 528–533.

Reid, D. T., & Renwick, R. M. (1994). Preliminary validation of a new instrument to measure life satisfaction in adolescents with neuromuscular disorders. *International Journal of Rehabiltation Research, 17,* 184–188.

Testa, M. A., & Lendering, W. R. (1995). Quality of life considerations in AIDS clinical trials. In D. M. Finklestein & D. A. Schoenfeld (Eds.), *AIDS clinical trials: Guidelines for designing and analysis* (pp. 213–241). New York: Wiley.

Usherwood, T. P., Scrimgeour, A., & Barber, J. H. (1990). Questionnaire to measure perceived symptoms and disability in asthma. *Archives of Disabled Children, 65,* 779–781.

Varni, J. W., Katz, E. R., Seid, M., Quiggins, D. J., Friedman-Bender, A., & Castro, C. M. (1998). The Pediatric Cancer Quality of Life Inventory (PCQL). I. Instrument development, descriptive statistics, and cross–informant variance. *Journal of Behavioral Medicine, 21,* 179–204.

Wiklund, I., Wiren, L., Erling, A., Karlberg, J., & Albertsson-Wikland, K. (1994). A new self-assessment questionnaire to measure well-being in children, particularly those of short stature. *Quality of Life Research, 3,* 449–455.

Wildrick, D., Parker-Fisher, S., & Morales, A. (1996). Quality of Life in children with well-controlled epilepsy. *Journal of Neuroscience in Nursing, 28,* 192–198.

2

Adherence

Maureen A. Frey
Children's Hospital of Michigan

INTRODUCTION

One of the most daunting challenges facing health care providers and researchers is assisting families and children to adhere to recommendations for managing acute and chronic conditions. Despite varying rates of non-adherence across conditions and components of management, a conservative estimate is about 50% underuse of medications and even lower rates of non-adherence to recommendations other than medication (Riekert & Drotar, 2000), such as behavioral changes.

The consequences of non-adherence for children, families, and the health care system in the care of chronic childhood conditions in childhood such as asthma, cystic fibrosis, diabetes, and HIV are well documented in the literature. However, an understanding of non-adherence and the factors that influence it in pediatric populations lags far behind. The conceptual and methodological issues that limit adherence research have been reviewed in the literature (Drotar et al., 2000; Frey & Naar-King, 2001; LaGreca, 1990). These include terms and definitions, the lack of agreed upon standards of care, single sources of data, and use of multiple disease specific scales that often lack adequate reliability and validity. In this chapter, we present several strategies to measure adherence that can be used across diagnostic groups. These strategies can be used in whole or in part for clinical interviews, as well as research. In addition, the strategies can be adapted to specific conditions and management protocols. Disease-specific adherence measures that are used frequently are listed at the end of this chapter.

The 24-Hour Recall Interview (Freund, Johnson, Silverstein, & Thomas, 1991), Daily Phone Diary (Quittner & Opipari, 1994), and Family Responsibility Questionnaire (FRQ; Anderson, Auslander, Jung, Miller, & Santiago, 1990), are self-report strategies. Self-report, the most frequently used strategy for assessing adherence, is cost-effective, flexible, easy to administer, and useful for individual, group, or telephone data collection. However, data based on self-report is often biased. Children, adolescents, and parents tend to overestimate their own adherence behaviors while parents tend to underestimate their child–adolescent's behavior. Potential reasons for this are social desirability, displaced confidence, lack of knowledge about child–adolescent illness management behaviors, or all of the aforementioned.

The quality of self-report data is improved when questionnaires are administered by interview rather than paper and pencil methods, when items ask about specific tasks and activities rather than global ratings of behaviors, when the time window is short and specific, when data are collected from more than one person, and when the same question is asked in different ways. The 24-Hour Recall Interview, Daily Phone Diary, and Family Responsibility Questionnaire incorporate these strategies. In addition, the Daily Phone Diary goes beyond adherence activities to include all activities that last more that 5 minutes. As noted, these recalls techniques have been used with children as young as 6 years of age. All of the measures can be administered to more than one family member. Both the Family Responsibility Questionnaire and 24-Hour Recall Interview have some evidence of validity when scored for two different respondents.

The Medical Compliance Incomplete Stories Test (MCIST; Koocher, Czajkowski, & Fitzpatrick, 1990) is a strategy that shows great promise, especially with younger children. Administration and scoring combine projective techniques, non-direct probing, and quantitative scoring based on objective criteria. Sensitivity, reliability, and validity have been investigated in several studies and there is also a parent version (MCIST-PF).

Despite recognition that multiple different behaviors contribute to illness management, measuring the amount of medication that has been taken is a useful way to assess adherence. The accuracy of medication measurement—if subjects can be relied upon to actually bring medication to the clinic or research interview—has been greatly improved by microelectronic technology. The medication electronic monitoring system (MEMS; Aprex Corporation) is a microelectronic medication bottle cap that records each time the bottle is opened and closed. Additional information about administration can be programmed and stored for later retrieval. Information on missed doses and dose-interval errors has a high degree of accuracy. In addition to individual and population medication adherence rates, studies using electronic monitoring confirm that patient self-report and other approaches to counting pills overestimate adherence. Although the fact that MEMS caps are highly accurate, patients can still manipulate adherence behavior (i.e., dispose of medication after it is removed from the bottle), the cost is very high, and they cannot be used for liquid medications.

Despite the issues and limitations involved in measuring adherence, it remains a cornerstone of clinical care and research. Most experts agree that measuring adherence can be improved by the use of multiple measurement strategies, the use of more than one informant, and by using similar measures across diagnostic groups (Drotar, et al., 2000). Taken together, this multi-method–multi-trait approach facilitates research findings and contributes to improved clinical care.

REFERENCES

Anderson, B. J., Auslander, W. F., Jung, J., Miller, J. P., & Santiago, J. V. (1990). Assessing family sharing of diabetes responsibility. *Journal of Pediatric Psychology, 15,* 477–492.

Drotar, D., Riekert, K.A., Burgess, E., Levi, R., Nobile, C. Kaugars, A.S., & Walders, N. (2000). Treatment adherence in childhood chronic illness: Issues and recommendations enhance practice, research, and training. In D. Drotar (Ed.), *Promoting adherence to medical treatment in chronic childhood illness concepts, methods, and interventions* (pp. 455–478). Mahwah, NJ: Lawrence Erlbaum Associates.

Freund, A., Johnson, S.B., Silverstein, J., & Thomas, J. (1991). Assessing daily management of childhood diabetes using 24-hour recall interviews: Reliability and stability. *Health Psychology, 10,* 200–208.

Frey, M.A., & Naar-King, S. (2001). The challenge of measuring adherence in children and adolescents. *Journal of Child and Family Health, 4,* 296–300.

Koocher, G. P., Czajkowski, D. R., & Fitzpatrick, J. R. (1990). Manual for the Medical Compliance Incomplete Stories Test. Unpublished Manuscript.

LaGreca, A. M. (1990). Issues in adherence with pediatric patients. *Journal of Pediatric Psychology, 4,* 423–436.

Quittner, A. L., & Opipari, L. C. (1994). Differential treatment of siblings: Interviews and diary analysis comparing two family contexts. *Child Development, 65,* 800–814.

Riekert, K.A., & Drotar, D. (2000). Adherence to medical treatment in pediatric chronic illness: Critical issues and answered questions. In D. Drotar (Ed.), *Promoting adherence to medical treatment in chronic childhood illness concepts, methods, and interventions* (pp. 3–32). Mahwah, NJ: Lawrence Erlbaum Associates.

DAILY PHONE DIARY

Source

Quittner, A. L., & Opipari, L. C. (1994). Differential treatment of siblings: Interviews and diary analyses comparing two family contexts. *Child Development, 65,* 800–814.

Availability

From the first author. Alexandra L. Quittner. Department of Clinical and Health Psychology, College of Health Professions, 1600 SW Archer Road, Room DG-136, Gainesville, Florida, 32610–0165.

Purpose.   The Daily Phone Diary (DPD) was initially developed to collect daily activity reports for families with children with cystic fibrosis, but the measure is adaptable to other populations. In addition to adherence activities, the DPD measures other daily activities, such as recreational and family interactions.

Description.   A trained interviewer contacts the parent, teen, or both in the evening and asks the parent to report all activities in the past 24 hours that lasted more than 5 minutes. A script for the interviewer is provided in the manual. For each activity, the respondent reports the type of activity, the duration, who else was present, and whether the activity was positive or negative. After the initial recall, the interviewer prompts to make sure that all target activities were reported. For example, if taking medication is being targeted, the interviewer might prompt by asking about administration during the prior 24 hours. The DPD is computerized, and the interviewer enters the information directly into the computer during the interview. Specific activity codes are entered for type of activity, which fall under seven general activity codes: Child Care, Medical Care, Household Tasks, Recreation-Home, Recreation-Outside, Self-Care, Work, and Sleep. The interviewer may code seven general categories of activity with specific sub-categories also specified. The interviewer subsequently calls the family on the two following evenings. The interview takes 15–20 minutes to complete.

Standardization and Norms.   There are no published norms. Due to the fact that most of the pilot work has been done with the cystic fibrosis population, the samples have been predominantly Caucasian.

Reliability and Validity.   The authors report high levels of inter-rater agreement and test-retest reliability. The authors reported construct validity data at a conference presentation, but this data has not been published. Criterion validity has been reported in a number of studies (see references), though the studies have focused on family interactions and division of parental responsibility for medical care as opposed to adherence.

Summary of Strengths and Limitations.   The DPD shows the strengths and weaknesses inherent in this measurement approach (see aforementioned introduction), but may be more standardized than other recall procedures. While reliability appears to be strong and validity promising, further studies applying the measure to other chronic illness populations and to more diverse groups are necessary to fully evaluate the measure.

Additional Readings

Quittner, A. L., Espelage, D. L., Ievers-Landis, C., & Drotar, D. (2000). Differential treatment of siblings: Interviews and diary analysis comparing two family contexts. *Journal of Clinical Psychology in Medical Settings, 7,* 41–54.

Quittner, A. L., Espelage, D. L., Opipari, L. C., Carter, B., & Eid, N. (1998). Role strain in couples with and without a child with chronic illness: Associations with marital satisfaction, intimacy, and daily mood. *Health Psychology, 17,* 112–124.

Quittner, A. L., Opipari, L., Regoli, M. H., Jacobsen, J., & Eigen, H. (1992). The impact of caregiving and role strain on family life: Comparisons between mothers of children with cystic fibrosis and matched controls. *Rehabilitation Psychology, 37,* 275–289.

FAMILY RESPONSIBILITY QUESTIONNAIRE

Reference

Anderson, B. J., Auslander, W. F., Jung, K. C., Miller, J. P., & Santiago, J. V. (1990). Assessing family sharing of diabetes responsibilities. *Journal of Pediatric Psychology, 15,* 477–492.

Availability

From the first author. B. J. Anderson, Mental Health Unit, Joslin Diabetes Center, One Joslin Place, Boston, MA 02215.

Purpose. The authors developed the Diabetes Family Responsibility Questionnaire (DFRQ) to provide a clinically useful research tool to assess family members' perceptions of who takes responsibility for illness management and health behaviors. The measure was initially developed to diabetes, but can be adapted to other chronic conditions. The measure has been successfully adapted for cystic fibrosis (Drotar & Ievers, 1994), pediatric asthma (McQuaid et al., 2001) and pediatric HIV (Naar-King, Frey, Harris, & Secord, 1998).

Description. Parents and children ages 6 and older respond to a list of 17 tasks related to diabetes care and general health care. Subjects rate who is responsible for each task most of the time: the parent, the child, or the parent and child share. The pilot measure included 22 items. Results of a principal components analysis of parents' responses demonstrated that 17 items uniquely fell on three factors: General Health (7 items), Regimen Tasks (6 items), and Social Presentation (4 items). The authors report that factor analysis of the child data did not yield these factors. Three patterns emerge when comparing parent and child responses: perfect agreement when parent and child agree; overlap when parent and child both claim to take responsibility; no one takes responsibility when one member reports that the other shares or takes full responsibility but the other reports no responsibility. The authors believe the latter may be the most clinically relevant pattern when assessing adherence. Thus, they use a count of the number of items where this pattern is evident as the total score. A zero means there are no items where no one takes responsibility based on parent–child agreement, and a 17 means that no one takes responsibility for each of the 17 items. There is also an alternative scoring strategy to measure child autonomy based on a single respondent (parent or child). A response indicating child responsibility is scored a 3, a response of sharing responsibility is scored a 2, and parent taking responsibility is scored a 1. Items are summed with higher scores indicating greater child responsibility or autonomy. Responses of "No One" are not included in the score. The cystic fibrosis version, the Cystic Fibrosis Family Responsibility Questionnaire (CFFRQ; Drotar & Ievers, 1994) is scored similarly, and includes 17 items corresponding to three subscales similar to the DFRQ. McQuaid et al. (2001) used this alternate scoring procedure but with a 5-point scale ranging from 1 (parent completely responsible) to 5 (child completely responsible, with a score of 3 indicating equal responsibility. This asthma version, the Asthma Responsibility Questionnaire, includes 10 items on a single scale. The HIV version includes 10 items on a single scale.

Standardization and Norms. The original sample included 121 children ages 6 to 21 with insulin-dependent diabetes and their mothers. The sample was 54% female and 84% Caucasian. The majority of families scored in the middle SES group. While there are no published norms, older children were significantly more likely to assume greater responsibility, and mothers reported that females took more responsibility than males.

Reliability and Validity. The measure shows satisfactory internal consistency for the total scale (alpha = .84). Cronbach's alphas for the subscales ranged from .69 to .79. The measure has good content validity as the items were generated from interviews with providers and families. As an example of criterion validity, mothers who reported their children took more responsibility also reported greater family independence on the Family Environment Scale. Drotar & Ievers (1994) reported good internal consistency reliability for the CF version total scale (Cronbach's alpha = .92), but did not report information on the subscales. As evidence of criterion validity, they found that independence in illness management as measured by both the DFRQ and the CFFRQ was associated with a measure of independence in non-illness activities. McQuaid et al. (2001) reported adequate internal consistency reliability for the asthma version. Construct validity was also reported with mother's reports of increased child independence and children's reports of increased self-efficacy associated with increased autonomy. In addition, all studies showed that scores increased with age.

Summary of Strengths and Limitations. The FRQ shows significant promise as an assessment of disease management. The single scale score seems to demonstrate the strongest reliability and validity. Psychometric properties of the subscales are unclear. Further research on psychometric properties with other chronic illnesses is necessary.

Additional Readings

Drotar, D., & Ievers, C. (1994). Age differences in parent and child responsibilities for management of cystic fibrosis and insulin-dependent diabetes. *Journal of Developmental and Behavioral Pediatrics, 15,* 265–272.

McQuaid, E., Penza-Clyve, S. M., Nassau, J.H., Fritz, G., Klein, R., O'Connor, S., Wamboldt, F., & Gavin, L. (2001). The Asthma Responsibility Questionnaire: Patterns of family responsibility for asthma management. *Children's Health Care, 30,* 183–199.

Naar-King, S., Frey, M., Harris, M., & Secord, E. (1998). *Measuring adherence to treatment of pediatric HIV.* Unpublished manuscript.

MEDICATION ELECTRONIC MONITORING SYSTEM

Availability

From APREX, 1430 O'Brien Drive, Suite F, Menlo Park, CA 94025–1486, 650–614–4100, Fax: 650–614–4110, *www.aprex.com.* Copyrighted.

Purpose. The MEMS is designed to estimate adherence to medical regimens by electronically recording every time a medication bottle is opened.

Description. The MEMS is a medication bottle cap containing microelectronics that records each time the bottle is opened and closed. It can also store information about the patient and the medication. Patient instruction sheets educate the patient on how to use and care for the cap. The patient is explicitly instructed to only open the container when taking the dose of medication for that specific time. The MEMS have two product lines, both of which are available in child-resistant caps. The MEMS TrackCap is a standard white cap that performs the basic tracking functions. In addition to tracking medication events, a more advanced model, the MEMS SmartCap, also displays the number of times the bottle was opened in a day and the number of hours since the last opening. The SmartCap also has an optional audible reminder to take medications. The dosing time data are transferred to a communicator. This data can then be accessed by MEMS software to generate adherence information and reports in a variety of formats. These data result in two variables: missed doses and dose-interval errors. In addition, patterns of non-adherence can be assessed by tracking medication events over a given time period.

Reliability and Validity. Over 300 studies have been published using the MEMS, and APREX provides a reference list free of charge. Most studies suggest that patient report and pill counts overestimate adherence when compared to the MEMS. Many authors believe that the MEMS is more accurate than drug assays because patient adherence increases prior to the visits when drug assays are scheduled.

Summary of Strengths and Limitations. Although the MEMS cannot measure ingestion of the medication, it appears to be one of the more accurate estimates of adherence available. This is a significant limitation in pediatrics when older children and adolescents look for ways to hide non-adherence. In addition, the cost of the system is a serious limitation to widespread use.

Additional Readings

Cramer, J. A., Mattson, R. H., Prevey, M. L., Scheyer, R. D., & Ouellette, V. L. (1989). How often is medication taken as prescribed? A novel assessment technique. *Journal of the American Medical Association, 261,* 2373–3277.

Lee, J. Y., Kusek, J. W., Greene, P. G., Bernhard, S., Norris, K., Smith, D., Wilkening, B., & Wright, J. T. (1996). Assessing medication adherence by pill count and electronic monitoring in the African American study of kidney disease and hypertension (AASK) pilot study. *American Journal of Hypertension, 9,* 719–725.

Straka, R. J., Fish, J. T., Benson, S. R., & Suh, J. T. (1997). Patient self-reporting of compliance does not correspond with electronic monitoring: An evaluation using isosorbide dinitrate as a model drug. *Pharmacotherapy, 17,* 126–132.

Waterhouse, D. M., Calzone, K. A., Mele, C., & Brenner, D. E. (1993). Adherence to oral tamoxifen: A comparison of patient self-report, pill counts, and microelectronic monitoring. *Journal of Clinical Oncology, 11,* 1189–1197.

MEDICAL COMPLIANCE INCOMPLETE STORIES TEST

Source

Koocher, G. P., Czajkowski, D. R., & Fitzpatrick, J. R. (1990). *Manual for the Medical Compliance Incomplete Stories Test.* Unpublished Manuscript.

Availability

From the first author. Gerald P. Koocher, Ph.D., Department of Psychiatry, Children's Hospital, 300 Longwood, Boston, MA 02115. Instrument and manual available at no charge. The measure is copyrighted.

Purpose. MCIST assesses the attitudes of children and adolescents toward medical compliance situations. It is meant to provide an estimate or prediction of adherence, not an assessment of adherence behavior. The measure was developed for research purposes, but may be used as a screening measure for adherence concerns. While the measure may yield clinical data, the authors caution that the measure has not been validated for clinical use. The measure was developed with a sample of children with cystic fibrosis. However, the stories are generic and can be used with any chronic illness population.

Description. School-age children and adolescents (ages 5–20) complete five stories in which the main character is confronted with a choice of behavioral responses to medical advice. Administration is similar to projective measures, but the administrator reads the beginning of a story instead of presenting a picture. The instructions must be given verbatim, and each answer is recorded verbatim. The administrator may probe using non-directive questions to obtain necessary information for scoring. Each story is scored along three dimensions based on a 3-point scale using objective criteria. The scoring of each story yields a Compliance score, a Health Optimism score, and a Self-Efficacy score. Scores for each dimension are summed across the five stories yielding a scale score from 0 to 10 where higher scores indicate a more positive attitude. The three scale scores are summed to yield a total competency–compliance score ranging from 0 to 30. A parent version (MCIST-PF) with similar format for administration and scoring has been developed, and reliability and validity studies are underway.

Standardization and Norms.   The original sample included 40 children ages 13 to 23 with cystic fibrosis, and 35% were considered compliant based on observational data during an inpatient hospitalization. Data were collected at a large urban pediatric hospital, but other demographic data for the sample were not reported. The mean MCIST total score was 27.37 for "compliant" patients and 20.15 for "noncompliant" patients. Gudas, Koocher, & Wypij (1991) used the measure with 100 cystic fibrosis patients ages 5 through 20, and reported a mean MCIST total score of 24.68. D'Angelo, Woolf, Bessette, Rappaport, & Ciborowski (1992) reported a mean MCIST total score of 26.41 for hemophilic boys ages 8 to 18 in the same urban hospital setting.

Reliability and Validity.   The authors report inter-rater reliability ranging from .81 to 1.0 for individual story scores, and .98 for the three scale scores and the total score. While inter-item reliability was low for the subscores (.28 to .76), the three scale scores were highly correlated with the total score (.74 to .91). As evidence of validity, the authors report that the scale scores and total score significantly correlated with observed compliance in patients with cystic fibrosis. Results of discriminant analysis indicated that the MCIST correctly classified 97% of patients into compliant and noncompliant groups defined by observational data. D'Angelo et al. (1992) found that MCIST compliance scale scores were significantly associated with medical professionals' ratings of adherence in hemophilic boys and were inversely related to the number of monthly bleeding episodes. However, the other two scale score were not related to these indices, and these scales may be better interpreted as attitudinal measures rather than predictors of adherence behavior.

Summary of Strengths and Limitations.   The measures shows significant promise as a tool in cross-categorical adherence research. It is easy to administer and is reliably scored. The measure has strong validity, but internal consistency is weak and should be studied further if scale scores are to be interpreted meaningfully. Although the measure was developed using an urban population, ethnicity and SES data were not reported. Due to the fact that the measure has been predominantly used in the CF population, further research with more ethnically diverse samples representing a variety of chronic conditions is necessary. The measure may be used to screen for adherence concerns, and applications to clinical settings and treatment outcome studies should be studied to extend the utility of the measure.

Additional Readings

Czajkowski, D. R., & Koocher, G. P. (1986). Predicting medical compliance among adolescents with cystic fibrosis. *Health Psychology, 5,* 297–305.

Czajkowski, D. R., & Koocher, G. P. (1987). Medical compliance and coping with cystic fibrosis. *Journal of Child Psychology and Psychiatry, 28,* 311–319.

D'Angelo, E., Woolf, A., Bessett, J., Rappaport, L., & Ciborowski, J. (1992). Correlates of medical compliance among hemophilic boys. *Journal of Clinical Psychology, 48,* 672–680.

Gudas, L. J., Koocher, G. P., & Wypij, D. (1991). Perceptions of medical compliance in children and adolescents with cystic fibrosis. *Journal of Developmental and Behavioral Pediatrics, 12,* 236–242.

Developer's Comments

Copies of the manual including the instrument and scoring criteria are available free of charge from Dr. Koocher. A parent version is included. Users need to provide copies of research reports and publications in return. Such reports are routinely added to the reference list of the manual.

TWENTY-FOUR-HOUR RECALL INTERVIEW

Source

Johnson, S. B., Silverstein, J., Rosenbloom, A., Carter, R., & Cunningham, W. (1986). Assessing daily management in childhood diabetes. *Health Psychology, 5,* 545–564.

Availability

From the first author. Suzanne Bennett Johnson, Department of Psychiatry, Box J-234, JHMHC, Gainesville, Florida, 32610–0234. Not copyrighted.

Purpose.   The 24-hour recall interview was designed to be a practical, general adherence assessment strategy that improves upon self-report measures. The authors hope to improve accuracy by focusing on specific behaviors during a recent, time-limited period, and by using multiple informants on multiple occasions. The measure was designed to assess daily management of childhood diabetes, but the assessment strategy is easily adapted to other medical regimens.

Description.   The 24-hour recall interview was adapted from the standard dietary assessment technique. All daily parent and child adherence behaviors are recorded. Subjects are asked to recall all behaviors over the previous 24 hours. The interview is conducted in temporal sequence, from the time that the child wakes in the morning until bedtime. Although subjects report all of the day's activities, only adherence behaviors are recorded. Interviewers are trained to prompt for adherence behaviors if the subject does not spontaneously report them. Subjects should be interviewed about three 24-hour periods including one weekday and one weekend day. Percent of adherence is calculated by dividing what was actually done by what was prescribed. For example, if the child completed blood glucose testing two times and was instructed to complete testing four times, percent adherence for blood testing would be 50%. Subjects' responses are averaged across the three time periods, and parent and child responses may also be averaged. Subsequent research suggested that children as young as 6 years can complete the interview, though they may not be able to report timing of activities with accuracy. The authors caution against creating a single adherence measure from different adherence activities, because factor analyses suggest that subjects do not adhere consistently across dimensions of adherence. For diabetes, 13 behaviors fell on five factors accounting for over 70% of the variance (Exercise, Injection, Eating Frequency, Calories Consumed, and Type of Calories Consumed). The measure is currently being piloted with an HIV population, and the hypothesized dimensions are doses taken, dose timing, and compliance with special instructions (e.g., taking medications with food).

Reliability and Validity.   The authors report significant parent–child agreement as an index of reliability and validity. Glasgow and colleagues (cited in Johnson, 1991) demonstrated adequate test-retest reliability over a 2-month period in adolescents and adults, but reliability estimates for a 6-month interval were lower. As evidence of construct validity, Reynolds and associates (cited in Johnson, 1991) compared child reports to observer ratings and found significant agreement with the exception of underestimation of dietary behaviors and exercise intensity. The factor analyses previously described are further evidence of construct validity. Criterion validity has been demonstrated in studies of predictors of adherence and associations between adherence and metabolic control (e.g., Johnson et al., 1992).

Summary of Strengths and Limitations. The 24-hour recall interview is a reliable and valid adherence assessment strategy that is brief and easy to administer. While the strategy may improve upon the accuracy of self-report, a social desirability factor can still lead to an overestimation of adherence. The need for follow-up phone contact also limits its utility, particularly with inner-city families who may not have phones or be transient. Reliability and validity studies need to be replicated with other chronic illness populations.

Additional Readings

Johnson, S. B. (1991). Compliance with complex medical regimens. *Advances in Behavior Assessment of Children and Families, 5,* 113–137.

Johnson, S. B., Kelly, M., Henretta, J. C., Cunningham, W. R., Tomer, A., & Silverstein, J. H. (1992). A longitudinal analysis of adherence and health status in childhood diabetes. *Journal of Pediatric Psychology, 17,* 537–553.

Reynolds, L. A., Johnson, S. B., & Silverstein, J. (1990). Assessing daily diabetes management by 24-hour recall interview: The validity of children's reports. *Journal of Pediatric Psychology, 15,* 493–509.

TABLE 2.1
Disease-Specific Measures

Disease	Measure	Reference
Asthma	Asthma Family Management System	Klinnert, McQuaid, & Gavin (1997)
Cystic Fibrosis	Treatment Adherence Questionnaire–Physician Form	Ievers et al., (1999)
	Treatment Adherence Questionnaire	Quittner et al. (1996)
Diabetes	Self Care Inventory	Greco et al. (1990)
	Self-Care Adherence Inventory	Hanson et al. (1996)
	Diabetes Self-Care Practices Instrument	Frey & Fox (1990)
	Situational Obstacles to Dietary Adherence Questionnaire (SODA)	Schlundt et al. (1996)
Spina Bifida	Parent Report of Medical Adherence in Spina Bifida Scale	Holmbeck et al. (1998)

References

Frey, M. A., & Fox, M. A. (1990). Assessing and teaching self-care to youth with diabetes mellitus. *Pediatric Nursing, 16,* 597–599.

Greco, P., LaGreca, A. M., Auslander, W. F., Spetter, D., Skyler, J. S., Fisher, E., & Santiago, J. V. (1990). Assessing adherence in IDDM: A comparison of two methods. *Diabetes, 40,* 108A.

Hanson, C. L., DeGuire, M., Schinkel, A., Kolterman, O., Goodman, J., & Buckingham, B. (1996). Self-care behaviors in insulin-dependent diabetes: Evaluative tools and their associations with glycemic control. *Journal of Pediatric Psychology, 21,* 467–482.

Holmbeck, G. N., Blevedere, M., Christensen, M., Czerwinski, A. M., Hommeyer, J. S., Johnson, S., & Kung, E. (1998). Assessment of adherence with multiple informants in pre-adolescents with spina bifida: Initial development of a multidimensional multitask parent report questionnaire. *Journal of Personality Assessment, 70,* 427–441.

Ievers, C. E., Brown, R. T., Drotar, D., Caplan, D., Pishevar, B. S., & Lambert, R. G. (1999). Knowledge of physician prescriptions and adherence to treatment among children with cystic fibrosis and their mothers. *Journal of Developmental and Behavioral Pediatrics, 20,* 335–343.

Klinnert, M., McQuaid, E. L., & Gavin, L. (1997). Assessing the family asthma management system. *Journal of Asthma, 34,* 77–88.

Quittner, A. L., Tolbert, V. E., Regli, M. J., Orenstein, D., Hollingsworth, J. L., & Eigen, H. (1996). Development of the Role-play Inventory of Situations and Coping Strategies (RISCS) for parents of children with cystic fibrosis. *Journal of Pediatric Psychology, 21,* 209–235.

Schlundt, D. G., Rea, M., Hodge, M., Flannery, M. E., Kline, S., Meek, J., Kinzer, C., & Pichert, J. W.(1996). Assessing and overcoming situational obstacles to dietary adherence in adolescents with IDDM. *Journal of Adolescent Health, 19,* 282–288.

Pain Management

Jocelyn McCrae
Children's Hospital of Michigan

INTRODUCTION

Pain is an unpleasant sensory, emotional, and cognitive event. It may be experienced with or without actual tissue injury. Even when pain is reported in the absence of a clear physiological basis, it should still be accepted by clinicians as pain (IASP Task Force on Taxonomy, 1994). Children and adolescents learn about pain through direct experience, as well as others' pain-related reports and expressions (Gil, Williams, Thompson, & Kinney, 1991).

Individual children differ in their experiences of pain. Some of this individual variation can be attributed to physiological factors, such as type or degree of tissue injury. However, much of the individual variation in pain experience cannot be explained on the basis of biological factors alone. Pain responses are often the outgrowth of a complex interplay of child factors (e.g., anxiety level, perceptions of control) and environmental factors (e.g., family members' anxiety or distress reactions; McGrath, 1990).

In pediatric settings, pain may arise in association with unpleasant medical procedures, bodily injury, or disease. A goal of pain measurement is to understand child's experience of pain, including any relevant moderating influences (McGrath, 1996). With thorough assessment, interventions can be developed to reduce pain and its concomitant costs. To understand the child's experience of pain, it is useful to gather qualitative, as well as quantitative information from multiple sources (child, caregivers, and medical staff). The specific characteristics of the child's pain (location, frequency, duration, and sensory qualities), the cognitive, emotional, and behavioral responses of the child and her caregivers, as well as relevant environmental and cultural factors that may modify the experience or expression of pain should be assessed. The impact of the pain on the child's functioning is also relevant to the assessment process (Gil et al., 1991; McGrath, 1990, 1996) as either acute or chronic pain experiences may have a significant impact on quality of life (see chapter 1).

When selecting a pain measure, instrument reliability, validity, and utility are critical considerations. Reliable assessment tools yield reproducible pain measurements that are not significantly affected by extraneous respondent or situational factors. Valid assessment devices accurately measure pain and are not confounded by the emotional or behavioral reactions that can accompany pain (McGrath, 1990). This task is more difficult, however, when evaluating pain in children because they often cannot differentiate the emotional components of pain (e.g. anxiety) from the sensory components.

Selected pain assessment tools should be appropriate for the age and cognitive level of the child. Physiological measures (e.g., heart and respiration rates) and behavioral observations (e.g., crying and stalling) are useful with infants or very young children who lack the verbal skills to adequately communicate about their pain (McGrath, 1990). A limitation of behavioral and physiologic assessment strategies, however, is their sensitivity to pain-related emotional distress over and above actual pain experienced (McGrath, 1990, 1996). Practicality is also a concern when choosing physiological or behavioral indices because raters typically need to be trained to use these assessment tools. Nevertheless, assessment of behavioral and physiological responses may provide important information about the pain experienced, as well as the effectiveness of treatment (McGrath, 1990). Self-reports of pain, whether from interviews, questionnaires, or facial and visual analog scales are considered to be the gold standard of pediatric pain assessment when children are old enough to provide a self-report (Varni, Blount, Waldron, & Smith, 1995).

Although the number of assessment measures available for measuring acute pediatric pain has burgeoned in recent years, there remains a paucity of reliable and valid measures specifically designed to assess chronic pain in children (McGrath, 1996). Due to the fact that chronic pain varies over time, continuous tracking is required for its measurement. Pain diary approaches are often used in an attempt to gather such information. To determine the impact of chronic pain on the child, it is also necessary to assess general functioning, including involvement in family, school, and peer activities, as well as medication usage and health care contacts.

Pain management in pediatric health settings is often collaborative and may include a team consisting of physicians, nurses, and other medical staff. Therefore, there is often a need for pain assessment in clinical settings to be time-limited and cost-efficient. Assessment strategies should be practical and lead to the development of effective interventions to treat pediatric pain.

Subsequent pages review several pain assessment tools that are used in pediatric health care settings. These measures are reviewed with respect to their psychometric properties (reliability and validity), strengths, limitations, and utility (time and administration requirements). It is hoped that this information will be useful when selecting measures to accurately evaluate and effectively treat children's pain.

REFERENCES

IASP Task Force on Taxonomy. (1994). IASP pain terminology. In H. Merskey and N. Bogduk (Eds.), *Classification of chronic pain* (2nd ed., pp. 209–214). Seattle, WA: IASP Press.

Gil, K., Williams, D., Thompson, R., & Kinney, T. (1991). Sickle cell disease in children and adolescents. The relation of child and parent pain coping strategies to adjustment. *Journal of Pediatric Psychology, 16*, 643–663.

McGrath, P. A. (1990). *Pain in children.* New York: Guilford Press.

McGrath, P.A. (1996). There is more to pain management than "ouch." *Canadian Journal of Psychology, 37*(2), 63–75.

Varni, J., Blount, R., Waldron, S., & Smith, A. (1995). Management of pain and distress. In M. C. Roberts (Ed.), *Handbook of pediatric psychology* (2nd ed., pp. 105–123). New York: Guilford Press.

BIERI FACES SCALE

Source

Bieri, D., Reeve, R., Champion, G. D., Addicoat, L., & Ziegler, J. B. (1990). The Faces Pain Scale for the self-assessment of the severity of pain experienced by children: Development, initial validation and preliminary investigation for ratio scale properties. *Pain, 41*, 139–150.

Availability

From the last author, Division of Paediatrics, Prince of Wales Children's Hospital, High Street, Randwick, N.S.W., 2031, Australia.

Purpose. The Bieri Faces Scale was designed to obtain children's self-ratings of pain intensity. The authors developed the scale with the intent of optimizing the scale properties of the set of faces. In particular, they attempted to develop a faces scale where there were equal pain intervals between each face and where the first face measured no pain.

Description. The Bieri Faces Scale consists of seven cartoon faces, with the first face depicting a neutral expression and the next six faces depicting increasing amounts of pain. Children choose the one face that best represents the amount of pain they experience.

Standardization and Norms. The instrument was developed using an Australian sample of schoolchildren in first through third grades.

Reliability and Validity. The authors assessed scaling properties in a number of ways. First, they developed several potential sets of faces, then had subjects place them in order from most to least painful. The set with the highest percent of agreement in ordering was the one chosen for the Bieri Faces Scale. Second, children were asked to place the faces along a line according to the degree of pain they depicted. Children were found to display good approximation to the positions that would be predicted if the scale had equal interval properties. Test-retest reliability of the instrument was established by having children rate the amount of pain that would be experienced in several hypothetical situations. Results indicated adequate test-retest reliability ($r = .79$). Face validity of the scale was established by using faces that were derived from those drawn by first through third graders asked to depict children in pain. Construct validity of the Bieri Faces Scale has been established by showing that children being treated for leukemia are able to use the measure to discriminate between a variety of painful medical procedures (e.g., venipuncture was rated as less painful than an injection of local anesthetic). Research comparing the Bieri Faces Scale to faces scales that begin with a smiling face rather than a neutral face suggest that it is less likely to be biased in the direction of inflation of pain scores.

Summary of Strengths and Limitations. The Bieri Faces Scale offers several advantages to researchers over other available faces pain ratings scales. These include data supporting the Bieri scale as a ratio scale rather than an ordinal scale. Advantages over pain rating scales that use facial photographs may include a lower potential for children (or staff) to try to match their own face to those shown on the scale. The brevity of the scale and ease of administration give it clear clinical applications. However, the scale was not validated with young children and its psychometric properties with preschoolers are unknown.

Additional Readings

Chambers, C. T., Giesbrecht, K., Craig, K. D., Bennett, S. M., & Huntsman, E. (1999). A comparison of faces scales for the measurement of pediatric pain: Children's and parent's ratings. *Pain, 83,* 25–35.

CHILD-ADULT MEDICAL PROCEDURE
INTERACTION SCALE-REVISED

Source

Blount, R., Sturges, J., & Powers, S. (1990). Analysis of child and adult behavioral variations by phase of medical procedure. *Behavior Therapy*, *21*, 33–48.

Availability

From the first author, Department of Psychology, University of Georgia, Athens, Georgia, 30602.

Purpose. The Child-Adult Medical Procedure Interaction Scale–Revised (CAMPIS–R) was designed to measure distress behaviors displayed by children during painful medical procedures. However, unlike other measures of behavioral distress, it also measures the coping and nondistress behaviors displayed by children at such times. In addition, the CAMPIS–R allows the behavior displayed during painful procedures by adults—such as parents and medical staff—to be quantified.

Description. The CAMPIS–R is a revised version of the CAMPIS. The CAMPIS consists of 35 observational codes. These codes were re-grouped into six categories in the CAMPIS–R. The six categories are: Child Coping (e.g., humor by child), Child Distress (e.g., verbal resistance), Child Neutral (e.g., requests relief from nonprocedural discomfort), Adult Coping Promoting (e.g., commands to use coping strategies), Adult Distress Promoting (e.g., criticism) and Adult Neutral (e.g., nonprocedural talk to adults). The CAMPIS–R is coded from audio or videotapes of the painful procedure. Coders must be formally trained.

Standardization and Norms. The instrument was developed and validated with children aged 4–13 who were undergoing a variety of painful medical procedures (e.g., injections, lumbar punctures, and bone marrow aspirations). Samples appear to have been primarily Caucasian.

Reliability and Validity. Inter-rater reliability of the CAMPIS–R has been reported to be good to excellent in many publications by the first author. However, no data on internal consistency of the measure has been reported. Criterion validity has been established by comparing CAMPIS–R ratings to ratings on other observational measures of distress, child self-ratings of anxiety and pain, and parent–staff ratings of distress, anxiety, and pain. Both child and adult CAMPIS–R Coping and Distress codes have been found to be significantly correlated with these other measures. However, inverse relationships were found between child and adult Neutral codes and the validity measures. The authors also point out that the majority of subjects in the validity study were aged 4–7, which means that the validity of the CAMPIS-R for older adolescents is not known.

Summary of Strengths and Limitations. The measure generally appears to have strong psychometric properties which gives it high potential research utility. It is also the only behavioral measure of distress that allows quantification of behaviors of individuals other than the child, such as parents and staff. It should be noted, however, that the CAMPIS–R is used to code vocal behaviors rather than motoric behaviors; therefore, it does not allow quantification of the role of such factors in the expression of pain behaviors and/or coping behaviors. In addition, extensive training of coders is required to use the CAMPIS–R system. Users should be careful to view the CAMPIS–R as a measure of behavioral distress during painful procedures rather than a direct measure of subjective pain.

Additional Readings

Blount, R., Cohen, L., Frank, N., Bachanas, P., Smith, A., Manimala, M. R., & Pate, J. (1997). The Child-Adult Medical Procedure Interaction Scale–Revised: An assessment of validity. *Journal of Pediatric Psychology, 2,* 73–88.

CHILDREN'S HOSPITAL OF EASTERN ONTARIO PAIN SCALE

Source

McGrath, P. J., Johnson, G., Goodman, J. T., Schillinger, J., Dunn, J., & Chapman, J. (1985). CHEOPS: A behavioral scale for rating postoperative pain in children.

Availability

From the first author, Psychology Department, Dalhousie University, Halifax, Nova Scotia, B3H 4J1. Copyrighted.

Purpose. The CHEOPS was designed to measure post-operative pain in young children who are unable to provide accurate self-reports of pain. It is a multidimensional behavioral rating scale that requires brief ratings from coders in several behavioral domains.

Description. The CHEOPS codes six behavioral responses: Cry, Facial, Child Verbal, Torso, Touch, and Legs. For each behavior response, several ratings exist, along with verbal descriptors. Ratings are not ordinal (e.g., for Torso, Neutral is coded as 1 and Shifting, Tense, Shivering, Upright, and Restrained are all coded as 2). However, the total score for the CHEOPS is ordinal and ranges between 4 and 13. In the initial validation study, the CHEOPS was primarily coded from bedside observations.

Standardization and Norms. The instrument was developed using a sample of children aged 1 to 7 from the recovery room of a tertiary care hospital. Children had undergone a variety of surgical procedures including circumcision, tonsillectomy, and hypospadias repair.

Reliability and Validity. Initial item selection for the CHEOPS was carried out by surveying experienced recovery room nurses who were asked to identify behaviors indicative of pain in children. Inter-rater reliability of the CHEOPS ranged from .90 to .99. Construct validity for the measure was established by assessing changes in CHEOPS scores before and after an analgesic was administered to children experiencing post-surgical pain. Scores varied in the expected direction, although raters were not blind to analgesic administration. In order to assess criterion validity, experienced nurses assigned a pain score to the child during post-surgical care using a visual analogue scale (VAS); raters simultaneously assigned a CHEOPS score. Nurses' VAS score was found to be significantly correlated with coders' CHEOPS score (.52–.81).

Summary of Strengths and Limitations. The CHEOPS coding system is simple and easy to use and requires little time for coders to master. In addition, preliminary psychometric properties appear sound. Therefore, the measure has good research utility. Nevertheless, since discriminant validity has not been established, the CHEOPS should be viewed as a measure of behavioral distress during painful procedures rather than a direct measure of subjective pain. The measure is simple to use and was developed as a bedside coding system. Therefore it may also have clinical use as a method of identifying and managing pain in children. However, clinical utility, such as the development of norms that might be used to make decisions regarding pain management, has not yet been established.

NEONATAL FACIAL CODING SYSTEM

Source

Grunau, R.V.E., & Craig, K. (1987). Pain expression in neonates: facial action and cry. *Pain, 28*(3), 395–410.

Availability

From the first author, Research Institute for Children's and Women's Health Rm L408, 4480 Oak Street, Vancouver, BC V6H 3V4.

Purpose. The Neonatal Facial Coding System (NFCS) is a unidimensional behavioral measure of pain during infancy. It was derived from the Facial Action Coding System (FACS), a comprehensive measure of infant emotional state that was designed to capture all possible infant facial movements. It codes infant facial actions in order to provide an objective description of infants' reactions to painful events.

Description. Ten facial actions are rated by a coder observing the infant during exposure to a painful stimulus. These actions are Brow Bulge, Eye Squeeze, Naso-labial Furrow, Open Lips, Stretch Mouth (horizontal), Stretch Mouth (vertical), Lip Purse, Taut Tongue, and Chin Quiver. The instrument has been used with both preterm and term newborns undergoing painful procedures, such as heel lances. Coders must be formally trained in use of the system. Coding is completed either from videotapes of the infant or at the bedside.

Standardization and Norms. The instrument was developed using a sample of 140 neonates from the well-baby unit of a maternity hospital. Sixty-three percent of the infants were Caucasian. The NFCS has subsequently been used with older infants and toddlers.

Reliability and Validity. Initial studies with the NFCS were carried out using videotapes of infants undergoing painful procedures. Interrater reliability was computed on a randomly selected 20% of subjects and was reported to be .88. Factor analyses suggested good construct validity for the measure, with all facial movements loading on one factor. Subsequent research investigating the utility of the NFCS as a measure of pain with infants and toddlers has also replicated this factor structure. Additional evidence of construct validity comes from studies using the NFCS that show that the instrument differentiates between infants who receive pharmacologic intervention during painful procedures and those who do not. The authors have established the criterion validity of the NFCS by comparing it to the FACS. The relationship between the NCFS and similar facial actions on the FACS was .89.

Reliability and validity of the NFCS when used at the bedside in real time has also been established. Coders trained in the NFCS coding system were able to demonstrate a high degree of inter-rater reliability (.83) when using the instrument at the bedside. Construct validity was established in this context by showing that the NFCS differentiated between infants during various stages of a heel lance procedure.

Summary of Strengths and Limitations. The measure is one of the few tools for the assessment of pain in infants with established reliability and validity data. The fact that the coding system also has strong psychometric properties when used with older infants increases its utility. As compared with more comprehensive systems for coding infant facial activity that can potentially be used to rate pain, the measure requires relatively less time for coders to master. Therefore, the measure has good research utility. The authors suggest that the measure may also have clinical use as a method of identifying and managing pain in infants. Psychometric properties of the instrument when used at the bedside have been established, suggesting that the instrument has the potential for translation to clinical practice. However, clinical utility, such as the development of norms that might be used to make decisions regarding pain management, has not yet been established.

Additional Readings

Grunau, R. E., Oberlander, T., Holsti, L., & Whitfield, M. (1998). Bedside application of the Neonatal Facial Coding System in pain assessment of premature neonates. *Pain, 76,* 277–86.

Lilley, C., Craig, K., & Grunau, R. E. (1997). The expression of pain in infants and toddlers: Developmental changes in facial action. *Pain, 72,* 161–170.

NEONATAL INFANT PAIN SCALE

Source

Lawrence, J., Alcock, D., McGrath, P., Kay, J., MacMurray, S. B., & Dulberg, C. (1993). The development of a tool to assess neonatal pain. *Neonatal Network, 12,* 59–66.

Availability

From the first author, Children's Hospital of Eastern Ontario, 401 Smyth Road, Ottawa, Ontario, K1H 8L1. Copyrighted.

Purpose. The Neonatal Infant Pain Scale (NIPS) was designed to measure pain in premature and full-term neonates. It is a multidimensional behavioral rating scale that requires brief ratings from coders in several behavioral domains. Items were derived from the CHEOPS, a behavioral measure of pain in older children and from a survey of neonatal nurses. The NIPS was intended to provide an objective measure of pain response as differentiated from other distress responses such as hunger.

Description. The NIPS codes six behavioral responses: Facial Expression, Cry, Breathing Patterns, Arms, Legs, and State of Arousal. Each behavior except Cry is coded 0 or 1. Cry may be coded 0, 1, or 2. The total score for the NIPS therefore ranges between 0 and 7. In the initial validation study, the NIPS was coded from videotapes of infants.

Standardization and Norms. The instrument was developed using a sample of 38 neonates from the neonatal intensive care unit of a tertiary care hospital. These infants underwent 90 painful procedures. Sixty-seven of the procedures were performed on preterm infants and 23 were performed on full-term infants.

Reliability and Validity. Initial item selection for the NIPS was carried out by surveying experienced neonatal nurses who were asked to identify behaviors indicative of pain in infants undergoing painful procedures. A pilot study indicated that two behaviors initially included in the NIPS (Facial Color and Torso Movement) were either difficult to code or confounded with other distress states. Therefore, they were not included in the final version of the instrument. Inter-rater reliability of the NIPS was calculated for a randomly selected subset of videotapes and ranged from .92 to .97. In addition, the NIPS was found to have high internal consistency with Cronbach's alpha ranging from .95 to .88. Construct validity for the measure was established by assessing changes in NIPS scores before, during, and after needle punctures. These scores varied in the expected direction. In order to assess criterion validity, experienced nurses separately assigned a pain score to the infant during the needle puncture procedure using a visual analogue scale. Nurses' scores were found to be significantly correlated with coders' NIPS score (.53–.84)

Summary of Strengths and Limitations. The measure is one of the few tools for the assessment of pain in neonates with established reliability and validity data. The coding system is simple and easy to use, therefore it requires little time for coders to master. Hence, the measure has good research utility. However, as compared with more comprehensive systems for coding infant pain, the measure may be less sensitive to subtle signs of pain, particularly chronic pain. This issue is also reflected in the limited gradations within behavioral response categories (e.g., can only be rated from 0–2). The authors suggest that the measure may also have clinical use as a method of identifying and managing pain in infants. However, clinical utility, such as the development of norms that might be used to make decisions regarding pain management, has not yet been established.

OBSERVATIONAL SCALE OF BEHAVIORAL DISTRESS

Source

Elliott, C., Jay, S., & Woody, P. (1987). An observational scale for measuring children's distress during medical procedures. *Journal of Pediatric Psychology, 12,* 543–551.

Availability

From the second author. Behavioral Sciences Program, Division of Hematology–Oncology, Children's Hospital of Los Angeles, 4650 Sunset Boulevard, Los Angeles, CA 90027.

Purpose. The Observational Scale of Behavioral Distress (OSBD) was designed to measure children's behavioral responses during painful medical procedures. It allows the observer to record the occurrence of a variety of distress-related behaviors that are hypothesized to signal the presence of pain in children.

Description. The OSBD is a revision of the Procedure Behavior Rating Scale (PBRS). The OSBD differs from the PBRS in that: (a) behavior is recorded continuously in 15-second intervals during the painful procedure, and (b) each behavioral category on the scale is weighted based on the severity of distress it represents (e.g., Flail is weighted more heavily than Information Seeking). Eight behaviors are rated: Information Seeking, Cry, Scream, Physical Restraint, Verbal Resistance, Seeks Emotional Support, Verbal Pain, and Flail. The authors also note that users of the OSBD may chose to code only occurrence–nonoccurrence of the eight behaviors during a painful procedure rather than using the continuous behavioral coding strategy. Coders must be formally trained. Coding may be completed during the actual procedure.

Standardization and Norms. The instrument was developed using a sample of 55 children aged 3–13 with leukemia undergoing bone marrow aspirations as part of their medical treatment. Fifty-five percent of the children were Caucasian, 25% were Hispanic, 13% were African American, and 7% were Asian.

Reliability and Validity. The authors conducted an item analysis of the OSBD and subsequently eliminated 3 of the original 11 scales. Internal consistency of the scale was subsequently reported to be .72. Inter-rater reliability of the scale was reported to be acceptable ($r = .98$; percent agreement = 84%). Acceptable inter-rater reliability has also been established when using the scale to rate distress among children undergoing other types of painful procedures such as intramuscular injections (Powers et al., 1993). Criterion validity was established by comparing OSBD ratings with several measures of pain and distress including ratings of distress by nurses, fear and pain ratings by children, heart rate, and blood pressure. The OSBD was significantly correlated with all measures except child's self-ratings of pain and post-procedural blood pressure for all age groups and correlated with all measures except post-procedural blood pressure for children over the age of 7.

Summary of Strengths and Limitations. The measure appears to have strong psychometric properties that gives it high potential research utility. However, training coders to use the system may be a relatively lengthy process, as the authors cite periods of 6–8 weeks to establish 75% reliability. Training of coders may be simplified by dropping the use of continuous behavioral coding and coding only for occurrence–non-occurrence of distress behaviors during the painful procedure. Users should be careful to view the OSBD as a measure of behavioral distress during painful procedures rather than a direct measure of subjective pain.

Additional Readings

Jay, S. M., & Elliott, C. H. (1984). Behavioral observation scales for measuring children's distress: The effects of increasing methodological rigor. *Journal of Consulting and Clinical Psychology, 52,* 1106–1107.

Powers, S. W., Blount, R. L., Bachanas, P. J., Cotter, M. W., & Swan, S. C. (1993). Helping preschool leukemia patients and their parents cope during injections. *Journal of Pediatric Psychology, 18,* 681–696.

OUCHER

Source

Beyer, J., Denyes, M., & Villarruel, A. (1992). The creation, validation and continuing development of the Oucher: A measure of pain intensity in children. *Journal of Pediatric Nursing, 7,* 335–346.

Availability

From the first author, School of Nursing, University of Missouri at Kansas, 2220 Holmes St., Kansas, MO 64108–2676. Copyrighted.

Purpose. The Oucher was designed to obtain children's self-ratings of pain intensity using visual analogues.

Description. The Oucher consists of two scales: a 0–100 numerical pain-rating scale that can be used with older children and a six-picture photographic scale for younger children. The photos are of children experiencing increasing levels of pain. Versions are also available for African-American and Hispanic children.

Standardization and Norms. The Oucher was originally developed and validated with a sample of 3–12-year-old children who were primarily Caucasian. Subsequently, extensive validation of two alternative forms for children of African-American and Hispanic ethnicity has been undertaken with children ages 3–12.

Reliability and Validity. Reliability of the Oucher has been indirectly assessed by showing children pictures of cartoons depicting young children in potentially painful situations, then asking children to use the Oucher to rate the degree of pain experienced. Moderately high internal consistency and test-retest reliability was established. Validity studies of the Oucher have been conducted with both the photographic scale and the numeric scale. To determine content validity of the photographic scale, the authors conducted several analyses to ascertain that photos appeared in the correct sequence (i.e., children agreed that each face in the sequence demonstrated a greater degree of pain than the last). Children allowed to place the photos in order themselves were significantly more likely than chance to place them in the same order as they appear on the Oucher; 86% of 7-year-olds were able to match the sequence with less than half of 3- to 4-year-olds able to do so. Parallel studies of content validity of the alternative versions of the Oucher for children of different ethnicities have replicated these findings. Construct validity of the Oucher has been established by showing that children who are experiencing pain rate their pain higher before receiving analgesics and lower afterwards. Children admitted for surgery also have increasingly lower scores on the Oucher during successive post-operative days (Caucasian Oucher only). Discriminant and convergent validity were established by demonstrating significant, large-order correlations between the Oucher and other pain-rating scales and low-order correlations between the Oucher and ratings of fear.

Summary of Strengths and Limitations. The measure appears to have strong psychometric properties that give it high research utility. Given that the Oucher utilizes a photographic scale, the availability of versions for use with African-American and Hispanic children is important, as is the instrument's established validity with these populations. The brevity of the instrument and ease of administration give it clear clinical applications as well. Suggestions for determining whether to use the photographic or numeric scale during clinical pain assessment are available in the user manual. Although the Oucher does include a numerical pain-rating scale, the photographic scale is more salient. Since the photos are of young children, the Oucher may be most appropriate for preschool and school aged children.

Additional Readings

Beyer, J., & Aradine, C. R. (1986). Content validity of an instrument to measure children's perceptions of the intensity of their pain. *Journal of Pediatric Nursing, 1,* 386–395.

Beyer, J., & Aradine. C. (1988). The convergent and discriminant validity of a self-report measure of pain intensity for children. *Children's Health Care, 16,* 274–282.

Villaruel, A. M., & Denyes, M. J. (1991). Pain assessment in children: Theoretical and empirical validity. *Advances in Nursing Science, 14,* 31–39.

Developer's Comments

The description of the Oucher provides an accurate summary of the reliability and validity of the tool to date. Psychometric studies are continuing, including an alternate forms reliability study to demonstrate the ability of children to reliably use smaller formats of all versions of the Oucher. This tool is being developed by Pain Associates in Nursing (PAIN). PAIN is currently in the process of developing a website for the Oucher (*www.OUCHER.org*), in digitalizing the photographs for clearer facial images and in reducing the size of the Oucher even further.

PEDIATRIC PAIN QUESTIONNAIRE

Source

Varni, J., Thompson, K., & Hanson, V. (1987). The Varni-Thompson Pediatric Pain Questionnaire. I. Chronic musculoskeletal pain in juvenile rheumatoid arthritis. *Pain, 28,* 27–38.

Availability

From the first author, Center for Child Health Outcomes, Children's Hospital and Health Center, 3020 Children's Way MC 5053, San Diego, CA 92123 or *www.PedsQL.org.* Copyrighted.

Purpose:. The Pediatric Pain Questionnaire (PPQ) was designed to measure chronic pain in children. It is intended to measure the intensity of pain; the sensory, emotional, and evaluative components of pain; and the location of pain in a fashion that is developmentally appropriate and easily understood by children.

Description. The PPQ was modeled after the McGill Pain Questionnaire, an instrument widely used for the assessment of chronic pain in adults. The PPQ has three parts: (a) a visual analogue scale (VAS) for rating present and worst pain intensity in the past week; (b) a color-coded, pain-rating scale to measure pain intensity–location where the child colors a body outline with crayons and then matches the chosen colors with pain descriptors; and (c) a list of pain descriptors that are circled by the child to best describe his pain. The corresponding parent version of the PPQ includes the VAS, the list of pain descriptors, and a family history section that asks questions about pain history and treatment, family pain history, and socio-environmental situations that may influence pain perception or reports of pain.

Standardization and Norms. The instrument was developed and validated on several groups of children aged 4–16 with various rheumatoid diseases, mostly juvenile rheumatoid arthritis (JRA). The only demographic data reported was that the average annual family income was between 10,001 and 30,000 dollars (52% of the sample).

Reliability and Validity.   The authors reported data on the stability of scores on the VAS portion of the PPQ over a 6-month period. Although the amount of pain experienced by children with JRA would be expected to vary, children participating in the study were described as having relatively stable disease. Therefore, stability of VAS scores can be considered to be an index of reliability. Child and parent ratings of pain on the VAS at baseline were significantly related to their VAS scores 6 months later. Considerable data does support the validity of the VAS portion of the PPQ as a pain measure. VAS scores of parents and children have been found to be significantly and positively correlated with one another and also with ratings of the child's disease activity and functional status.

Summary of Strengths and Limitations.   This measure has the advantage of having both clinical and research utility. Two portions of the questionnaire, the color-coded pain ratings and list of pain descriptors, do not have proven psychometric properties. However, they are valuable as a means for assessing an individual child's cognitions about pain and as a mechanism for developing intervention strategies. For instance, the authors suggest that patient-generated color associations may be useful when developing imagery-based interventions for pain control. The VAS portion of the measure appears to have strong psychometric properties that give it high potential research utility. The availability of both a parent and child version is also appealing. Further studies with other pediatric populations are necessary.

Additional Readings

Gragg, R., Rapoff, M., Danovsky, M., Lindsley, C.B., Varni, J., Waldron, S., & Bernstein, B. (1996). Assessing chronic musculoskeletal pain associated with rheumatic disease: Further validation of the Pediatric Pain Questionnaire. *Journal of Pediatric Psychology, 21,* 237–250.

WALDRON-VARNI PEDIATRIC PAIN COPING INVENTORY

Reference

Varni, J., Waldron, S., Gragg, R. A., Rapoff, M. A., Bernstein, B. H., Lindsley, C. B., & Newcomb, M. D. (1996). Development of the Waldron-Varni Pediatric Pain Coping Inventory. *Pain, 67,* 141–150.

Availability

From the first author, Center for Child Health Outcomes, Children's Hospital and Health Center, 3020 Children's Way MC 5053, San Diego, CA 92123 or at *www.PedsQL.org.* Copyrighted.

Purpose. The Pediatric Pain Coping Inventory (PPCI) was developed with the goal of better understanding individual differences in pain perception and pain behavior. In particular, it was designed to assess children's perceptions of coping mechanisms that they use when experiencing pain. It was modeled after measures used in the adult chronic pain literature that assess pain coping strategies (i.e., the Coping Strategies Questionnaire).

Description. The PPCI is a 41-item instrument. The respondent is asked to rate whether or not a coping strategy is used when "[I] feel hurt or pain." Response format is from 0 ("never") to 2 ("a lot"). Both a parent-report version and a child self-report version are available. Furthermore, the child version is available in both child and adolescent forms that are written in developmentally appropriate language. The PPCI can be scored using five theoretically derived scales (Cognitive Self-Instruction, Problem Solving, Distraction, Seeks Social Support, and Catastrophizing–Helplessness) or five empirically derived scales (Cognitive Self-Instruction, Seek Social Support, Strive to Rest, Cognitive Refocusing, and Problem Solving Self-Efficacy).

Standardization and Norms. The instrument was developed using a sample of children aged 5 to 16 years of age with chronic musculoskeletal pain seen at tertiary medical care centers. The sample was largely Caucasian. The developers report the mean Hollinghead four-factor index was 44.4 (SD = 13.1), indicating on average the sample was middle-class SES.

Reliability and Validity. Content validity was established by generating items for the measure from the adult and pediatric pain-coping literature, then soliciting item review from pediatric pain experts. Pilot testing of the measure was also completed and four items that were difficult for respondents to interpret were dropped. Internal consistency for the overall PPCI was reported to be high (.85). Internal consistency for the theoretically derived scales was moderately strong (.57–.74). Factor analysis suggested a five-factor solution for the PPCI (scales are previously described), with internal consistency ranging from .67–.77 for the empirically derived scales. Criterion validity was established by comparing ratings on the PPCI with pain ratings and ratings of externalizing and internalizing behavior problems. Children who scored higher on a PPCI scale measuring active coping strategies scored lower on self-reported worst-ever pain and depression, while those who scored higher on a PPCI scale measuring passive coping strategies scored higher on self-reported present pain, worst ever pain, depression, and anxiety. Findings were similar for the parent report version.

Summary of Strengths and Limitations. The PPCI is one of the only instruments available that was specifically designed to assess pain-coping strategies in the pediatric population. Limited psychometric data is available at present, although preliminary studies suggest adequate internal consistency and construct validity. The availability of child, adolescent, and parent versions is a strength of the instrument. Because the PPCI was initially designed for use in a research context and norms are not available, clinical utility is currently limited.

TABLE 3.1
Disease-Specific Measures

Disease	Measure	Reference
Gastroenter-ology	Pain-Response Inventory for Children	Walker, Smith, Garber, & Van Slyke (1997)
Juvenile Rheumatoid Arthritis	Child Health Assessment Questionnaire	Billings, Moos, Miller, & Gottlieb (1987)
Immunizations	Behavioral Approach-Avoidance and Distress Scale	Bachanas & Blount (1996)
Oncology	Perception of Procedures Questionnaire	Kazak, Penati, Waibel, & Blackall (1996)
Sickle Cell	Coping Strategies Questionnaire	Gil, Williams, Thompson, & Kinney (1991)
Surgery Anticipation	Modification of Procedure Behavior Rating Scale	Altshuler, Genevro, Ruble, & Bornstein (1995)

References

Altshuler, J. L., Genevro, J. L., Ruble, D. N., & Bornstein, M. H. (1995). Children's knowledge and use of coping strategies during hospitalization for elective surgery. *Journal of Applied Developmental Psychology, 16*, 53–76.

Bachanas, P. J., & Blount, R. L. (1996). The behavioral approach-avoidance and distress scale: An investigation of reliability and validity during painful medical procedures. *Journal of Pediatric Psychology, 21*, 671–81.

Billings, A., Moos, R., Miller, J., & Gottlieb, J. (1987). Psychosocial adaptation in juvenile rheumatic disease: A controlled evaluation. *Health Psychology, 6*(4), 343–359.

Gil, K., Williams, D., Thompson, R., & Kinney, T. (1991). Sickle cell disease in children and adolescents: The relation of child and parent pain coping strategies to adjustment. *Journal of Pediatric Psychology, 16*(5), 643–663.

Kazak, A. E., Penati, P., Waibel, M. K., & Blackall, G. F. (1996). The Perception of Procedures Questionnaire. *Journal of Pediatric Psychology, 21,* 195–207.

Walker, L. S., Smith, C. A., Garber, J., & Van Slyke, D. A. (1997). Development and validation of the pain response inventory for children. *Psychological Assessment, 9,* 392–405.

4

Child Behavior

Arthur Robin
Wayne State University

INTRODUCTION

You are a clinician or researcher in a pediatric health care setting. When you arrive at the office on a Monday morning, you find one or more of the following requests for assistance on your desk:

1. The hemophilia clinic staff have been noticing that an abnormally large number of their patients exhibit Attention Deficit/Hyperactivity Disorder (ADHD) symptoms. They have checked with their colleagues around the country and found that others have also noticed the high number of ADHD symptoms in children with hemophilia. The clinic wants to start screening all of their patients for ADHD symptoms to help them determine when to refer the patients for a full evaluation. They want the parents to complete a brief screening instrument in the waiting room before clinic visits. They are asking you to help them select an appropriate screening tool.

2. The attending neurologist on the inpatient pediatric unit is asking you to do a consultation on Nicole Buttress, a 15-year-old female, to determine whether there is a psychogenic component to her "seizures." Several times per week, Nicole goes into brief, trance-like states during which she is unresponsive to all external stimulation, loses all muscle tone, and stares off in space. Extensive medical work-ups, including normal and sleep-deprived electroencephalograms (EEGs), have not revealed any evidence of a seizure disorder. However, Nicole's 10-year-old sister has grand mal seizures.

3. Dr. Jones wants to evaluate the effectiveness of several complementary and alternative medicine interventions for helping children with ADHD. He wants to compare the effectiveness of blue-green algae and mega-vitamins to Concerta and a placebo, using a between-group design. The children in each group will receive a pre-assessment, 10 months of intervention, a post-assessment, and a 6-month follow-up assessment. He asks you to help him select the dependent measures, some of which will be rating scales.

The behavioral screening measures described in this chapter can play a helpful role in each of these situations. How does the pediatric health care professional decide which of these screening measures to use in each situation? The selection of an appropriate screening instrument depends upon a number of important factors: (a) the purpose of the assessment measure—screening, diagnosis, treatment planning, serving as a dependent measure in a research study, or all; (b) who will rate the child–parent, teacher, the child, physician, nurse, psychologist, or other allied medical staff; (c) the nature and band-width of the assessment targets—narrow band-width targets, such as illness-specific behavior problems, ADHD symptoms, or depression versus wide band-width" targets, such as all DSM-IV Axis I diagnoses; (d) the psychometric characteristics of the measure—reliability and validity; and (e) ease of use of the measure—length, readability, etc.

HEMOPHILIA CLINIC

In the case of the hemophilia clinic, the purpose of the assessment is to screen patients for possible ADHD. Parents rate their children in the waiting room, which means a short, easy-to-use measure is needed. A narrow band-width instrument is needed for a single target area, ADHD symptoms, and high discriminant validity is the most important psychometric characteristic. Four of the instruments described in this chapter have scales that measure attention problems, hyperactivity, or both: the Child Behavior Checklist (CBCL), the Conners' Rating Scales (CRS), the Pediatric Behavior Scale (PBS), and the Behavior Assessment System for Children (BASC). The PBS has limited norms and limited psychometric data available, with no information about the validity of its scales for screening purposes. The CBCL and BASC are wide-band width instruments designed to assess a variety of behavioral problems, including ADHD characteristics. Although easy for parents to understand, the CBCL and BASC are longer and take 10–20 minutes for parents to complete. Both instruments have excellent psychometric properties, and in the case of the

CBCL researchers have developed criteria for using the instrument to distinguish ADHD from non-ADHD children (Biederman et al., 1993).

The BASC does have an associated BASC ADHD Monitor that is a 47-item teacher and parent-rating scale assessing attention and hyperactivity. It has been shown to discriminate well between children with and without ADHD. This is not reviewed in the current chapter, but would be an acceptable screening tool. The Revised Conners' Parent and Teacher Rating Scales have a 12-item ADHD Index specifically constructed to discriminate well between children with and without ADHD. This would be the best choice of the measures reviewed in this chapter because of its brevity, ease of use, and psychometrics designed specifically for screening purposes.

SEIZURE CONSULT

In the case of the consult to address a possible psychogenic component to seizures, the purpose of the assessment is to answer a differential diagnostic question about the seizure behavior. The health care professional would review the medical chart and then conduct comprehensive interviews with Nicole and her parents. Although the interviews may provide important information by which to address the referral question, questionnaires and rating scales can provide helpful data. Ideally, the questionnaires should be completed and scored before the interviews are conducted, so the resulting profiles might provide fruitful hypotheses to test through while interviewing. The health care professional might wish to use behavioral screening tools to survey a wide spectrum of possible behavioral and emotional conditions, with at least one instrument including a somatization scale. It would be useful to have Nicole and her parents complete the measures to get multiple vantage points.

The BASC and the CBCL provide broad surveys of internalizing and externalizing behavioral problems. Both include scales assessing somatization, and have associated measures that Nicole can complete, for example, the Youth Self-Report Form and the Self-Report of Personality. In addition, two of the measures discussed in this chapter were specifically designed to assess the behavior of chronically ill children: the PBS and the Pediatric Inpatient Behavior Scale (PIBS). Although the psychometrics of these measures are not as strong as others such as the CBCL and the BASC, they do sample the relevant content domains. The PIBS was normed with nursing staff as raters in a pediatric hospital setting and includes scales for Oppositional–Noncompliant Behavior and Positive–Sociability. The medical staff working with Nicole would complete the

PIBS. The PBS was normed with parents as raters and includes scales such as Conduct, Deviation, and Health. Nicole's parents would complete the PBS. It may also be useful to assess Nicole's self-esteem using the Piers-Harris Self-Esteem Inventory or the Harter Perceived Self-Competence Scale for Children.

ALTERNATIVE MEDICINE RESEARCH PROJECT

As noted in the hemophilia clinic example, the investigator has a choice of the CBCL, the CRS, the PBS, or the BASC as dependent measures that include ADHD symptoms and behaviors. The matter is discussed further with Dr. Jones. He indicates that he wants to measure as many different facets of ADHD as possible, but that he is also interested in measuring other behavior problems such as oppositional behavior. In addition, he wants to look at other problems experienced by children with ADHD, such as anxiety, depression, and self-esteem deficits. He is not concerned about the length of the assessment because he is going to pay the subjects for completing the dependent measures. In addition, he wishes to collect data from teachers and parents, and to compare the impact of the interventions on teacher versus parent ratings. The PBS is eliminated because it does not have comparable teacher and parent versions, as do the other three instruments. Only the long versions of the parent and teacher CRS tap multiple aspects of ADHD symptoms. They yield scores for Oppositional, Cognitive Problems, Hyperactivity, the ADHD Index, the Global Index—Restless–Impulsive, the Global Index—Emotional Lability, the DSM-IV Inattention Symptom Score, the DSM-IV Hyperactive Impulsive Symptom Score, and the DSM-IV Total Symptom Score. Dr. Jones should include the Conners' Parent and Teacher Rating Scales—Revised Long Forms.

However, the CRS do not adequately tap depression, anxiety, and social withdrawal. The CBCL has scales for anxious–depressed and social problems, but anxiety and depression are not separated from each other. The BASC has separate scales for anxiety, depression, and withdrawal. Again, the Piers-Harris or Harter self-esteem measures can be used to assess improvements in self-concept after intervention implementation.

The four assessment examples discussed illustrate how the pediatric health care professional can balance information about the purpose of the assessment, who will rate the child, the band-width of the target behaviors, the psychometric characteristics of the measure, and the ease of use of the measure when selecting a behavioral screening measure. The guidelines are based upon a rational-deductive analysis of the assessment task and familiarity with the assessment measures. It would be preferable to have specific guidelines based upon empirical research with various pediatric health care assessment tasks. No such research currently exists. Future research may assist in evaluating the contribution of rating scales and questionnaires to the clinical, consultative, and research tasks of the pediatric health care clinician or researcher.

REFERENCES

Biederman, J., Faraone, S. V., Doyle, A., Lehman, B. K., Kraus, I., Perrin, J., & Tsuang, M. T. (1993). Convergence of the Child Behavior Checklist with structured interview-based psychiatric diagnoses of AD/HD children with and without comorbidity. *Journal of Child Psychology and Psychiatry, 34,* 1241–1251.

BEHAVIORAL ASSESSMENT SYSTEM FOR CHILDREN

Source

Reynolds, C. R., & Kamphaus, R. W. (1998). *BASC: Behavior Assessment System for Children Manual.* Circle Pines, MN: American Guidance Service.

Availability

American Guidance Service, Inc. 4201 Woodland Rd, Circle Pines, MN 55014–1796. Copyrighted.

Purpose. The BASC was developed as a screening measure of child and adolescent behavioral adjustment. The BASC differs from other screening measures of child adjustment because the scales were conceptually rather than empirically derived. The intent was to create an instrument that had a high degree of utility in clinical assessment settings. Items on the BASC load on only one scale, which also increases ease of clinical interpretation of scales.

Description. The BASC is available in three versions: parent report (BASC-PRS), teacher report (BASC-TRS), and child self-report (BASC-SRP). A structured developmental history (SDH) interview and a system for making classroom observations of the child are also available to be used in conjunction with the formal assessment measures.

BASC-PRS. The BASC-PRS assesses both child adaptive behaviors and problem behaviors. Response format is from 0 ("never") to 3 ("almost always"). Three different forms are available depending on the age of the child (preschool, child, adolescent). The BASC-PRS consists of three broad composite scales (Externalizing Problems, Internalizing Problems, and Adaptive Skills) and 12 subscales. The Behavioral Symptom Index (BSI) assesses the overall level of problem behaviors (adaptive behaviors are not included). In addition, the BASC-PRS includes an "F" index that serves as a validity check for negative response sets. A Spanish version of the BASC-PRS is available.

BASC-TRS. The BASC-TRS is very similar to the parent-report version. The main difference is scale composition. The BASC-TRS consists of four broad composite scales (Externalizing Problems, Internalizing Problems, School Problems, and Adaptive Skills) and 14 subscales. Again, the BSI assesses the overall level of problem behaviors and an "F" index is available as a validity check. Validity scales are also available and vary by the age version used.

BASC-SRP. The BASC-SRP has two different forms depending on the age of the child (child or adolescent). Response format is true or false. The BASC-SRP consists of three broad composite scales: School Maladjustment, Clinical Maladjustment, and Personal Adjustment. The Emotional Symptoms Index (ESI) assesses the overall level of adjustment (both problem scales and adaptive scales are included).

All three BASC versions are scored for clinical purposes by converting raw scores to T scores and percentile scores

Standardization and Norms. The instrument was standardized at 116 sites across the United States. The sample was representative of the population of U.S. children aged 4 to 18 in terms of gender and ethnicity. The manual includes three sets of norms: general population norms, general population norms that are gender specific, and clinical norms. Clinical norms were derived from clinical samples in outpatient mental health centers, inpatient psychiatric settings, residential schools, and school programs for children with emotional disorders.

Reliability and Validity. Test-retest reliability for the BASC-PRS was reported to range from .70 to .88, and for the BASC-TRS was reported to range from .82 to .91 across the three different age versions. Test-retest reliability for the BASC-SRP was reported to be .76. Internal consistency of the composite scales, BSI and ESI was reported to be high across all three versions and ranged from .85 to .97. Inter-rater reliability was reported to be high for the BASC-TRS and moderate for the BASC-PRS. Findings of only moderate agreement between fathers and mothers are consistent with previous reports of discrepancies in parents' views of the severity of child behavior problems.

Content validity was established by generating an initial item pool for the measure from clinicians, teachers, and students, as well as from existing child assessment measures. Two item tryouts were completed as part of preliminary scale construction, with subsequent item analyses completed to be sure that all retained items contributed to measurement and discrimination.

Factor analyses of the BASC-PRS, BASC-TRS, and BASC-SRP indicated that the conceptually derived composite scales for each form adequately fit the data. This supports the construct validity of the instrument. However, in each case, model testing less clearly supported loading of subscales onto theorized composite scales. In addition, BASC-PRS, BASC-TRS, and BASC-CRP ratings were obtained for children with a variety of psychiatric diagnoses, such as depression or conduct disorder. High concurrence between diagnostic category and elevated scale ratings (i.e., those with a diagnosis of major depression scored highest on the depression scale) also supports the construct validity of the instrument.

Criterion validity was established by comparison of BASC-PRS and BASC-TRS ratings to ratings on a variety of well-established parent and teacher behavior rating scales and comparison of the BASC-SRP to ratings on a variety of well-known adolescent personality inventories and behavioral rating scales. The instruments were consistently moderately to highly correlated. Criterion validity of the BASC-PRS has also been established in another study by examining the instrument's ability to predict membership in three mutually exclusive diagnostic groups. The BASC-PRS was found to have adequate utility in discriminating between groups.

Summary of Strengths and Limitations. The BASC is an excellent tool for assessing child behavior problems in the general population. Psychometrics of the instrument appear to be sound. The fact that scales were rationally rather than empirically derived makes the measure easier to interpret. Availability of parent, teacher, and child versions allow for cross-informant ratings that may be useful to both researchers and clinicians. However, a limitation of the scale when used in child health care settings is that it was not designed to assess children with medical illnesses. Therefore, several biases are possible, including inflated ratings on scales that rate somatization or include somatic symptoms. In addition, assessment of behavioral difficulties particular to children with medical disorders (e.g., cooperation during medical procedures) is not within the scope of the instrument.

Additional Readings

Doyle, A., Ostrander, R., Skare, S., Crosby, R., & August, G. (1997). Convergent and criterion-related validity of the Behavioral Assessment System for Children-Parent Rating Scale. *Journal of Consulting and Clinical Psychology, 26*, 276–284.

CHILD BEHAVIOR CHECKLIST

Source

Achenbach, T. M., & Rescorla, L. A. (2001) *Manual for ASEBA School Age Forms & Profiles*. Burlington, VT: University of Vermont Research Center for Children, Youth and Families.

Availability

From ASEBA, Room 6436, 1 South Prospect St. Burlington, VT 05401–3456. Copyrighted.

Purpose

The CBCL was developed as a general assessment instrument for child behavioral–emotional problems and competencies. It is a multiaxial assessment instrument that allows data to be obtained from multiple sources (i.e., child, parent, and teacher). The CBCL underwent a significant revision in 2001 (called the CBCL/6–18). The goal of this revision was to derive scales that were common across informants, as well as across gender and age, making cross-informant comparisons easier.

Description. The CBCL is available in three versions: parent report (CBCL/6–18, for 6–18 year olds), teacher report (TRF, for 6–18 year olds) and adolescent self-report (YSR, for 11–18 year olds). In addition, parent and caregiver–teacher report forms for 18 month to 5-year-olds are available. A semi-structured clinical interview (SCICA) and a system for making classroom observations of the child (DOF) are also available and can be used in conjunction with the questionnaire assessment measures. Recent revisions of the instrument include the addition of Diagnostic and

Statistical Manual (DSM) scales that are scored from the forms and allow users to view children's problems in terms of DSM diagnostic categories. The DSM-oriented scales are comprised of the Achenbach System of Empirically Based Assessment (ASEBA) items that experts from 16 cultures rated as very consistent with particular DSM diagnoses. Thus, ASEBA items can now be viewed in terms of both DSM-oriented and empirically derived scales for the same child.

All questionnaire scales for the instrument were empirically derived via factor analyses. The instrument's developers utilized an empirical rather than a theoretical approach to scale construction due to concerns about the limited knowledge available regarding the taxonomy of child mental health problems.

CBCL/6–18. The CBCL/6–18 assesses both child adaptive behaviors and problem behaviors. There are 112 items that assess problem behaviors and 20 items that assess adaptive behavior. Response format for problem behaviors is from 0 ("not true") to 2 ("very true"). The problem behavior items load onto two broad-band scales (Internalizing and Externalizing) and eight narrow-band scales (Rule Breaking, Aggressive Behavior, Withdrawn–Depressed, Somatic Complaints, Anxious–Depressed, Social Problems, Thought Problems, and Attention Problems). The adaptive behavior items load onto three scales: Activities, Social Competence, and School Competence. A Total Competence and Total Behavior Problems score are also provided.

TRF. The TRF is similar to the CBCL/6–18. There are 112 items that assess problem behaviors (95 are shared with the CBCL) and 16 items that assess academic performance and adaptive behavior. Response format for problem behaviors is the same as for the CBCL/6–18. Problem behavior items load onto the same scales as found on the CBCL/6–18. Other items load onto two scales: Adaptive Functioning and Academic Functioning.

YSR. Items on the YSR are similar to those on the CBCL/6–18. There are 105 problem behavior items (all are shared with the CBCL) and 14 adaptive behavior items. Response format for problem behaviors is the same for the CBCL/6–18. Problem behavior items load onto the same scales as found on the CBCL/6–18. Adaptive items load onto an Activities Scale and a Social Competence Scale. A Total Competence score is also provided.

All three versions of the CBCL are scored for clinical purposes by converting raw scores to T scores and percentiles. T scores of 70 are considered clinically significant for all scales. In order to facilitate comparison across different informants' versions of the CBCL, cross-informant scoring packages are also available that provide Q-correlations for scales across all informants.

Standardization and Norms. Two sets of norms are provided for the CBCL: general population and clinical norms. The normative sample for the 2001 revision of the CBCL was drawn from a national probability sample assessed in 1999. The sample was obtained in a fashion that ensured appropriate representation of the U.S. population with regard to ethnicity, SES, and geographical locale. Children referred for mental health services in the previous year were excluded. Approximately 2,000 CBCLs were utilized to derive norms for the general population sample. A clinical sample was also obtained. Children in the clinical sample were drawn from a variety of mental health and special education settings, including school special education programs, community mental health settings, child guidance centers, and residential treatment facilities. They were matched with children in the non-referred sample on the basis of gender, age, SES, and ethnicity.

Reliability and Validity. One week test-retest reliability for the CBCL/6–18 was reported to range from .80 to .94, and 2-week test-retest reliability for the TRF was reported to range from .60 to .95. Longer-term stability of the CBCL/6–18 was assessed in a study of low-birth weight children. One- to 2-year stabilities ranged from .43 for the Social Competence Scale to .82 for the Externalizing Scale. Stability of the TRF was also adequate across a 2-month interval for the majority of scales with the exception of Somatic Complaints. Internal consistency was generally reported to be high across all versions given that scales were derived via factor analysis techniques. Inter-rater reliabilities were obtained for the CBCL/6–18 by having two parents each complete a rating of their child. Reliabilities ranged from moderate to high, with the highest agreement obtained on scales assessing externalizing behavior. Inter-rater reliability was reported to be low to moderate for the TRF when teacher–teacher-aide ratings on the same student were compared, with the highest concordance again found on scales rating externalizing behavior.

Content validity for the original version of the CBCL was established by generating an initial item pool for the measure from clinicians and from the extant research literature. Pilot versions of the CBCL were tested with parents and revisions were made. Items were modified for the TRF and YSR and also pilot tested for appropriateness. Changes on six YSR and three TRF items were made for the 2001 revision of the forms. Children in the clinical (referred) sample scored significantly higher on the CBCL, TRF, and YSR than the non-referred sample, supporting the construct validity of the instrument. Criterion validity was established by comparing CBCL, TRF, and YSR ratings to ratings on a variety of well-established parent and teacher behavior rating scales. Correlations were consistently moderate to high on analogous scales.

Summary of Strengths and Limitations. The CBCL is an excellent tool for assessing child behavior problems in the general population. Empirical rather than rational derivation of scales makes the measure more difficult for clinicians to interpret. However, DSM-oriented scales are provided for scoring the 2001 version, which significantly improves usability for clinicians. Psychometrics of the instrument are sound and have been demonstrated in multiple studies. Availability of parent, teacher, and child versions allows for cross-informant ratings that may be useful to both researchers and clinicians. However, a limitation of the scale when used in child health care settings is that it was not designed to assess children with medical illnesses. Therefore if the instrument is used with a child with a health problem, several biases are possible. These include inflated ratings on scales that rate somatization or include somatic symptoms, despite the fact that CBCL somatic items are worded to avoid such misinterpretation by respondents. In addition, assessment of behavioral difficulties particular to children with medical disorders (e.g., cooperation during medical procedures) is not within the scope of the instrument. Finally, as the measure was designed to assess clinically significant behavioral disorders, it may have decreased sensitivity for identification of less serious behavior problems that are more characteristic of children with chronic medical illnesses.

Additional Readings

Achenbach, T. M., & Rescorla, L. A. (2000). *Manual for the ASEBA Preschool Forms and Profiles.* Burlington, VT: University of Vermont Research Center for Children, Youth and Families.

Achenbach, T. M., & Ruffle, T. M. (2001). *Medical Practitioners Guide for the Achenbach System of Empirically Based Assessment* (2nd ed.). Burlington, VT: University of Vermont Research Center for Children, Youth and Families.

Developers' Comments

The empirically based ASEBA syndromes are derived from bottom-up analyses that identify actual associations among problems reported for large samples of children. Some empirically based syndromes reflect distinctions that are not made in DSM diagnoses. For example, statistical analyses have repeatedly distinguished between aggressive and unaggressive conduct problems, such as lying, stealing, and associating with delinquent peers. This distinction is embodied in separate ASEBA syndromes designated as Aggressive Behavior and Rule-Breaking Behavior. The DSM combines both kinds of conduct problems in its criteria for conduct disorder. Clinicians who wish to evaluate children in relation to separate national norms for aggressive and rule-breaking behavior can view children in terms of their scores on the two syndromes. Clinicians can also evaluate children in terms of normed scores on the DSM-oriented ASEBA Conduct Problems scale.

The 1991 empirically based syndromes combined anxiety and depression into a single syndrome, which reflects general disposition toward what has come to be known as negative affect. The 2001 empirically based syndromes and DSM-oriented scales scored from the school-aged forms distinguish more clearly between the anxious and depressive aspects of negative affect (i.e., factor analyses have separated the more anxious aspects of negative affect into the Anxious–Depressed syndrome on the one hand and the more depressed aspects into the Depressed–Withdrawn syndrome on the other).

To avoid inflating scores on the ASEBA Somatic Complaints syndrome and DSM-oriented Somatic Problems scale when assessing children with physical illnesses, users can omit all somatic items related to a child's illness. The value of ASEBA instruments for assessing diverse kinds and degrees of behavioral–emotional correlates of medical conditions has been demonstrated in hundreds of studies of over 100 medical conditions.

CONNERS' PARENT RATING SCALE– REVISED

Source

Conners, C. K., Sitarenios, G., Parker, J. D., & Epstein, J. (1998). The revised Conners' Parent Rating Scale (CPRS-R): Factor structure, reliability and criterion validity. *Journal of Abnormal Child Psychology, 26,* 257–268.

Availability

Multi-Health Systems, 9008 Niagara Falls Blvd., North Tonawanda, NY 14120–2060. Copyrighted.

Purpose. The original Connors' Parent Rating Scale (CPRS) was developed as a screening measure of child and adolescent behavioral adjustment. A recent revision of the CPRS, the CPRS-R, was intended to address several deficits in the original instrument including use of a small, non-representative normative sample, a factor structure that varied across studies, and outdated content. The revised CPRS was also designed to facilitate diagnosis of ADHD and therefore may be most useful as a screening measure of ADHD versus other disruptive behavior disorders.

Description. The CPRS-R is a parent-report scale that can be used with children aged 3 to 17. Response format is from 0 ("not at all true") to 3 ("very much true"). It is available in both a short (27 item) and long version (80 items). The long version of the CPRS-R is comprised of the following scales: Oppositional, Cognitive Problems, Hyperactivity–Impulsivity, Anxious–Shy, Perfectionism, Social Problems, Psychosomatic, an ADHD Index, three DSM-IV Symptom scales, and the Conners Global Index. The DSM-IV Symptom scales are comprised of 18 items that were worded to conform to the DSM-IV criteria for ADHD and can therefore be used to facilitate formal psychiatric diagnoses. A teacher version, the Conners' Teacher Rating Scale–Revised (CTRS-R), is also available. The factor structure of the CTRS-R is the same as that of the parent version with the exception that the Psychosomatic scale is not included. This allows direct comparisons of behavior in the home and school context. The CPRS-R and CTRS-R are scored by converting raw scores to T-scores.

Standardization and Norms. Scoring for the CPRS-R was developed using a normative sample of 2,200 children attending 200 schools throughout the United States and Canada that served as recruitment sites. An additional clinical sample consisted of 91 children who had been referred to an outpatient ADHD clinic or who had been diagnosed with ADHD. Norms are available by age and by gender.

Reliability and Validity. Six week test-retest reliability for the CPRS-R was reported to be moderately strong for most scales, although stability of the perfectionism scale was weak (.13). Test-retest reliability of the CTRS-R was relatively better, with reliability scores ranging from .86 to .47. Internal consistency for the CPRS-R scales ranged from .75 to .94 and for the CTRS-R ranged from .73 to .95. Inter-rater reliability of the CPRS-R was not reported.

Content validity was established by generating an initial item pool and by conducting an item tryout as part of preliminary scale construction. Subsequent item analyses were completed to be sure that all retained items contributed to measurement and discrimination. Factor analysis was used to confirm scale structure of the instrument. Criterion validity of the CPRS-R and CTRS-R has been established by examining the instruments' ability to differentiate between children with and without formal ADHD diagnoses. Children with ADHD diagnoses scored significantly higher on several CPRS-R and CTRS-R scales. Discriminant function analyses suggested that sensitivity of the CPRS-R for ADHD was 92.3% and specificity was 94.5%. For the CTRS-R, sensitivity was 78.1% and specificity was 91.3%.

Summary of Strengths and Limitations. The revised CPRS-R has improved psychometric properties as compared to the original version, including a more representative normative sample and a stable factor structure with increased empirical support. However, stability of some of the CPRS-R scales (i.e., Social Problems) is low. Although the CPRS-R does provide information on a range of child behavior problems, the revised measure was primarily intended as a screening measure for ADHD, and therefore it may be less valid for assessing other behavior disorders. Comparability of the factors structure of the parent and teacher rating scales is useful in both a clinical and research context, as it allows the child's behavior to be compared across multiple contexts. A limitation of the scale when used in child health care settings is that it was not designed to assess children with medical illnesses. Therefore, several biases are possible, including inflated ratings on scales that rate somatization or include somatic symptoms.

Additional Readings

Conners, C. K., Sitarenios, G., Parker, J. D., & Epstein, J. (1998). Revision and restandardization of the Conners Teacher Rating Scale (CTRS-R): Factor structure, reliability and criterion validity. *Journal of Abnormal Child Psychology, 26,* 279–291.

Parker, J. D., Sitarenios, G., & Conners, C. K. (1996). Abbreviated Conner's Rating Scales revisited: A confirmatory factor analytic study. *Journal of Attention Disorders, 1,* 55–62.

PEDIATRIC BEHAVIOR SCALE

Source

Lindgren, S., & Koeppl, G. (1987). Assessing child behavior problems in a medical setting: Development of the Pediatric Behavior Scale. In R. J. Printz (Ed.), *Advances in behavioral assessment of children and families* (Vol. 3, pp. 57–90). Greenwich, CT: JAI.

Availability

From the first author, Department of Pediatrics, 345 CDD, University of Iowa College of Medicine, Iowa City, IA 52242.

Purpose.   The PBS was designed to assess the behavior of children seen in a medical setting. The PBS includes items that are not found on traditional child behavior rating scales, such as those that assess non-compliance with medical regimen, because it was designed for children with a medical illness. PBS scales were also conceptually rather than empirically derived. The intent was to create an instrument that had a high degree of clinical utility in pediatric settings. Therefore, items that rate cognitive development and school performance were included.

Description.   The PBS is a 165-item parent rating scale. Each item is rated on a 4-point scale ranging from 0 ("almost never or not at all") to 3 ("very often or very much"). The PBS is comprised of 24 subscales that assess problems in six domains: Conduct, Attention Deficits, Depression-Anxiety, Deviation, Health, and Cognition. Subscale scores may be totaled to calculate a score in each of these six domains. A Total Behavior Problems score may also be calculated. The PBS can be used with children aged 6–16. A teacher version of the PBS is also available. Raw scores may be converted to T-scores for the 24 subscales. Alternatively, raw scores for each of the 24 subscales, the six domains, and Total Behavior Problems may be compared to clinical cutoffs derived from a normative sample.

Standardization and Norms.   The authors indicate that normative data used to develop T-scores and clinical cutoffs were collected on 600 Iowa children who had no medical behavioral or learning problems. These children were between the ages of 6 and 12, with sampling stratified by age and gender. The sample included children of predominantly middle to upper middle class SES. Approximately 12% were minorities.

Reliability and Validity.   All available psychometric data reported on the PBS are for the school-aged version of the parent-rating scale. Psychometrics were established using a sample of 106 children seen in the divisions of pediatric neurology, pediatric psychology, and developmental disabilities at the University of Iowa. No information on the test-retest reliability (i.e., stability) of the PBS was reported. Internal consistency of the PBS was moderately strong for most subscales (median coefficient alpha = .83) and strong for the domain scores (median coefficient alpha = .91). Inter-rater reliability was estimated from a subsample of 33 children who had both parents complete the PBS. Reliabilities for the six domain scores ranged from .79 to .51, with relatively higher reliability coefficients obtained for scales that assess externalizing behavior problems.

Content validity was established by generating an initial pool of 400 items for the measure from pediatric psychologists. Items were eliminated, simplified or combined based upon further review by pediatric psychologists and pilot testing with parents. This resulted in a 165-item scale. Criterion validity was established by comparing the PBS scores of children with different psychiatric and medical diagnoses. For instance, children with ADHD scored significantly higher on the Attention, Impulsivity, Hyperactivity, Social Isolation, and Inappropriate Social Behavior subscales than did children with either neurological disorders (e.g., seizures) or specific developmental disorders, such as learning disabilities. Construct validity requires further study.

Summary of Strengths and Limitations. The PBS is one of the only instruments available that was specifically designed to measure child behavior problems among children seen in outpatient medical settings. It has the advantage of including items not found on traditional child behavior rating scales that are important when assessing medically compromised children (i.e., poor adherence to medical regimen). The available psychometric data on the instrument are preliminary but appear generally promising. However, until more extensive data are available, norms should be used with caution.

Additional Readings

Max, J. E., Castillo, C., Lindgren, S., & Arndt, S. V. (1998). The neuropsychiatric rating schedule: Reliability and validity. *Journal of the American Academy of Child and Adolescent Psychiatry, 37,* 297–304.

McCarthy, A. M., Lindgren, S., Mengeling, M. A., Tsalikian, E., & Engvall, J. C. (in press). Effects of diabetes on learning in children. *Pediatrics.*

Developers' Comments

As noted in the description of the PBS, it is one of the few measures designed to assess behavior problems in children treated in medical settings. It also assesses a wider range of cognitive and executive functions than is typical of broad-band behavioral rating scales. Several PBS subscales correlate well with data from neuropsychiatric interviews sensitive to changes in behavior, mood, and executive functioning following brain injury (Max, Castillo, Lindgren, & Arndt, 1998). Briefer screening versions of the PBS have been developed, including a 50-item scale assessing four empirically defined factors (i.e., Aggression–Opposition, Hyperactivity–Inattention, Depression–Anxiety, and Physical Complaints), as well as items assessing specific problems associated with diabetic children (including mood variability, fatigue, compliance, and learning; McCarthy, Lindgren, Mengeling, Tsalikian, & Engvall, in press).

PEDIATRIC INPATIENT BEHAVIOR SCALE

Source

Kronenberger, W. G., Carter, B. D., & Thomas, D. (1997). Assessment of behavior problems in pediatric inpatient settings: Development of the Pediatric Inpatient Behavior Scale. *Children's Health Care, 26,* 211–232.

Availability

From the first author, Riley Child Psychiatry Clinic, Riley Children's Hospital, 702 Barnhill Drive, Indianapolis, IN 46202–5200. Copyrighted.

Purpose. The PIBS is a structured behavior rating scale that was designed to provide a quantitative measure of children's behavior in an inpatient hospital setting. Because traditional behavior checklists have not been developed for use with pediatric inpatients, norms from such instruments may not be applicable to an inpatient population and instrument content may not include hospital-specific adjustment problems. The PIBS was intended to facilitate clinical care of physically ill children admitted to hospitals and to facilitate research with such populations. The PIBS was designed for use by hospital staff (i.e., nurses) and is therefore a staff-rating scale rather than a parent-rating scale.

Description. The PIBS is a 47-item instrument. Although the majority of PIBS items are problem behaviors, several are adaptive or prosocial behaviors. The respondent is asked to rate the frequency with which a child exhibits a given behavior. Response format is from 0 ("never") to 2 ("often"). The rating scale is appropriate for use with school-aged and adolescent children. The PIBS can be scored using 10 factor-analytically derived subscales (Oppositional–Non-compliant, Positive–Sociability, Withdrawal, Conduct Problems, Distress, Anxiety, Elimination Problems, Overactive, Self-Stimulation, and Self-Harm.) Subscale scores are calculated by averaging the items that load on each scale.

Standardization and Norms. The instrument was developed at two pediatric tertiary care hospitals in the midwestern United States. Two hundred twenty-one 5–18-year-old children admitted to these facilities had PIBS ratings completed by nursing staff who had assumed primary care for the child for at least a full shift. Children's medical diagnoses were varied and included hematology–oncology, pulmonary, diabetes, traumatic accidents, etc. PIBS ratings were obtained on two different samples of children: those who were referred to the pediatric psychology–psychiatry consultation liaison service (clinical sample) and those who were not referred (general pediatric sample). Means and standard deviations on the PIBS are provided for these two samples, but standard scores are not provided and would have to be derived. In addition, although there is some indication that PIBS scores may differ by age (i.e., younger children score higher), separate normative data for school-aged children and adolescents is not presented.

Reliability and Validity. No data on the test-retest reliability (i.e., stability) or internal consistency of the PIBS was reported. Inter-rater reliability on the PIBS was obtained by having two nurses provide independent ratings of 11 children that they cared for during the same shift. Acceptable inter-rater reliability ranging from .70 to .78 was obtained for four scales (oppositional, positive–sociable, distress, and overactive). The inter-rater reliability of four scales (conduct problems, elimination problems, self-stim, and self-harm) was assessed by calculating percent agreement due to a high frequency of scores of zero that made calculation of correlational reliability problematic. Percent agreement ranged from 91–100%.

Content validity was established by generating an initial item pool for the measure from pediatric care specialists who provided examples of specific behaviors exhibited by hospitalized children. Items were eliminated or combined based upon further review by pediatric psychologists, social workers, and nurses. This resulted in a 47-item scale. Construct validity of the PIBS was assessed in two ways. First, the general pediatrics sample was dichotomized based upon nurse ratings of degree of need for psychological intervention. Children who were classified as having a high need for intervention scored significantly higher on 7 of 10 PIBS subscales than children rated as having a low need for intervention. However, it should be noted that the same nurse provided both the PIBS rating and the rating of need for psychological intervention. This raises the possibility that findings are accounted for by method bias. Second, children in the clinical sample were compared with a subsample of the general pediatric sample matched for gender, diagnosis, and age. Children in the referred sample scored significantly higher on 2 of the 10 PIBS subscales than non-referred children.

Summary of Strengths and Limitations. The PIBS is one of the only instruments available that was specifically designed to measure child behavior in an inpatient pediatric setting. It has the advantage of including items not found on traditional child behavior rating scales that are highly salient for hospital staff caring for sick children (i.e., uncooperative with medical procedures). The available psychometric data on the instrument are preliminary, but appear generally promising. The PIBS may be particularly useful in general research on behavioral adjustment of inpatient pediatric populations or for program evaluation to determine the efficacy of inpatient consultation-liaison intervention services. However, the lack of extensive standardization makes its clinical utility limited at the present time.

Additional Readings

Kronenberger, W. G., Causey, D., & Carter, B. D. (2001). Validity of the Pediatric Inpatient Behavior Scale in an inpatient psychiatric setting. *Journal of Clinical Psychology, 57,* 1421–1434.

Developers' Comments

The PIBS has been used as a clinical, research, and program evaluation instrument in pediatric and psychiatric hospital settings. In studies conducted following the original scale development research projects, significant relationships have been found between PIBS scores and DSM-IV diagnoses (both on pediatric and psychiatric hospital units), clinician ratings of severity of behavior problems, pre-hospitalization child behavior problems, and family stress. Additionally, internal consistency of all subscales has been shown to be greater than .70 in a pediatric sample. Currently, we are completing a project studying a second large nonreferred sample of hospitalized physically ill children to replicate the norms from the 1997 study.

PEDIATRIC SYMPTOM CHECKLIST

Source

Jellinek, M. S., Murphy, J. M., & Burns, B. J. (1986). Brief psychosocial screening in outpatient pediatric practice. *Journal of Pediatrics, 109,* 371–378.

Availability

From the first author, Child Psychiatry Service, ACC 725, 15 Parkman St., Massachusetts General Hospital, Boston, MA 02114–3117.

Purpose. The Pediatric Symptom Checklist (PSC) is a brief behavioral screening questionnaire that was originally designed to measure children's behavioral adjustment during routine pediatric office visits. The PSC was intended to improve pediatricians' ability to recognize children with psychosocial impairments by providing a quantitative measure of behavior that can be completed in a short period of time. The PSC has subsequently been used in a variety of other settings, including schools.

Description. The PSC is a 35-item parent-rating scale. The respondent is asked to rate the frequency with which a child exhibits a given behavior. Response format is from 0 ("never") to 2 ("often"). The authors state that the scale is appropriate for use with children 4–16, although the majority of the PSC validation studies have not included children older than 12. It should also be noted that when used with preschoolers, the four PSC items that rate school behavior problems are not included. A total score on the PBS is obtained by summing all items. A cut-off score of 28 is used to identify school-aged children at risk for psychosocial difficulties and a cut-off score of 24 is used for preschoolers. A self-report version of the PSC, the PSC-Y, is also available for adolescents. Use of a cut-off score of 30 on the PSC-Y is recommended to identify adolescents with mental health problems.

Standardization and Norms. Cut-off scores for the PSC were initially generated using a sample of 206 6–12-year-old children seen in suburban pediatric practices in the eastern United States. The majority of these children were middle or upper class. However, findings have subsequently been replicated in other samples, including 123 children seen in an inner-city community clinic who were largely lower SES, minority, or both.

Reliability and Validity. Test-retest reliability for the PSC was calculated on a sample of 48 school-aged children over an interval of 4 months. The correlation coefficient for the total score was .86, suggesting parent ratings tended to be stable over time. Test-retest reliability for the PSC-Y was calculated on a sample of 90 adolescents over an interval of 4 months. The correlation coefficient for the total score was .45, while the kappa for the categorical agreement of PSC-Y scores was .50. This suggests only moderate stability for PSC-Y scores. Internal consistency for the PSC total score was calculated to be .89 when used with school-aged children and .78 when used with preschoolers (4- and 5-year-olds).

Content validity was established by generating an initial item pool from the Washington Symptom Checklist. The measure was then piloted on a general pediatrics inpatient unit in a tertiary care facility to determine whether it could distinguish children in need of psychiatric consultation. Construct validity of the PSC is supported by several studies that suggest that children with more risk factors for mental health difficulties (e.g., living in poverty, higher levels of family stress, or family history of mental health problems) are more likely to score in the clinically significant range on the PSC. Numerous studies of the criterion-related validity of the PSC have been undertaken. PSC scores have been found to be significantly related to ratings by mental health professionals on the Children's Global Assessment Scale, parent report of mental health problems on the Diagnostic Interview for Children and Adolescents, and school guidance counselor ratings of the need for school-based mental health intervention. Sensitivity and specificity scores have ranged from 87–95% and 68–100%, respectively. Again, criterion validity of the instrument has been demonstrated for children of a variety of socioeconomic and ethnic backgrounds. Criterion validity of the PSC-Y was established by comparing PSC-Y scores to scores on the Child Depression Inventory (CDI) and Revised Children's Manifest Anxiety Scale (RCMAS). The agreement in case classification between the CDI and PSC-Y was 84% and between the PSC-Y and RCMAS was 83%.

Summary of Strengths and Limitations. The PSC's brevity and ease of administration give it high clinical utility as a screening device. Several studies suggest that it improves recognition of children with mental health problems when compared with brief interview-type screening by physicians and that it identifies children in clinic and school settings who had not previously come to the attention of care providers. Psychometrics of the parent-report version of the PSC appear sound. This is generally true of the adolescent self-report version, although stability of scores is more questionable. In keeping with the developers' intent, the PSC provides information only with regard to the presence of mental health problems and does not provide any significant detail regarding the nature of these difficulties (e.g., whether they are externalizing or internalizing in nature, how severe they are). Therefore, its most obvious clinical application is as a mechanism for identifying children at risk for psychosocial difficulties who need comprehensive mental health assessment. The PSC has also been used in this fashion in research attempting to establish base rates of mental health problems in different populations (i.e., children with dermatologic conditions).

Additional Readings

Jellinek, M. S. (1998). Approach to the behavior problems of children and adolescents. In T. A. Stern, J. B. Herman, & P. L. Slavin (Eds.), *MGH Guide to psychiatry in primary care* (pp. 437–442). New York: McGraw-Hill.

Little, M., Murphy, J. M., Jellinek, M., Bishop, S., & Arnette, H. (1994). Screening 4 and 5 year old children for psychosocial dysfunction: A preliminary study with the Pediatric Symptom Checklist. *Developmental and Behavioral Pediatrics, 15,* 191–197.

Pagano, M., Cassidy, L., Little, M., Murphy, M., & Jellinek, M. (2000). Identifying psychosocial dysfunction in school-aged children: The Pediatric Symptom Checklist as a self-report measure. *Psychology in the Schools, 37,* 91–106.

Developers' Comments

The goal of the PSC is to alert the pediatrician to children with psychosocial dysfunction in major areas of their life (family, friends, school activities or self-esteem). Therefore, the PSC is not meant as a one stop screening instrument from office to mental health referral, but is designed to alert the care provider to the need to confirm the symptoms and complete a short functional interview. The most recent studies of the PSC show that in large populations, children who score higher on the PSC have higher primary care utilization. This work suggests that in addition to individual child screening, the PSC may be useful in populations to identify children who are "high utilizers" of primary care and specialty pediatric services.

PIERS-HARRIS 2

Source

Piers, E. V., & Herzberg, D. S. (2002). *Piers-Harris 2: Piers-Harris Children's Self Concept Scale* (2nd ed.) Western Psychological Services, Los Angeles, CA.

Availability

From the publisher, Western Psychological Services, 12031 Wilshire Blvd, Los Angeles CA 90025–1251. Copyrighted.

Purpose. The Piers-Harris 2 is a self-report, screening measure of self-concept in child and adolescents. The Piers-Harris 2 measures children's conscious self-perceptions. Self-concept is viewed as a relatively stable set of self-attributions that develops and stabilizes over the course of childhood.

Description. The Piers-Harris 2 is a 60-item scale that can be used with children aged 7 to 18. Response format is "yes–no." The Piers-Harris 2 consists of six subscales (Behavioral Adjustment, Intellectual and School Status, Physical Appearance and Attributes, Freedom From Anxiety, Popularity, Happiness, and Satisfaction) and a total score. In addition, two clinical validity indices, the Response Bias Index and Inconsistency Index, can be obtained. The Piers-Harris 2 is scored by converting raw scores to percentiles, T-scores, or both. The measure may be scored manually, by computer, or by mailing or faxing in forms to the publisher.

Standardization and Norms. Norms for the Piers-Harris were originally derived from two different samples. The sample used to derive norms for the total score consisted of 1,183 school-aged children from a rural area of Pennsylvania. Data from this sample were collected during the 1960s. The sample used to derive norms for the six subscales consisted of 485 school-aged children. The Piers-Harris 2 incorporates a new, nationally representative normative sample based on 1,387 students that closely resemble 2001 census data.

Reliability and Validity. Test-retest reliability for the Piers-Harris over intervals of 2 to 5 months was reported to be moderately strong and ranged from .71 to .75. Stability with ethnically diverse populations has been explored in several studies. Reliability coefficients for these groups are in the same range as those for Caucasian children. Internal consistency for the total score and the six subscale scores ranged from .76 to .93 in the 1996 sample.

Content validity was established by generating an initial item pool of 164 items and conducting an item tryout as part of preliminary scale construction. Items that were consistently endorsed positively or negatively by the majority of the sample (low discriminatory power) were dropped, whereas those that discriminated between children with very high or low scores on the Piers-Harris were retained. Construct validity was established by conducting factor analyses of the Piers-Harris in a number of different samples. Such analyses have generally supported the six-scale structure of the instrument, although it should be noted that the behavior, intellectual status, and physical appearance scales have the most consistent support. Criterion-related validity of the Piers-Harris has been established by examining the instrument's relationship to other measures of self-esteem and measures of behavioral and emotional functioning. The Piers-Harris has been found to be positively and significantly related to children's ratings on measures of self-esteem such as the Coopersmith Self-Esteem Inventory, Children's Self-Concept Scale, and negatively and significantly related to measures of anxiety and neuroticism.

Summary of Strengths and Limitations. The Piers-Harris has been extensively used as a screening measure of children's self-esteem. It is easy to administer and relatively brief. Concerns regarding the possibility of social desirability biases that are common to many self-esteem measures have been offset by the inclusion of clinical validity indices. The Piers-Harris 2 alleviates the concern regarding the original instrument's dated normative sample. As with all self-esteem instruments, users who intend to use the Piers-Harris in a research context should carefully consider theoretical issues related to the stability of the self-concept construct when deciding whether the total score or subscale scores are the most appropriate outcome measure. Finally, the manual includes studies of the Piers-Harris with special populations, such as children with developmental disabilities and chronic medical conditions.

SELF-PERCEPTION PROFILE FOR CHILDREN

Source

Harter, S. (1985). *Manual for the self-perception profile for children.* Denver, CO: University of Denver.

Availability

From the first author, University of Denver, Department of Psychology, 2155 S. Race Street, Denver, CO 80208–0204. Copyrighted.

Purpose. The author of the Self-Perception Profile for Children (SPPC) views self-concept as a construct that can be either domain specific (i.e., concept of self in the academic vs. athletic arena) or global (i.e., general self-worth). Children are believed to make different self-appraisals in different areas of competence. Therefore, the SPPC allows the user to measure perceived competence in a variety of domains and to obtain an independent measure of global self-esteem. As a result, more comprehensive data on self-worth can be obtained than would be available from a single self-concept score.

Description. The SPPC is a 36-item child self-rating scale. It is a revision of the Perceived Competence Scale for Children (PCSC). The SPPC can be used with children aged 8–15. A unique item response format is used to reduce social desirability biases. For each item, the child is first asked to choose which of two descriptors is most like them (i.e., "Some kids find it hard to make friends; some kids find it's pretty easy to make friends"). The child then rates whether the chosen descriptor is "sort of true" or "really true" of them. Each item is then rated on a 1 to 4 scale where a 1 indicates low perceived competence and a 4 indicates high perceived competence. The SPPC is comprised of five subscales that assess perceived competence in five specific domains (Scholastic Competence, Social Acceptance, Athletic Competence, Physical Appearance, and Behavioral Conduct) and a global self-worth scale. The original PCSC, in contrast, contained only three domain subscales (Cognitive, Social, and Physical Competence). Subscale scores are calculated by averaging the items that load on each scale.

A teacher version of the SPPC is available for use, although teachers rate only the five domain-specific scales. An instrument to assess perceived competence in younger children, the Pictorial Scale of Perceived Competence and Social Acceptance, is also available.

Standardization and Norms. The instrument was developed with four school-aged samples of 1,543 children residing in Colorado. Although limited information is available regarding these samples, children were predominantly middle class and 90% were Caucasian. Means and standard deviations on the SPPC are provided for these two samples, but standard scores are not provided and would have to be derived. SPPC scores appear to differ by age and gender (i.e., boys rate themselves more highly on the athletic competence scale than girls) and therefore normative data are presented by grade and gender.

Reliability and Validity. No data on the test-retest reliability (i.e., stability) of the SPPC were reported, although 3- and 9-month test-retest reliabilities for the original PCSC scale were reported to be adequate (.69–.87). Internal consistency of the SPPC was moderately strong for all subscales and ranged from .71 to .86.

Content validity for the original PCSC scale was established by generating an initial pool of 40 items for the measure from interviews with children and existing scales. Subsequent item analyses were completed to be sure that all retained items contributed to measurement and discrimination, resulting in a 28-item scale. However, specific information regarding the development of new items and revision of items for the SPPC is not provided.

Factor analyses generally suggested good construct validity for the SPPC. Each subscale was found to define its own factor, with all items loading substantially on the appropriate subscale and negligible cross-factor loading apparent. Again, no data on criterion validity of the SPPC were provided, although a variety of studies with the original PSCS suggest that the appropriate domain scores are significantly correlated with children's academic performance, sociometric status, and teacher ratings of athletic prowess.

Summary of Strengths and Limitations.   The SPPC is a useful scale for conducting research on self-esteem in children. Efforts have been made by the author to eliminate the social desirability biases inherent when obtaining reports of self-esteem. In addition, significant time was spent developing an instrument for which self-worth domain scores would be psychologically meaningful (i.e., academic domain, social domain, etc.) Those psychometric properties of the SPPC that are reported are generally sound, although limited information is available, particularly regarding criterion validity. Extensive information is available on the psychometrics of the scale's predecessor, the PCSC. However, given changes in items on the SPPC and addition of two new scales, the instruments cannot be considered to be synonymous. The SPPC has limited utility in a clinical context given the dearth of normative data available, although review of scores may yield qualitative information that helps direct further assessment or evaluation.

Additional Readings

Harter, S. (1982) The Perceived Competence Scale for Children. *Child Development, 53,* 87–97.
Harter, S., & Pike, R. (1984). The Pictorial Scale of Perceived Competence and Social Acceptance for Younger Children. *Child Development, 55,* 1969–1982.

TABLE 4.1
Disease-Specific Measures

Disease	Measure	Reference
Asthma	Asthma Problem Behavior Checklist (Revised)	Creer et al., 1989
	Childhood Asthma Symptom Checklist	Fitz & Overholser (1989)
	Usherwood Questionnaire	Usherwood, Scrimgeour, & Barber (1990)

(Continued)

TABLE 4.1 *(Continued)*

Disease	Measure	Reference
Cystic Fibrosis	Cystic Fibrosis Problem Checklist	Sanders, Gravestock, Wanstall, & Dune (1991)
Diabetes	Diabetic Adjustment Scale	Sullivan (1979, 1989)
	Diabetes Coping Measure	Welch (1994)
	Diabetes Pictorial Scale	Garrison & Biggs (1990a, 1990b)
	Teen Adjustment to Diabetes Scale	Wysocki (1993)
	Problem Areas in Diabetes Scale	Welch, Jacobson, & Polonsky (1997)
Oncology	Deasy-Spinetta Behavioral Questionnaire	Deasy-Spinetta (1981)

References

Creer, T. L., Wigal, J. K., Tobin, D. L., Kotses, H., Snyder, S. E., & Winder, J. A. (1989). The Revised Asthma Problem Behavior Checklist. *Journal of Asthma, 26*, 17–19.

Deasy-Spinetta, P. (1981). The school and the child with cancer. In J. J. Spinetta & P. Deasy-Spinetta (Eds.), *Living with childhood cancer* (pp. 153–168). St. Louis, MO: C. V. Mosby.

Fitz, G. K., & Overholser, J. C. (1989). Patterns of response to childhood asthma. *Psychosomatic Medicine, 51*, 347–355.

Garrison, W. T., & Biggs, D. (1990a). The Diabetes pictorial scale: A direct measure of young children's knowledge, attitudes, and behavior relevant to their insulin-dependent diabetes mellitus. *The Diabetes Educator, 16*, 21–22.

Garrison, W. T., & Biggs, D. (1990b). Young children's subjective reports about their diabetes mellitus: A validation of the diabetes pictorial scale. *The Diabetes Educator, 16*, 304–308.

Sanders, M. R., Gravestock, F. M,. Wanstall, K., & Dune, M. (1991). The relationship between children's treatment-related behaviour problems, age and clinical status in cystic fibrosis. *Journal of Pediatric Child Health, 27*, 290–294.

Sullivan, B. (1979). Adjustment in diabetic adolescent girls: I. Development of the diabetic adjustment scale. *Psychosomatic Medicine, 41*, 119–126.

Sullivan, B. (1989). Adjustment in diabetic adolescent girls. II. Adjustment, self-esteem, and depression. *Psychosomatic Medicine, 41*, 127–138.

Usherwood, T. P., Scrimgeour, A., & Barber, J. H. (1990). Questionnaire to measure perceived symptoms and disability in asthma. *Archives of Disabled Children, 65*, 779–781.

Welch, G. W. (1994). The Diabetes Coping Measure: A measure of cognitive and behavioral coping specific to diabetes. In C. Bradley (Ed.), *A guide to psychological measurement in diabetes research and practice* (pp. 391–404). London: Harwood Academic.

Welch, G. W., Jacobson, A. M., & Polonsky, W. H. (1997). The problem areas in diabetes scale: An evaluation of its clinical utility. *Diabetes Care, 20*, 760–766.

Wysocki, T. (1993). Associations among parent-adolescent relationships, metabolic control and adjustment to diabetes in adolescents. *Journal of Pediatric Psychology, 18*, 443–454.

5

Child Development

Michelle Macias
Medical University of South Carolina, Department of Pediatrics

Conway F. Saylor
The Citadel Department of Psychology

INTRODUCTION

Throughout a child's early years, reliable monitoring of developmental milestones is necessary to identify global delay or a specific delay in areas such as receptive language, expressive language, social skills, and fine or gross motor functioning. The goal of early developmental screening is to identify problems at the earliest stage of development, when treatment is more effective (Frankenburg, 1994). Additionally, developmental screening is used to monitor progress, detect changes in developmental rate, or identify a loss of skills over time.

Public Law 99–457, subsequently reauthorized under the Individuals with Disabilities Education Act (IDEA; Pub. L. 105–17), mandates the identification and placement in early intervention programs of young children with developmental disabilities. Accurate identification of those in need of services based on a prenatal and perinatal history alone is difficult. Thus, a critical component of pediatric care is developmental screening or assessment, but the choice of an appropriate screening instrument is often difficult. Many measures are characterized by poor standardization, lengthy administration time, inadequate instructions and scoring criteria, lack of interpretive guidelines, and questionable reliability and validity (Glascoe, Martin, & Humphrey, 1990). Ideal screening measures are easily administered, brief, inexpensive, norm-referenced, given in a standardized manner, objective, reliable, and valid. Too often the professional has the dilemma of choosing between a measure that is more psychometrically sound and one that is more practical within the primary pediatric care setting.

Despite widespread acceptance of the need for early detection of developmental and behavioral problems in children, developmental screening instruments are not routinely used in many pediatric settings (Casey & Swanson, 1993). Reasons include inadequate time available for administration, inadequate training in their use, uncertainty about disposition with undesirable results, and lack of knowledge of the usefulness of early identification and subsequent intervention (Casey & Swanson, 1993). In addition, no consensus exists on how to optimally perform early identification (Glascoe & Dworkin, 1995). In general practice, a well-founded rationale exists for use of developmental surveillance–monitoring or prescreening rather than full developmental testing because of these constraints and concerns (Squires, Nickel, & Eisert, 1996).

Prevention includes any process that can limit the progression of disease at an earlier stage. Developmental screening is therefore preventative in nature, as the primary goal is to identify deviations from normal earlier than they would usually be determined. Primary prevention is complete prevention of disease occurrence. Secondary prevention is early detection of a problem before the obvious symptom stage. Tertiary prevention is identification and treatment of a problem after recognizable symptoms exist. Developmental screening is generally felt to be a form of secondary prevention (Lesser, 1972).

LEVELS OF DEVELOPMENTAL EVALUATION

Different levels of assessment can be utilized depending on the purpose of the evaluation. "Developmental surveillance" utilizes caretaker report, making accurate longitudinal observations of children, and obtaining a relevant developmental history as a method of evaluating developmental progress (Glascoe & Dworkin, 1993). "Prescreening" requires caretaker completion of a brief questionnaire or short, structured interview to identify children needing further screening testing (Squires et al., 1996). "Developmental screening" is a brief, hands-on evaluation (usually administered by a physician, nurse, or psychologist), intended to identify those children with deviations from normal, who will need a more detailed and definitive developmental assessment for diagnosis. "Assessment" involves the use of more detailed testing, and results in a diagnosis (Aylward, 1997).

DOMAINS OF DEVELOPMENT

Early development is usually divided into four main domains: (a) motor skills (fine and gross motor); (b) language (receptive, expressive, and speech); (c) cognitive (non-verbal problem solving); and (d) personal-social–adaptive (self-help); (Capute & Accardo, 1996). These areas generally conform to those identified by IDEA (Pub. L. 105–17) as needing early identification of delays. One of the difficulties of developmental assessment, particularly at earliest stages, is that most observable behaviors involve more than one domain. If one domain is compromised due to a disabling condition, it can be difficult to accurately determine function in others. For example, in the first 2 years of life, many of the cognitive abilities of infants are inferred from their visual-motor responses to a problem-solving task with objects such as cubes and rings. Therefore, a fine motor impairment will interfere with accurate assessment of early cognitive abilities. Toddlers who lack expressive language likewise have difficulty demonstrating their cognitive capacities for verbal problem-solving tasks. Another trade-off professionals have to make in selecting measures is to get accurate measures of only a few domains, or to try to document overall function by measuring performance on tasks that require integration of more than one domain.

SELECTION OF INSTRUMENTS
FOR DEVELOPMENTAL SCREENING

The selection of appropriate assessment and screening tests is based on child age and stage of development, as well as practical and psychometric considerations. The following six criteria can be utilized to assess various screening tests:

1. Acceptability: The screening test must be acceptable to the child screened and their family, the professionals who receive referrals, and the community.

2. Simplicity: Screening tests should be easy to teach, learn, and administer.

3. Cost: The cost includes the equipment, personnel time, personal costs to the individual being screened, cost of inaccurate results, and the total cost of the test relative to the benefits of early recognition of a developmental problem.

4. Appropriateness: Appropriateness is based on its applicability of the screening test to the population being screened.

5. Reliability (precision): Screening tests should generate consistent results in repeated trials or when administered by different professionals.

6. Validity (accuracy): Screening tests should give a true measure of the characteristic or developmental skill being tested (Stangler, Huber, & Routh, 1980).

Sensitivity and specificity are the most important indicators of concurrent and predictive validity, especially for developmental screening instruments. Sensitivity (true positives) is a measure of how well the screening measure identifies the children with developmental problems. Children with developmental problems who are not identified by the screening test are known as false negatives. Specificity (true negatives) refers to the proportion of children who do not have a developmental problem and whom the test appropriately identifies as normal. Normal children incorrectly identified by the test as being delayed are known as false positives. Specificity is therefore a measure of how well the screening test identifies appropriately developing children as normal. Sensitivity is calculated by dividing the number of delayed children correctly identified (true positives) by the number of correctly identified plus number of delayed children not identified by the test (true positives + false negatives), multiplied by 100. Specificity is calculated by dividing the number of children correctly identified as being normal (true negatives) by the number of correctly identified normal children plus those incorrectly identified by the screening test as being delayed (false positives), multiplied by 100 (Aylward, 1994, 1997). Arguments have been made to more correctly term sensitivity as co-positivity and specificity as co-negativity because of the lack of a true gold standard in developmental assessment (Aylward, 1997).

A trade-off exists between sensitivity and specificity. That is, if the sensitivity of a measure is high (designed to maximally identify children with delays), the specificity will be lower, and vice-versa (Aylward, 1997). Sensitivity rates of 70% and specificity rates of 60–70% are generally felt to be acceptable values in developmental screening (Glascoe, 1997)

Positive and negative predictive values are also important concepts to consider in developmental screening. The predictive validity of either a positive or negative screening test indicates how accurate the screening result is according to the screening test. The positive predictive value is the proportion of children with a positive test result who are actually delayed. The negative predictive value is the proportion of children with a negative test result who are truly developing normally. The positive predictive value may be calculated as the number of correctly identified delayed children (true positives), divided by the number of correctly identified delayed children plus those incorrectly identified as being delayed (false positives). The negative predictive value is calculated as the number of correctly identified normal children, divided by the number of correctly identified normal children plus those children incorrectly identified as developing normally (false negatives). In developmental screening, a positive predictive value of 50% is felt to be acceptable (Glascoe, 1997).

The purpose of this chapter is to present a logical and systematic approach to the evaluation of child development screening tests used in a pediatric setting. Currently, multiple instruments exist that can be used in screening for developmental delays. The reviews that follow highlight the logistics of administration, domains, psychometric properties, strengths, and liabilities for many of the most commonly recommended tests. Researchers and clinicians need to weigh the areas of strength of each test against their purposes in testing to select the instruments best suited to their populations and missions.

REFERENCES

Aylward, G. (1994). *Practioner's guide to developmental and psychological testing.* New York: Plenum.

Aylward, G. (1997). Conceptual issues in developmental screening and assessment. *Journal of Developmental and Behavioral Pediatrics, 18*(5), 50–59.

Casey, P., & Swanson, M. (1993). A pediatric perspective of developmental screening in 1993. *Clinical Pediatrics, 32,* 209–212.

Capute, A. J., & Accardo, P. J. (1996). A neurodevelopmental perspective on the continuum of developmental disabilities. In A. J. Capute, P. J. Accardo, & J. Pasquale (Eds.), Developmental disabilities in infancy and childhood (pp. 7–41). Baltimore, MD: Brooks Publishing Co.

Frankenburg, W. (1994) Preventing developmental delays: Is developmental screening sufficient? *Pediatrics 93*(4), 586–593.

Glascoe, F. P. (1997). Parents' concerns about children's development: Prescreening technique or screening test? *Pediatrics, 99,* 522–528.

Glascoe, F. P., & Dworkin, P. H. (1993). Obstacles to effective developmental surveillance: Errors in clinical reasoning. *Journal of Developmental and Behavioral Pediatrics, 14,* 344–349.

Glascoe F. P., & Dworkin, P. H. (1995). The role of parents in the detection of developmental and behavioral problems. *Pediatrics, 95,* 829–836.

Glascoe, F. P, Martin, E. D., & Humphrey, S. (1990). A comparative review of developmental screening tests. *Pediatrics, 86,* 547–554.

Lesser, K. (1972). Health and education screening of school-age children-definition and objectives. *American Journal of Public Health, 62,* 191–198.

Squires, J., Nickel, R., & Eisert, D. (1996) Early detection of developmental problems: Strategies for monitoring young children in the practice setting. *Journal of Developmental and Behavioral Pediatrics, 17,* 420–427.

Stangler, S. R., Huber, C. J., & Routh, D. K. (1980). *Screening, growth and development of preschool children: A guide for test selection.* New York: McGraw-Hill.

AGES AND STAGES QUESTIONNAIRES

Source

Squires, J., Bricker, D., & Potter, L. (1997). Revision of a parent-completed developmental screening tool: Ages and Stages Questionnaire. *Journal of Pediatric Psychology, 22,* 313–328.

Availability

From the publisher, Brookes Publishing Co, P.O. Box 10624 Baltimore MD 21285–0624. Copyrighted.

Purpose. The Ages and Stages Questionnaires (ASQ) are screening questionnaires designed to identify infants and young children with developmental delays. They are revised versions of the Infant-Child Monitoring Questionnaires. The ASQ were developed in order to allow a child's caregivers to provide quantitative information regarding developmental abilities. Such a screening system was viewed as an economical means of identifying children at risk for developmental difficulties.

Description. The ASQ are a series of 19 developmental assessment questionnaires that can be administered at 2- to 6-month intervals when the child is between 4 and 60 months of age. The measure has been recently revised to improve readability and eliminate items that were rarely endorsed. Each questionnaire is comprised of three parts: demographic information, 30 developmental items, and seven open-ended questions about the child's behavior and development. The response format for the 30 developmental items is "yes" (child performs the item) "sometimes" (child performs the item, but not consistently) or "not yet" (child does not yet perform the item). The developmental items load onto five scales: Gross Motor, Fine Motor, Communication, Problem Solving, and Personal-Social. Scales were theoretically rather than empirically derived. Cut-off scores are provided for each subscale so that the child can be identified as at risk for developmental delays or not.

Standardization and Norms. Raw scores on the ASQ are not converted to standard scores. Rather, the child's score is judged relative to whether it falls above or below a cut-off score indicative of likely developmental delay (and clinically of the need for further assessment). Cut-off scores are those that fall two standard deviations from the mean within each domain at each age. Cutoff scores were derived using a sample of 2,008 children. The sample included children chosen due to medical risk factors (e.g., NICU admission), children chosen due to environmental risk factors (e.g., child protective services involvement) and a normative group with no known risk factors. The authors report the following distribution of annual income of families: $5,000 (13%); $5,001–10,000 (13%); $10,001–$15,000) (12%); $15,001–$20,000 (15%); $20,001–$25,000 (14%); and more than $25,000 (32%). Receiver operating characteristics (ROC) analyses were used to determine cut-off points that provided optimal sensitivity and specificity for the ASQ.

Reliability and Validity. Test-retest reliability of the ASQ was established using a subset of 175 parent ratings. Two-week stability of ASQ ratings as measured by percent agreement on the child's classification (delayed–not delayed) was reported to be 94% overall. Data were not provided regarding any variability in test-retest reliability based upon the age of the child being rated. Internal consistency of the ASQ was reported to be moderately strong. Coefficient alphas ranged from .49–.87. Internal consistency appeared to be poorest for the Personal–Social scale. Inter-rater reliability was also established on a subsample of 112 children. Although it should be noted that examiner ratings were completed up to 2 weeks apart from those of parents, parents and professional examiners both rated children. Percent agreement on the child's classification (delayed–not delayed) was 94% overall. In another study, inter-rater reliability was established for both a low-income and middle-income group of parents. Percent agreement between parent and professional examiner in the low-income group was 85% overall, suggesting that the instrument can be used reliably with persons of various socio-economic backgrounds.

Limited information regarding the establishment of content validity of the ASQ is available. An item pool for the original Infant-Child Monitoring Questionnaires was developed by using items from existing developmental questionnaires and assessment instruments. Subsequently, items were assigned to questionnaires based upon their potential ability to discriminate children performing below the norm. Eight items were eliminated and replaced with more easily understood items in the construction of the ASQ. No information is presented regarding the construct validity of the instrument. Criterion validity was established by comparing the child's classification based upon the ASQ (i.e., delayed–not delayed) to his classification based upon standardized psychological testing. Sensitivity across all ages was calculated to be 75% and specificity was calculated to be 86%.

Summary of Strengths and Limitations. The ASQ have several strengths as a screening tool for assessing child developmental status.

Brevity and ease of administration makes them ideal as a clinical screening device. The ASQ also allow assessment of parent perceptions of child development. Psychometric properties appear to be promising, although relatively low internal consistency of some scales is of concern and additional information regarding validity (i.e., construct validity, predictive validity) is warranted. A potential drawback of the instrument is the 19 questionnaire structure, which means that children can only be assessed at predetermined ages. While ideal for clinical practices that schedule children for well-child checkups in such a fashion, this structure limits research utility when infants and young children of variable ages need to be assessed.

Additional Readings

Squires, J. K, Potter, L., & Bricker, D. D. (1998). Parent-completed developmental questionnaires: Effectiveness with low and middle income parents. *Early Childhood Research Quarterly, 13,* 345–354.

Developers' Comments

The ASQ were revised in 1999 to better accommodate the screening of young children between the ages of 4 months and 5 years. The 19 intervals of the ASQ allow for efficient and effective screening in both home and clinic settings. A companion tool to the ASQ, the Ages and Stages Questionnaires: Social-Emotional (ASQ: SE) was recently developed to identify young children with potential problems in social and emotional development.

AUTISM BEHAVIOR CHECKLIST

Source

Krug, D. A., Arick, J., & Almond, P. (1993). *Autism screening instrument for behavioral planning: 2nd Ed. Examiners' Manual.* Austin, TX: Pro-Ed.

Availability

From the publisher, Pro-Ed, 8700 Shoal Creek Boulevard, Austin, TX 78757. Copyrighted.

Purpose.   The Autism Behavior Checklist (ABC) is a screening checklist designed to identify persons with autism. It is one component of the

Autism Screening Instrument for Educational Planning-II, which contains five separately standardized subtests that can be used to make diagnoses and develop educational interventions for persons with autism.

Description. The ABC consists of 57 items rated as present or absent for a given child. Items fall on five subscales (Sensory, Relating, Body and Object Use, Language, and Social Interaction and Self-Help). Each item is assigned a differential weight depending on how highly related it is to the diagnosis of autism. Item weights are summed to calculate a total score. Although the ABC was originally designed to be completed by teachers, it has also been used with parents. A cut-off score is provided to allow interpretation of the ABC total score as indicative of autism or not.

Standardization and Norms. Three samples were used in the development of the ABC. Sample one consisted of 1,049 individuals from 18 months to 35 years of age including 172 persons with autism, 777 persons with other disabilities, and 100 with no disabilities. The second sample consisted of 63 autistic individuals aged 3 to 23 years. The third sample consisted of 953 adults of whom 95% had severe mental retardation. No other information regarding ethnicity SES or residence of the sample was provided. Normative data (i.e., means and standard deviations) are available for the sample, but standard scores are not provided and would have to be derived.

Reliability and Validity. Test-retest reliability for the ABC has not been reported. Internal consistency of the ABC total score has been reported to be adequately high (.87). However, internal consistency of the subscales is more variable. The authors evaluated inter-rater reliability in a sample of 42 raters who rated 14 children. Percent agreement was reported to be high (95%). However, other research on the inter-rater reliability of the ABC suggests that parents' and teachers' ABC ratings do not agree (e.g., $r = .08$ for the ABC total score).

Content validity was established by generating an initial item pool for the measure from other autism screening instruments and expert descriptions of autistic children. Subsequently items were reviewed by 26 experts in the field of autism and by 3,000 special educational professionals and final item revisions were made. Construct validity was established by comparing scores of autistic subjects with those of subjects with other disabilities and children that were not handicapped. The autistic group scored significantly higher than subjects with other diagnoses. Another study compared scores on the ABC of autistic subjects with scores of subjects with mental retardation, pervasive developmental disorder, language disorder, and schizophrenia. Again, autistic subjects had the highest scores. Criterion validity has been established by comparing ratings on the ABC to ratings on the Childhood Autism Rating Scale (CARS). Correlations between the ABC total score and the CARS total score were moderately strong (.67). A recent study also compared the ABC to the Pervasive Developmental Disorders Rating Scale (PDDRS). Correlations between the total scores for the two instruments were strong (.80). The phi coefficient assessing the relationship between the instruments' classification status was moderately strong (.68).

Summary of Strengths and Limitations. The ABC is administered in a questionnaire format that makes it easy to administer and score. This is a significant advantage given that many screening tools for autism require significant training on the part of the rater. The psychometric properties of the ABC are generally sound. However, the majority of reliability and validity studies have been completed with professionals rather than parents. This should be taken into account when deciding what type of informant to utilize.

Additional Readings

Eaves, R., Campbell, H., & Chambers, D. (2000). Criterion-related and construct validity of the Pervasive Developmental Disorders Rating Scale and the Autism Behavior Checklist. *Psychology in the Schools, 37,* 311–321.
Krug, D. A., Arick, J., & Almond, P. (1980). Behavioral checklist for identifying severely handicapped individuals with high levels of autistic behavior. *Journal of Child Psychology and Psychiatry, 21,* 221–229.

BAYLEY INFANT NEURODEVELOPMENTAL SCREENER

Source

Aylward, G. P. (1995). *Bayley Infant Neurodevelopmental Screener.* San Antonio, TX: Psychological Corporation.

Availability

From the publisher, The Psychological Corporation, 19500 Bulverde, San Antonio, TX 78259. Copyrighted.

Purpose. The Bayley Infant Neurodevelopmental Screener (BINS) is a screening test designed to identify infants and young children who are at risk for developmental and neurodevelopmental delays. It has primarily been used in settings where high-risk infants are followed (e.g., developmental follow-up clinics for children admitted to neonatal intensive care units at birth).

Description. The BINS consists of a subset of items from the Bayley Scales of Infant Development-II (BSID-II), but also includes items that measure neurological status (e.g., ratings of active and passive tone in arms and legs). It can be used with children between 3 and 24 months of age. Depending on the child's age, one of six item sets, each consisting of 11–13 items, is given. This allows for rapid administration (approximately 10 minutes). Four areas are assessed: Basic Neurological Functions–Intactness (e.g., muscle tone and head control), Receptive Functions (e.g., visual and auditory input), Expressive Functions (e.g., oral skills and motor skills), and Cognitive Processes (e.g, memory and problem solving). Items on the BINS are scored as "non-optimal" or "optimal." An overall score is derived by summing all items passed within the item set. Cut-off scores are provided so that the child can be identified as at high, moderate, or low risk for developmental delay.

Standardization and Norms. Two samples were utilized when standardizing the BINS and developing test norms. The first sample consisted of normal infants recruited so as to be demographically representative of the U.S. population with regard to gender, ethnicity, geographic location, and parents' educational level. The second clinical sample was recruited from neonatal intensive care units, and included children with a variety of medical problems such as prematurity.

Reliability and Validity. Test-retest reliability of the BINS was reported to range from .71 to .81 depending on child age. Internal consistency of the BINS was reported to be moderate to strong. Coefficient alphas ranged from .73-.85 across age. Inter-rater reliability was also established and ranged from .79 to .96.

In support of the construct validity of the BINS, scores have been found to be related to indices of severity of medical problems encountered by the child, although the magnitude of these correlations was relatively small. For example, in a population of children who had been hospitalized in a neonatal intensive care unit at birth, BINS scores were related to length of hospitalization and a medical risk index. Criterion validity of the BINS in a high-risk infant population was established by comparing BINS scores to those obtained using the BSID-II. When "high risk" categorization on the BINS was compared with Mental Development Index scores < 70 on the BSID-II, sensitivity and specificity were calculated to be

64% and 87%, respectively. Predictive validity has been established in at least two studies. The first compared BINS scores at 6 months to scores on the BSID-II scores at 1 year. BINS scores were significantly associated with scores on both the Mental and Psychomotor Development Indices. The second study investigated the relationship between infants' BINS categorization (i.e., low, moderate, or high risk) and their scores on intelligence tests at age 3. Children who scored in the high-risk group at 6, 12, or 24 months of age had significantly lower cognitive abilities at 3 years of age than children in either the moderate- or low-risk group.

Summary of Strengths and Limitations. The BINS is one of the few psychometrically sound tests available that allows examiners to screen young infants for developmental delays. It is also brief and easily administered by examiners with a variety of backgrounds (e.g., physicians, nurses, and psychologists). The BINS has a high degree of sensitivity, which is desirable in a screening instrument intended to be used in a high-risk population where underreferral for intervention services is problematic. A drawback of the instrument when used for clinical purposes is the three-tiered classification structure, since studies conducted to date on the BINS do not clarify whether children who fall into the moderate-risk group are in need of comprehensive developmental assessment or not. However, BINS scoring does allow infants in the moderate-risk group to be categorized as "high-moderate" or "low-moderate" risk, which may assist with referral decisions.

Additional Readings

Aylward, G. P., & Verhulst, S. J. (2000). Predictive utility of the Bayley Infant Neurodevelopmental Screener (BINS) risk status classification: Clinical interpretation and application. *Developmental Medicine and Child Neurology, 42,* 25–31.

Macias, M., Saylor, C., Greer, M. K., Charles, J. M., Bell, N., & Katikaneni, L. D. (1998). Infant screening: The usefulness of the Bayley Infant Neurodevelopmental Screener and the Clinical Adaptive Test/Clinical Linguistic Auditory Milestone Scale. *Developmental and Behavioral Pediatrics, 19,* 155–161.

CHILD DEVELOPMENT INVENTORY

Source

Ireton, H. (1992). *The Child Development Inventory Manual.* Minneapolis, MN: Behavioral Science Systems.

Availability

From the publisher, Behavioral Science Systems, P.O. Box 580274, Minneapolis, MN 55458. Copyrighted.

Purpose. The Child Development Inventory (CDI) is a parent-report measure for the assessment of developmental status of young children whose development is a concern. It was intended to provide a systematic approach to obtaining developmental information that would compliment professional observations and formal test results. In addition, it was designed to be easily understood by parents and to more systematically involve them in the assessment process.

Description. The CDI is a revision of the original 1972 Minnesota Child Development Inventory (MCDI). It can be used with children aged 15 months to 6 years. It consists of 270 developmental items and a 30-item problem checklist that covers health, development, and behavioral problems. The response format is "yes" (child performs the item) or "no" (child does not yet perform the item). The developmental items load onto nine scales: Social, Self-Help, Gross Motor, Fine Motor, Expressive Language, Language Comprehension, Letters, Numbers, and General Development. Scale scores are compared to cut-off scores that identify the child's development as falling in the normal, borderline, or delayed range. Items on the problem checklist are not scored, but can be reviewed for presence–absence. The CDI manual also provides information on the frequency with which these items were positively endorsed in the normative sample.

It should be noted that other screening versions of the CDI, covering smaller developmental windows, are also available. These include the Infant Development Inventory, the Child Development Review, and the Preschool Development Inventory.

Standardization and Norms. Norms for the CDI were derived from a sample of 568 children from South St. Paul, Minnesota aged 12 months to 6 years. This was a working-class community with an average parental education of 13 years and a mean IQ of 100 for elementary school children. The sample was 95% Caucasian. Children with major developmental disabilities were excluded from the normative sample. The authors note that because of the characteristics of the normative sample, the CDI should be used with caution for minority children or those where parents have fewer years of education. However, at least one other study has shown that the CDI can be used validly with parents with lower levels of education.

Norms are represented in mean scores by age level for each scale. A child's raw scores are plotted on the CDI Profile. Results are interpreted as: (a) functioning around mean score for age level (normal) and (b) borderline (only 70 to 80% of age level) or delayed (less than 70% of age level). The authors state that standard scores were not used so that results could be easily interpreted by both professionals and non-professionals.

Reliability and Validity.   Limited data on the reliability of the CDI are available. Test-retest reliability and inter-rater reliability were not reported. The author reported internal consistency data for the CDI for each scale by child age. Alpha coefficients for the General Development scale ranged from .69 to .90, with declines in internal consistency as the child's age increased. This may be due to the relatively lower number of items that are included in the scale at older ages.

Content validity was established for the original MCDI by generating an item pool of 673 questions that represented young children's developmental skills, were observable by parents, descriptive, clear, and had the potential to be age discriminating. Items were subsequently selected for inclusion based upon their ability to demonstrate systematic increases in the numbers of children passing them at each age. The author noted that similar analyses were used to select the CDI items, although details are not provided. Limited information is presented regarding the construct validity of the instrument, although it should be noted that scales were derived conceptually rather than empirically. As one indication of construct validity, the author reported correlation coefficients between raw scores on each scale and subject age. Correlations were strong and significant across scales (.70–.90). Criterion validity of the CDI has been established by comparing CDI parent ratings to ratings by pediatricians on developmental screening tests. Sensitivity of the CDI was reported to be 73%. Specificity was determined to be 87%. Additional data on criterion validity of the CDI when used with medically fragile children have been obtained by comparing CDI scores with those obtained on standardized biological tests. The CDI General Development Scale was significantly related to the General Cognitive Index of the McCarthy Scales of Abilities (r = .07) among children born of very low birth weight. tive validity of the CDI among children of kindergarten age lished by comparing the child's CDI scores at the time of school entry on standardized achievement tests obtained at the age. Scores on gross motor and social scales were found to be related to both reading and math achievement.

Summary of Strengths and Limitations.   The CDI is easier to administer as the "yes–no" response format and concrete items comprehensible for parents. The addition of problem behavior items to the CDI allows for clinical screening of parental concerns in domains outside of general development. Although the CDI is somewhat lengthy as compared to other developmental screening questionnaires, this may enhance its reliability. Psychometric properties appear to be promising although limited information is available, particularly regarding validity (i.e., construct and predictive validity). Extensive information is available on the validity of the scale's predecessor, the MCDI. However, given the substantial reduction in items on the CDI and differences in scale structure, the instruments cannot be considered to be synonymous.

Additional Readings

Ireton, H., & Glascoe, F. (1995). Assessing children's development using parents' reports: The Child Development Inventory. *Clinical Pediatrics*, *34*, 248–255.

Montgomery, M., Saylor, C. S., Bell, N. L., Macias, M. M., Charles, J. M., & Katikaneni, L. D. (1999). Use of the Child Development Inventory to screen high risk populations. *Clinical Pediatrics, 38*, 535–539.

Developers' Comments

The CDI is based on over 30 years of research and practice in education and health care. Briefer screening questionnaires are used in primary pediatric care and early childhood screening through the schools. The CDI is designed to obtain information from parents about their child's developmental status that is accurate and adds to assessment information generated directly by professionals through observation and testing. While some professionals object to the length of the CDI, concerned parents appreciate being involved in the assessment and treated as the expert on their child. Parent-professional collaboration is thereby enhanced.

DENVER II

Source

Frankenburg, W. K., Dodds, J., & Archer, P. *Denver II Technical Manual.* Denver, CO: Denver Developmental Materials Inc.

Availability

Denver Developmental Materials, Inc., PO Box 371075, Denver, CO, 80237–5075. 800–419–4729, 303–355–5622. Copyrighted.

Purpose. The Denver II is a revision of the widely used Denver Developmental Screening Test (DDST). The original DDST was designed to screen children for developmental delays either as part of an individualized assessment when developmental delay was suspected or as part of broader screening programs (e.g., identification of children eligible for early intervention services). However, the authors described the Denver II as a set of norms that define when children can be expected to accomplish certain developmental tasks and as analogous to a physical growth curve. Therefore, the Denver II does not provide a developmental quotient or age equivalent, and the authors cautioned against using it to predict later special educational placement or developmental disability. Rather, they recommended that the Denver II be used as a surveillance tool when monitoring children's development. In addition, they stated that decisions regarding the need for referrals for full developmental assessment should not be made solely on the basis of Denver II findings.

Description. The Denver II can be used with children from birth to 6 years of age. The instrument has 125 items that fall into four domains (Personal–Social, Fine Motor–Adaptive, Language, and Gross Motor). Each item is scored pass–fail or as refused. As with the DDST, some items can be scored as passed based upon parental report rather than examiner observation, although the total number of items where this is possible has been decreased as compared to the DDST. Pass–failure of items is then reinterpreted in light of Denver II normative data. Items that are failed are considered to indicate "delay" if 90% of same-aged children in the normative sample passed the item and to indicate "caution" if 75%–90% of same-aged children in the normative sample passed the item. Denver II results are classified as Normal, Suspect, or Untestable depending on the number of delays and cautions that are present. It should be noted that these criteria for test interpretation were established via the clinical judgment of the authors (see Reliability and Validity). Testing time is approximately 15–20 minutes, although a shortened administration is also available. Major changes from the DDST include a large increase in the number of items in the language domain, an updated normative sample, a decrease in the number of parent-report items, and better correspondence between the instrument's age scale and the schedule for well-child checkups recommended by the American Academy of Pediatrics.

Standardization and Norms. Two samples were utilized when standardizing the Denver II and developing test norms. The first sample consisted of 1,039 children residing in Denver County. The sample was stratified in order to obtain children from three different ethnic groups

(African American, Caucasian, and Hispanic) with varying levels of maternal education. The second sample consisted of 1,057 children from 20 other counties in Colorado that ranged in residential setting from urban to rural. This sample was stratified to obtain children from different residential settings with varying levels of maternal education. Obtaining a standardization sample that was more representative of the national population also allowed the instrument developers to identify items where age norms differed significantly across subgroups and to provide adjusted age norms for particular items as needed. Age norms that corresponded to 25%, 50%, 75%, and 90% pass rates for each item were obtained through logistic regression analyses and goodness of fit tests.

Reliability and Validity. Reliability of the Denver II is generally reported to be strong. Test-retest reliability was calculated for both 5–10 minute and 7–10-day intervals. Over these intervals and across domains, test-retest reliability was .90. Inter-rater reliability was calculated by comparing scores obtained by an examiner with those obtained by an observer who watched and then scored the same assessment. Inter-rater reliability averaged .99.

The Denver II is presented as a surveillance tool. Little information regarding test validity was reported by the authors, who argued that traditional indices of validity are not applicable to an instrument that they conceptualize as a formalized series of developmental tasks. Content validity for the Denver II was established by generating an item pool of 336 items that included many items from the DDST. The final 125 items were selected on the basis of a variety of criteria including ease of administration, ease of scoring (i.e., high inter-rater reliability), and low refusal rates. No statistical tests of item discrimination were used to make decisions to retain or reject items. The authors did not present any information regarding criterion validity of the Denver II scoring categories. They stated that criteria for the Normal and Suspect categories were established based upon clinical judgment and data from the standardization sample. However, at least one study investigated the sensitivity and specificity of the Denver II by comparing Denver II scores to formal diagnoses of developmental impairments including mental retardation, learning disabilities, language delays, and autism. Rates of sensitivity–specificity of the Denver II varied based upon how children with questionable scores were grouped. When questionable scores were grouped with abnormal scores, sensitivity was 83%, but specificity was 43%. This indicates that a large number of children for whom development was normal would be inaccurately found to be in need of further assessment based upon Denver II scores.

Summary of Strengths and Limitations. The Denver II attempts to remedy many of the problems of its predecessor, the DDST. It has been re-standardized using a contemporary and representative sample, has an increased number of language items and is easier to administer and score. In addition, the test has been found to be generally reliable. However, a major drawback is the lack of completion of a validity study as part of instrument development. As a result, item content and placement relative to child age may be problematic. In addition, one preliminary study suggests that use of the Denver II as an isolated developmental screening tool would result in a high rate of false positives and therefore many unnecessary referrals. In keeping with recommendations by the authors, the Denver II may best be viewed as systematized set of developmental screening items that can be used to monitor children's development in several domains. It can provide one indication that further development evaluation is needed, but should be used in conjunction with other sources of information to prevent false positives. Given the existing psychometric data, use of the Denver II in a research context should also be undertaken with caution.

Additional Readings

Frankenburg, W. K., Dodds, J., Archer, P., Shapiro, H., & Bresnick, B. (1992). The Denver II: A major revision and restandardization of the Denver Developmental Screening Test. *Pediatrics, 89,* 91–97.

Glascoe, F., Bryne, K., Ashford, L. G., Johnson, K., Chang, B., & Strickland, B. (1992). Accuracy of the Denver II in developmental screening. *Pediatrics, 89,* 1221–1225.

Developers' Comments

The Denver II has shifted its focus over the past 11 and a half years. The shift is from that of being a test to being used as a growth chart of development or a reference chart. It is for use by clinicians to compare the development of a specific child with that of children in the general population. It provides a quick overview of the child's general development and thereby serves as a useful tool in monitoring a child's development, which is referred to as developmental surveillance. Since the clinician's time is limited and the Denver II takes 15 to 20 minutes to properly administer, it is designed for use in conjunction with the Denver Pre-screening Developmental Questionnaire II, which only requires a few minutes to review. Only children who appear to be slow in their development are further evaluated with the Denver II.

The validity of the Denver II is only based upon its standardization. The standardization population, while selected in Colorado, did not differ significantly from the general population of the United States in terms of subgroup prevalence. Those items for which subgroup norms differ significantly from the composite norms have their norms tabulated separately in the Denver II Technical Manual.

DEVELOPMENTAL INDICATORS FOR THE ASSESSMENT OF LEARNING–3

Source

Mardell-Czudnowski, C., & Goldenberg, D. (1998). *Developmental Indicators for the Assessment of Learning–Third Edition (DIAL-3)*. Circle Pines, MN: American Guidance Systems.

Availability

From the publisher, American Guidance Systems, 4201 Woodland Rd, Circle Pines, MN 55014–1796. Copyrighted.

Purpose. The Developmental Indicators for the Assessment of Learning–3 (DIAL-3) is a revised version of its predecessors, the DIAL and DIAL-R. The original version of the DIAL was intended to be a brief screening test for developmental delays in preschoolers. In addition, it was designed to be multidimensional (i.e., cover multiple domains of development) and non-categorical (i.e., identify children at risk regardless of the etiology of the developmental lag) in nature.

Description. The DIAL-3 can be used to evaluate children aged 3 to 6. Five areas of development are assessed using the DIAL-3: Motor, Concepts, Language, Self-Help Developmental, and Social Development. The first three areas are assessed through formal testing procedures while Self-Help and Social Development are assessed via a parent-completed questionnaire. The parent questionnaire contains 35 questions with a 0–2 response format. The DIAL-3 can be scored in two ways: raw scores can be converted to scaled scores and then compared to cut-off scores to identify risk for developmental delay or they can be converted to percentiles and standard scores. The DIAL-3 is also available in a Spanish version that was separately normed on a national sample of Spanish-speaking children. The DIAL-3 is typically administered by a team (i.e., one administrator for each of the three formal testing areas). However, a shortened version of the DIAL-3, the Speed DIAL, can be given by one person.

Standardization and Norms. The DIAL-3 was normed and standardized on a national sample of 1,560 children stratified by age, gender, geographic area, ethnicity, and parental educational level. Ten percent of the standardization sample were children who received special educational services. The standardization sample for the Spanish DIAL consisted of 650 Spanish-speaking children.

Reliability and Validity. Test-retest reliability of the DIAL-3 was established using a subsample of 158 children (80 aged 3–6 to 4–5 and 78 aged 4–6 to 5–10) The average interval between test administrations was 28 days. Stability of the DIAL-3 total score for the two groups was .88 and .84. Median internal consistency of the DIAL-3 across ages was reported to range from .68 to .84 for the five subscales. Internal consistency for the total score was .88. The lowest coefficient alpha was found for the motor scale, which had particularly low internal consistency for 6-year-olds (.39). Reliability indices were also reported for the Speed Dial. While internal consistency was .80, median test-reliability across ages was .83.

Content validity of the DIAL-3 was initially established by utilizing items from the previous version of the DIAL. Administration and scoring of items were clarified where needed. Only items that demonstrated consistent increases in raw score across the age groupings of the DIAL-3 were retained in the final version. Construct validity of the DIAL-3 was established through factor analysis. Principle components factor analysis of the Motor, Concepts, and Language areas of the DIAL-3 found that a one-factor solution best fit the data. This indicates that DIAL-3 subscales load onto a construct assessing general development.

Criterion validity was established by comparing the DIAL-3 to previous versions of the DIAL and also to an intelligence test, the Differential Ability Scales (DAS). As expected, the DIAL-3 was significantly and positively related to the DIAL-R. Total scores for the two measures were correlated .91. The total score on the DIAL-3 was also significantly related to the General Conceptual Ability scale on the DAS (.75).

Summary of Strengths and Limitations. The DIAL-3 is a widely used screening tool for assessing child developmental status. Psychometric properties are generally sound, although internal consistency of the motor scale is not optimal. The availability of a Spanish version that is not simply a translation but has it own norms is highly beneficial for clinicians and researchers conducting developmental screening with preschoolers who are primarily Spanish speaking. The typical administration of the DIAL-3 (i.e., by a team) may be challenging to implement outside of a school setting. However, the existence of a brief version designed to be used by a single administrator offsets this concern.

Additional Readings

Chen, T., Wang, J., Mardell-Czudnowski, C., Goldenberg, D., & Elliott, C. (2000). The development of the Spanish version of the Developmental Indicators for the Assessment of Learning–Third Edition (DIAL-3). *Journal of Psychoeducational Assessment, 18,* 316–343.

Mardell-Czudnowski, C., & Goldenberg, D. (2000) A new test for assessing preschool motor development: DIAL-3. *Adapted Physical Activity Quarterly, 17,* 78–94.

EARLY SCREENING PROFILES

Source

Harrison, P. L. (1990) *AGS Early Screening Profiles Manual.* Circle Pines, MN., American Guidance Systems.

Availability

From the publisher, American Guidance Systems, 4201 Woodland Rd, Circle Pines, MN 55014–1796. Copyrighted.

Purpose. The Early Screening Profiles (ESP) is a brief developmental screening battery for young children. It was designed to provide a brief low-cost method of screening large numbers of children in order to identify children with possible developmental difficulties. In addition, the instrument is intended to provide a ecologically valid screening by gathering information on development from multiple sources (i.e., parents, teachers, and testers).

Description. The ESP can be used to evaluate children aged 2 to 6. Three scales, the Cognitive–Language Profile, Motor Profile, and Self-Help–Social Profile, each measure a major area of development. The Cognitive–Language Profile consists of two subtests that measure language and two subtests that measure non-verbal reasoning. The Motor Profile consists of a fine-motor and gross-motor subtest, and the Self-Help–Social Profile consists of four subscales (Communication, Daily Living Skills, Socialization, and Motor Skills). The three profile scores are combined to obtain a Total Screening Index. The first two profile scores are obtained through formal testing procedures while the Self-Help–Social score is obtained from a questionnaire that can be completed by either parents or teachers. The questionnaire contains 60 questions with a 0–2 response format (never performs activity to always performs activity). Two scoring systems, one of which is brief and one of which is detailed, are available for the ESP. In Level 1 scoring, raw scores are simply converted to numerical values of 1 to 6 with values of 1 and 2 indicating below average performance. In Level II scoring, raw scores can be converted to standard scores, percentile ranks, or age equivalents. In addition to the three profiles, the ESP system includes an Articulation Survey, Behavior Survey, Health History Survey, and Home Survey that can be used to gather additional information regarding the child's speech production, behavior, health history, and the amount of enrichment in the home environment.

Standardization and Norms. The ESP was normed and standardized on a national sample of 1,149 children. Initially, a probability sample of U.S. public school districts was selected with subjects chosen from these districts to approximate U.S. population variables such as child gender, child ethnicity, and parental educational level. Standard scores are available for the Total Screening Index based on administration of either two or three of the profiles.

Reliability and Validity. Test-retest reliability of the ESP was established using a subsample of 74 children. Test-retest data was characterized as either "immediate" (ESP re-administered within 5–21 days) or delayed (ESP re-administered within 22–75 days). Corrected reliabilities for immediate test-retest administration ranged from .70 to .90 for the three profiles to .87 for the Total Screening Index. Corrected reliabilities for delayed test-retest administration ranged from .55 to .81 for the three profiles to .83 for the Total Screening Index. Moderately strong stability was found for cognitive and social scales, but the stability of the motor scale was relatively poorer. Median internal consistency of the ESP profiles and Total Screening Index across child age ranged from .88 to .95 with the exception of the Motor Profile where internal consistency ranged from .60 to .78. Inter-rater-reliability data were obtained for some items on the motor profile that called for subjective judgements regarding score. Inter-rater reliabilities ranged from .80 to .99.

Content validity of the three profiles of the ESP was initially established by utilizing items from existing measures, such as the Kaufman Assessment Battery for Children, Bruininks-Oseretsky Test of Motor Proficiency, and Vineland Adaptive Behavior Scales. Field testing was undertaken for directly administered items and subsequently traditional item analytic techniques were used to select the final test items.

Construct validity of the ESP is supported by the fact that mean profile scores increase with age. Criterion validity was established by comparing scores on the ESP to scores on a variety of other measures of intelligence, receptive language, adaptive behavior, and motor proficiency. The ESP Total Screening Index was found to be correlated with scores on the Stanford-Binet (.77–.78) and Differential Abilities Scale (.78). Criterion validity was also assessed by investigating the ESP's ability to correctly characterize a child's current status with regard to receipt of special education services. Sensitivity and specificity were reported to be 92% and 77%, respectively, across children with a variety of handicapping conditions. Predictive validity was established by comparing ESP scores to those obtained on a variety of other measures of cognition up to a year after initial ESP administration. The ESP Total Screening Index was correlated with subsequent scores on the Otis-Lennon (.58–.63) and Stanford Achievement Test (.56–.65). Sensitivity and specificity of the ESP when considering ability to correctly predict later special educational status were 67% and 88%, respectively.

Summary of Strengths and Limitations. The ESP is a widely used screening tool for assessing child developmental status. It is easy to use and may be reliably administered by paraprofessionals with limited training in test administration. The inclusion of both directly obtained test data and parent–teacher report data enhances the ecological validity of the instrument. Psychometric properties are generally sound with the exception of the Motor Profile, which has relatively poorer internal consistency and stability. However, this may reflect the widely varied items included in this profile. In addition, specificity (i.e., correct classification of at-risk children) is somewhat lower than optimal, suggesting that the ESP may under identify children in need of comprehensive assessment.

Additional Readings

Gibney, L., Quinn, K., & Kundert, D. (2000). Concurrent validity of the Early Screening Profiles and the Differential Abilities Scales with an at risk preschool sample. *Psychology in the Schools, 37,* 201–207.

GILLIAM AUTISM RATING SCALE

Source

Gilliam, J. (1995). *The Gilliam Autism Rating Scale: Examiner's Manual.* Austin, TX: Pro-Ed.

Availability

From the publisher, Pro-Ed, 8700 Shoal Creek Boulevard, Austin, TX 78757. Copyrighted.

Purpose. The Gilliam Autism Rating Scale (GARS) is a behavioral checklist that identifies persons with autism. It was designed to be used by parents or teachers for the purpose of screening for autism.

Description. The GARS assesses autistic behaviors in persons aged 3 to 22. Forty-two items are rated on a 0–3 scale in terms of frequency of occurrence. The GARS has four subscales (Stereotyped Behaviors, Communication, Social Interaction, and Developmental Disturbances) that are summed to produce an omnibus score, the Autism Quotient. The same version of the GARS is used across all ages. Either parents or teachers may complete the rating scale.

Standardization and Norms. The instrument was normed and standardized using a sample of 1,092 autistic children and young adults. Seven hundred twenty teachers and 372 parents completed the GARS for the standardization sample. The sample was drawn from a variety of geographic regions of the United States. One set of norms is used regardless of the child's age or gender. Raw scores are converted to either standard scores or percentiles. Cut-off scores are provided to assist in making autism diagnoses.

Reliability and Validity. Test-retest reliability of the GARS was established using a small sample of teacher ratings (N = 11). Two-week stability of GARS subscale ratings was reported to range from .82 to .86, and was reported to be .88 for the Autism Quotient. Internal consistency of the GARS was reported to be high. Coefficient alphas for the subscales and Autism Quotient varied from .88 to .96. Inter-rater reliability was also established on a small sample. GARS ratings from two teachers were obtained for 12 subjects, ratings from two parents were obtained for 34 subjects, and ratings from a parent and a teacher were obtained for 11 subjects. Inter-rater reliabilities were reported to be high for teacher–teacher and teacher–parent ratings but only moderately strong for parent–parent ratings.

Content validity was established by generating an initial item pool for the measure from the DSM-IV diagnostic criteria for autism and autism descriptors provided by the Autism Society of America. Item difficulty and discrimination analyses were then completed to ensure that no items should be discarded. Construct validity was established by comparing scores of autistic subjects with those of subjects with other developmental disabilities and children that were not handicapped. The autism group scored significantly higher than subjects with other diagnoses. Subjects with learning disabilities and control subjects scored lowest. Criterion validity was established by comparing GARS scores to scores on the ABC. Correlations between the Autism Quotient of the GARS and the ABC total score were high (.94).

Summary of Strengths and Limitations. The GARS is one of only a few instruments that can be completed by raters that have limited expertise in the area of autism assessment (e.g., teachers). It has strong psychometric properties, including data from initial studies that suggest it can differentiate between children with autism and other developmental disabilities, such as mental retardation. The use of a large sample of autistic persons during the development of instrument norms also enhances the instrument's utility.

6

Child Coping

Anthony Spirito
Brown Medical School

INTRODUCTION

As pediatric health care has moved more and more to examining adaptive functioning in children with chronic and acute medical conditions, coping has become a common focus of empirical research. Coping is presumed to be an important mediator of the stress experienced by pediatric patients. For example, active coping strategies, such as problem solving, have been found to be related to better functioning when compared to less active strategies, such as distraction (Endler & Parker, 1990). Nonetheless, the assessment of coping in children and adolescents is in its infancy, at least in part because of varying theoretical conceptualizations of coping.

Many consider coping to be a process, rather than a trait, which varies by situation (Lazarus & Folkman, 1984). Given the many developmental phases that children experience as they transition from early to late childhood and from early adolescence to late adolescence, it seems unlikely that children and adolescents rely on one type of coping strategy for different stressors. Studies suggest that younger children use more behavioral strategies than older children and that children use more cognitive strategies as they get older (Brown, O'Keefe, Sanders, & Baker, 1986; Spirito, Stark, & Tyc, 1996).

Coping is likely to vary according to its function in a particular situation. Despite the use of different terminology, most studies distinguish between two basic types of coping: efforts to change the situation (labeled approach, active, primary control, or problem focused), and efforts to manage the emotions associated with a stressor (labeled avoidance, passive, secondary control, or emotion focused). For example, factor analyses of the Kidcope (Spirito, Stark, & Williams, 1988), a scale with 10 common coping strategies designed to cut across situations, have revealed both two-factor and single-factor structures, depending on the type of situation selected by chronically ill children. A two-factor structure (i.e., approach–avoidance) emerged when the problem selected involved aversive medical procedures, but a single-factor structure resulted when the stressor was an extended period of hospitalization. The changing factor structure reflects the fact that the function or classification of coping strategy (e.g., adaptive–nonadaptive) does not remain identical across situations. Variation in coping not only occurs across situations but may also be seen even as the demands of one stressful situation unfolds.

Conceptualizing coping as a relatively stable trait, which varies minimally across situations, has also been described. Repression–sensitization (Field, Alpert, Vega-Lahr, Goldstein, & Perry, 1988) and monitoring–blunting (Miller, Sherman, Combs, & Kruus, 1992) are examples of trait conceptualizations, which have been studied in pediatric populations. Trait conceptualizations have not been widely accepted in the study of children in general and pediatric patients in particular. Nonetheless, even when coping is conceptualized as a process, there is some consistency of coping across situations. Roecker, Dubow, and Donaldson (1996) used analyses of covariance to compare the coping patterns reported by children (ages 13–18) in response to interpersonal conflict between peers and interpersonal conflict between parents. The pattern of five coping responses (i.e., seeking support, problem solving, distancing, internalizing, externalizing) was remarkably consistent across the two situations. One exception was that internalizing was reported significantly more in response to parent, compared to peer, conflict. Donaldson, Prinstein, Danovsky, and Spirito (2000) reported similar coping consistency. In a study of children's patterns of coping with daily stressors, the patterns of coping strategy used were found to be similar across school, parents–family, siblings, and peer stressors. Wishful thinking, problem solving and emotional regulations were the most frequently used coping strategies. Adolescents tended to use a broader range of coping strategies than children regardless of type of stressor (Donaldson et al., 2000).

When constructing measures of coping appropriate for use with children, scale developers need to take into account the conceptual issues previously described. Researchers interested in examining coping have typically developed their own measures for a particular study. Most have not been particularly interested in testing the properties of their scales, and have not followed-up with a systematic line of scale development research. Consequently, a gold standard measure of coping in childhood has yet to emerge (Spirito, 1996).

Health researchers designing studies search for measures of coping that are appropriate for their particular study question. Unfortunately, there are relatively few measures from which to choose. In addition, given the rather limited state of psychometric sophistication in pediatric coping measures, the measure often chosen is less than perfect. Thus, this section of the volume gathers information on a number of coping scales in one place.

Information on seven scales assessing coping in childhood is presented here. The scales are quite diverse in their focus. Most are brief. Some assess coping strategies used in general situations, while others are specific to medical stressors. Most of the scales have been developed for children and young adolescents, but one is specific to older adolescents, and two are completed by caregivers. Most assess simply the frequency with which a coping strategy is endorsed, but several also examine perceived efficacy of the coping strategy. Some are situation specific, others refer to how a child generally copes with a medical condition. Some have a theoretical framework that guided item development, while others developed items based partially on theory and partially on pragmatics. They all define coping in slightly different ways, which has resulted in different measures that assess the same general coping strategy or style in different ways and with different items. On the one hand, the differences across the measures may be useful because it allows researchers to pick coping measures suited for a variety of questions related to coping. On the other hand, these measures, which may have served the original purpose of the study designers, have sufficient limitations that will likely preclude their widespread use by other researchers.

None of the scales reported here have very well developed psychometrics. There does not appear to be any group of researchers currently devoted to a systematic line of research on coping scale development. Why is this the case? Probably because the construct does not easily lend itself to objective measurement. Perhaps then we should abandon the search for a gold standard, self-report measure of coping. Instead, self-report measures may best be used as part of a comprehensive approach to assessing and understanding the coping of pediatric patients. In some studies, administering a self-report screening measure, and then interviewing children regarding their use of the most frequently reported coping strategies would be one way to thoroughly assess coping.

Interviewing children in depth about their coping strategies would be a much better way of understanding the nature of the coping process in childhood. However, interviews need to move beyond what specific coping strategies are used to a more sophisticated understanding of related concepts that affect coping. Such concepts include appraisal of control over the stressor; the emotional states that accompany the stressor and affect appraisal; the child's ability to generate a variety of related strategies; the sequence of coping strategies used; the simultaneous use or pattern of coping strategies; the ability of the child to choose the best strategy from among a variety of strategies and to implement the strategy in a given situation; and the perceived efficacy of these strategies. Only through the use of increasingly sophisticated questioning of children about their coping strategy use, in conjunction with the use of self-report measures, will our understanding of a pediatric patient's coping improve.

REFERENCES

Brown, J. M., O'Keefe, J., Sanders, S. H., & Baker, B. (1986). Developmental changes in children's cognition to stressful and painful situations. Journal of Pediatric Psychology, 11, 343–357.
Donaldson, D., Prinstein, M., Danovsky, M., & Spirito, A. (2000). Patterns of children's coping with life stress: Implications for clinicians. American Journal of Orthopsychiatry, 70, 351–359.
Endler, N., & Parker, J. (1990). Multidimensional assessment of coping: A critical evaluation. Journal of Personality Processes and Individual Differences, 58, 844–854.
Field, T., Alpert, B., Vega-Lahr, N., Goldstein, S., & Perry, S. (1988). Hospitalization stress in children: Sensitizer and repressor coping styles. Health Psychology, 7, 433–446.
Lazarus, R. S., & Folkman, S. (1984). Stress, appraisal, and coping. New York: Springer.
Miller, S., Sherman, H., Combs, C., & Kruus, L. (1992). Patterns of children's coping with short term medical and dental stressors: Nature, complications, and future directions. In A. M. LaGreca, L. J. Siegel, J. Wallander, & C. Walker (Eds.), Stress and coping in child health (pp. 157–190). New York: Guilford.
Roecker, C. E., Dubow, E. F., & Donaldson, D. L. (1996). Cross-situational patterns in children's coping with observed interpersonal conflict. Journal of Clinical Child Psychology, 25, 288–299.
Spirito, A. (1996). Commentary: Pitfalls in the use of brief screening measures of coping. Journal of Pediatric Psychology, 4, 573–575.
Spirito, A., Stark, L. J., & Tyc, V. (1996). Coping strategies described during hospitalization by chronically ill children. Journal of Clinical Child Psychology, 23, 314–322.
Spirito, A., Stark, L. J., & Williams, C. (1988). Development of a brief checklist to assess coping in pediatric patients. Journal of Pediatric Psychology, 13, 555–574.

ADOLESCENT COPING ORIENTATION FOR PROBLEM EXPERIENCES

Source

Patterson, J. M., & McCubbin, H. I. (1991). A-COPE adolescent coping orientation for problem experiences. In H. I. McCubbin & A. I. Thompson

(Eds.), *Family assessment inventories for research and practice* (pp. 235–254). Madison, WI: The University of Wisconsin–Madison.

Availability

From the first author. A single sample copy can be obtained for $5.00 from the Center for Excellence in Family Studies, Family Stress, Coping, and Health Project, University of Wisconsin–Madison, 1300 Linden Drive, Madison, WI 53706. The measure is copyrighted.

Purpose. The purpose of the Adolescent Coping Orientation for Problem Experiences (A-COPES) is to identify the behaviors adolescents find helpful in managing problems or difficult situations.

Description. The A-COPES consists of 54 behavioral items that represent 12 distinct patterns of coping. These patterns are: ventilating feelings; seeking diversions; developing self-reliance, optimism, and social support; solving family problems; avoiding problems; seeking spiritual and professional support; investing in close friends; engaging in demanding activity; and being humorous and relaxing. Adolescents are instructed to read each item and rate how often they use that behavior they find helpful to them in managing problems or difficult situations that happen to them or members of their family. Responses options are "never," "hardly ever," "sometimes," "often," and "most of the time." Responses are assigned values of 1 to 5. Summed scores and subscale scores are determined after reverse scoring several items. The A-COPES takes 15 to 20 minutes to complete, can be administered to individuals or groups, and is written at a sixth grade reading level. The conceptual basis for the A-COPES is the developmental needs of adolescents, primarily the need to become increasingly independent from the family.

Standardization and Norms. Initial construction, development, and testing of the A-COPES was done with several samples. The first sample consisted of 30 tenth, eleventh, and twelfth graders from a suburban midwestern high school. The second sample consisted of 467 junior and senior high school students from a suburban midwestern middle and high school. The third sample consisted of 709 adolescents who were enrolled in a HMO in a midwestern city. Females and males were represented in all samples. Eight percent of the sample was 11 years of age, 58% was 12–13 years of age, and the remaining 34% were between 14 and 18 years of age. All samples were predominately Caucasian (96%), two parent households (86%), and of relatively high SES. A third sample of males recruited from residential treatment programs included African-

American youth, but there was no reliability or validity data reported from this sample.

Reliability and Validity. Reliability and validity were evaluated in several studies. Internal consistency of the subscales, based on Cronbach's alpha, ranged from .50 to .76. The developing self-reliance and optimism, seeking professional help, engaging in demanding activity, and relaxing subscales all had alpha coefficients under .70. Others (Grey, Lipman, Cameron, & Thurber, 1997; Ryan-Wenger, 1996) have reported somewhat higher reliability for the subscales. The authors did not report internal consistency for the total scale for any evidence of test-retest reliability.

To ensure content validity, coping behaviors were identified following interviews with adolescents in the tenth, eleventh, and twelfth grade. Repeated factor analyses were used with the initial 95-item scale to find the most parsimonious set of items. The final 54-item scale had 12 factors with eigenvalues greater than 1 and item loadings greater than .40. The 12 factors accounted for 60.1% of the variance in the initial correlation matrix. Additional evidence of construct validity comes from hypotheses testing strategies. Adequate criterion validity has been demonstrated by significant relationships in the expected direction between the coping patterns, substance abuse, and psychological adaptation. Additional researchers have reported good reliability and validity with African-American and European-American adolescents from single and two parent families (see following additional readings).

Summary of Strengths and Limitations. The A-COPES has been extensively used by various disciplines to measure adolescent coping with general life stress. Schwartz and Schwartz (1996) recommended its use for adolescent stress and risk behavior research. The scale has been used with adolescents with chronic conditions and emotional disturbances, as well a community-based samples and is available in French, Japanese, Spanish, and Swedish. Limitations include the lack of theoretical foundation and the orientation to general rather than specific stressors, and the lack of a specified time frame for the respondent.

Additional Readings

Grey, M., Lipman, T., Cameron, M. E., & Thurber, F. W. (1997). Coping behaviors at diagnosis and in adjustment one year later in children with diabetes. *Nursing Research, 46,* 312–317.

Huth, M. M. (1999). Measurement of children's coping. *Journal of Child and Family Health, 2,* 215–221.

Ryan-Wenger, N. A. (1996). Children, coping, and the stress of illness: A synthesis of the research. *Journal of the Society of Pediatric Research, 1,* 126–138.

Schwartz, R., & Schwartz, C. (1996). A critical survey of coping instruments. In M. Zeidner & N. S. Endler (Eds.), *Handbook of coping: Theory, research, applications* (pp. 107–132). New York: Wiley.

THE CHILDREN'S COPING STRATEGIES CHECKLIST AND THE HOW I COPED UNDER PRESSURE SCALE

Source

Program for Prevention Research. (1999). *Manual for the Children's Coping Strategies Checklist and the How I Coped Under Pressure Scale.* Tempe, AZ: Arizona State University.

Availability

Tim S. Ayers (*Tim.Ayers@asu.edu*), Program for Prevention Research, Arizona State University, 900 S. McAllister Ave. Rm 205, PO Box 876005, Tempe, AZ 85287–6005. The measure is copyrighted.

Purpose. These measures were designed to test a multidimensional theory of children's coping strategies, as opposed to two-dimensional theories (e.g., active vs. passive, problem focused vs. emotion focused). The Childen's Coping Strategies Checklist (CCSC) measures dispositional coping behaviors or general coping style. The How I Coped Under Pressure Scale (HICUPS) measures situational coping behaviors in response to a stressful event.

Description. For both measures, children ages 9 to 13 respond to 45 items that form 10 subscales: Cognitive Decision Making, Direct Problem Solving, Seeking Understanding, Positive Cognitive Restructuring, Physical Release of Emotions, Distracting Actions, Avoidant Actions, Cognitive Avoidance, Problem-Focused Support, and Emotion-Focused Support. These scales form four factors: Active Coping Strategies, Distraction Strategies, Avoidance Strategies, and Support-Seeking Strategies. For the CCSC, children are asked to rate how often they do a behavior when faced with a problem. Items are rated on a 4-point likert scale from "never" to "most of the time." For the HICUPS, children are asked to focus on a single stressful event that occurred in the past 3 months. They then rate how often they did certain behaviors during this event from not at all to a lot.

Standardization and Norms. While the CCSC and HICUPS are not standardized, the authors have published means and standard deviations of the subscales using a diverse sample. The CCSC was first developed using a sample of 217 children from 10 schools in three different districts in a southwestern metropolitan area. Although the authors could not ask about ethnicity in this school context, other studies in the same districts suggested that the population was 43% Caucasian, 30% Hispanic, 20% African American, and 7% Native American. Income was not reported. In the second study, where the CCSC and the HICUPS were administered, the sample of 303 children was 53% Caucasian, 23% Hispanic, 13% African American, 4% Native American, and 2% of other ethnic status. The mean annual income was within the lower to middle class range, and 36% of parents were divorced or separated.

Reliability and Validity. Internal consistency reliability ranged from .51 to .72 for the CCSC scales and from .57 to .74 on the HICUPS scales. Cronbach's alphas were consistently higher on the HICUPS. To ensure content validity, items were constructed from a content analysis of semi-structured interviews with 57 children. A panel of faculty and graduate students studying children's coping were asked to categorize items into specific coping dimensions, and only those items where there was 80% agreement across raters were retained. Confirmatory factor analysis in two separate studies supported construct validity for the CCSC, and a separate factor analysis in the second study confirmed the factor structure of the HICUPS. Alternative two-dimensional models were not supported. Cronbach's alphas for the resulting four factor structure were .88 for active coping strategies, .72 for distraction strategies, .77 for avoidance strategies, .75 for support-seeking strategies for the CCSC. For the HICUPS, the Cronbach's alphas were .89 for active coping strategies, .80 for distraction strategies, .73 for avoidance strategies, and .78 for support-seeking strategies. Criterion validity was not assessed.

Summary of Strengths and Limitations. A key strength of the measure is its strong theoretical foundation and testing of its factor structure against other models of coping. In addition, the testing of its psychometric properties on a diverse population enhances its utility. While content and construct validity are very strong, reliability of some of the subscales may be less than adequate, and criterion validity requires further research. Some of the scales had only three items, which likely reduced reliability. Thus, reliability may be enhanced if the 10 subscales were summed to represent the four factors. The use of four superordinate scales would also simplify the use of the measure in data analyses, but the psychometric properties of this approach requires further study.

Additional Readings

Ayers, T. S., Sandler, I. N., West, S. G., & Roosa, M. W. (1996). A dispositional and situational assessment of children's coping: Testing alternative models of coping. *Journal of Personality, 64*(4), 923–958.

Sandler, I. N., Ayers, T. S., Wolchik, S. A., Tein, J.-Y., Kwok, O.-M., Haine, R. A., Twohey, J. L., Suter, J., Lin, K., Padgett-Jones, S., Weyer, J. L., Cole, E., Kriege, G., & Griffin, W. A. (in press). The Family Bereavement Program: Efficacy evaluation of a theory-based prevention program for parentally-bereaved children and adolescents. *Journal of Consulting and Clinical Psychology.*

Sandler, I. N., Tein, J., Mehta, P., Wolchik, S., & Ayers, T. (2000). Coping efficacy and psychological problems of children of divorce. *Child Development, 71*(4), 1099–1118.

Developer's Comments

Development of the CCSC and HICUPS is ongoing and at the time of publication we are currently using the second revision of each of the instruments (i.e., CCSC-R2 and HICUPS-R2). Through further work in the development of the instrument, there have been two major changes to the instruments. First, we have expanded our assessment of the positive cognitive restructuring coping components of the instruments and currently have three scales that assess coping in this area. positivity, optimism, and control. Second, we have reorganized and added items in our assessment of the support-seeking strategies. Instead of grouping items based on the function of the coping efforts (i.e., emotion-focused support or problem-focused support) we have found through additional factor analyses with these new items that the items are best grouped on the basis of the provider of the support. Thus, the current versions of the instruments have four short 4-item scales that assess support-seeking strategies from a parent–guardian, other adults, siblings, and peers. With these additional items, the current versions of the CCSC-R2 and HICUPS-R2 are 66 items in length. Information on ar⁻ᵈ copies of the latest version of the CCSC-R2 and the HICUPS-R2 are ε ιilable from the author previously listed.

COPING HEALTH INVENTORY
FOR CHILDREN

Source

Austin, J. K., Patterson, J. M., & Huberty, T. J. (1991). Development of the
coping health inventory for children. *Journal of Pediatric Nursing, 8*(3),
166–174.

Availability

From Joan K. Austin, DNS, FAAN, Indiana University School of Nursing,
111 Middle Drive, NU492, Indianapolis, IN, 46202-5107.

Purpose. The Coping Health Inventory for Children (CHIC) measures parent report of coping behaviors of 6- to 12-year-old children with a
chronic physical condition based on family stress theory (McCubbin &
Patterson, 1983), and Lazarus and Folkman's (1984) concept of coping.
Coping is viewed as the behaviors a child demonstrates in order to manage or reduce demands that can cause emotional distress. Behaviors are
distinct from resources, or what the child has, and adaptational outcomes
that are more global assessments of functioning. Although all behaviors
are intended to help manage distress, some are clearly more adaptive (i.e.,
develops optimism) than others (i.e., acts out).

Description. The CHIC consists of 45 behavioral items that represent
five conceptually distinct categories: develops competence and optimism;
feels different and withdraws; is irritable, moody and acts out; complies
with treatment; and seeks support. Each category represents a subscale. A
parent completes the inventory. Parents rate their child on each behavior
on 5-point scales of never, almost always, sometimes, often, and almost always. Although scoring instructions were not explicit, the authors present
mean scores for five subscales that they call coping patterns: Competence–
Optimism, Different–Withdraws, Irritable, Complies, and Seeks Support.

Standardization and Norms. The scale was tested in stages with 478
parents of children with asthma or epilepsy. The initial pretest was with
30 parents of 8–12-year-old children who had either epilepsy or asthma.
Following several revisions to provide more descriptions of behaviors
with examples, the scale was administered to another 74 parents with
children of the same age and diagnosis. This sample was also used to

establish test-retest reliability. A sample of 372 parents with children of the same age and diagnosis was used for validity studies. Demographic information about the sample was not reported.

Reliability and Validity.   Internal consistency reliability was greater than .70 for all subscales across all studies. Two- to 3-week test-retest reliability for all subscales ranged from .68 to .91 for mothers and .57 to .84 for fathers. There were moderate correlations among subscales. Bivariate correlation showed that positive type behaviors tended to be correlated with other positive type behaviors and visa versa for negative type behaviors.

The items were developed following literature review of adult and child coping, review of existing coping measures for children, interviews with parents of children with epilepsy, and interviews with children. A school psychologist, developmental psychologist, and nurse expert in childhood chronic illness evaluated content validity. Confirmatory factor analysis indicated a stronger factor structure if five of the items were included in more than one factor. Several items were also deleted. Subsequently, a five-factor solution showed acceptable fit with the data as evidence of construct validity.

Criterion validity was evidenced by the significant relationships in the expected direction between the CHIC subscales, and other measures of adaptation such as self-concept, home behavior, school behaviors, and attitude. Only one behavior distinguished the children with epilepsy from children with asthma. Children with asthma were significantly more likely to seek support. Children who reported a higher level of feeling different and withdrawal behavior had significantly more illness episodes. Coping strategies were also related to illness status. Parents who reported children's increased use of the more maladaptive coping patterns also reported an increase in seizure frequency and asthma episodes for the epilepsy and asthma subsamples, respectively.

Summary of Strengths and Limitations.   The CHIC has a strong theoretical and conceptual base. The clear focus on coping behaviors, rather than coping resources or strategies makes the scale attractive as a basis for planning interventions. It is short, easy to administer, and has evidence of reliability and validity. The scale is developed so that it could be used with almost any diagnostic group by naming the targeted condition. Overall, this scale has a great deal of potential for both research and clinical practice with children with chronic conditions.

Limitations include the lack of a specified window of time in responding to the items, no information on the length of time to complete, and the fact that the parent completes it. As such, it measures parent perception of children's coping behaviors. While parent report may be appropriate for younger school-aged children (i.e., 6–7-year-olds), other scales are available to directly measures coping behaviors for 8- to 12-year-olds. In addition, it must be noted that the race–ethnicity and family composition of the previous samples was not reported, which suggests that the samples lacked diversity on these important variables. More extensive use and evaluation of the CHIC with larger, more heterogeneous samples, and other diagnostic groups is warranted to further investigate psychometric properties and to increase generalizability of findings.

Additional Readings

Lazrus, R. S., & Folkman, S. (1984). *Stress, appraisal, and coping.* New York: Springer.
McCubbin, H. I., & Patterson, J. M. (1983). The family stress process: The Double ABCX model of adjustment and adaptation. *Marriage and Family Review, 6,* 7–37.

IMPACT ON FAMILY SCALE

Source

Stein, R.E.K., & Riessman, C. K. (1980). The development of an Impact-on-Family scale: Preliminary findings. *Medical Care, 18,* 465–472.

Availability

From the first author. Ruth E. K. Stein, M.D., Department of Pediatrics, Albert Einstein College of Medicine/Montefiore Medical Center; Centennial 1, 111 East 210th Street, Bronx, NY 10467.

Purpose. The Impact on Family scale was designed to quantify the impact of pediatric illness on a family along four dimensions identified from literature reviews and family interviews: Financial Burden, Social Impact, Family Impact, and the primary caregiver's Subjective Distress.

Description. Caregivers of children with medical conditions respond to 24 items rated on a 4-point likert scale from strongly agree to strongly disagree. The measure may be used for children of any age. Items are summed into four subscales: Financial Impact, Familial–social Impact,

Personal Strain, and Mastery. A summary of the score of all items may be used as a measure of overall impact.

Standardization and Norms. The Impact on Family Scale has not been standardized. The authors do not describe the first sample of 58 mothers other than to say that the data were collected in an urban setting. In the second sample of 100 mothers, 66% were Hispanic, 22% African American, and 11% Caucasian. Almost half the sample (44%) consisted of single mothers. Mothers were generally poor, and 66% did not graduate high school. The authors do not report the chronic conditions represented. The measure has also been used with Italian and Lebanese samples.

Reliability and Validity. A panel of experts evaluated the initial pool of items for face validity. Scales were revised based on factor analyses ensuring construct validity, and further construct validity data has been reported (Stein & Jessop, 1985). Internal consistency reliability based on Cronbach's alpha was adequate for all scales (.60 to .81) and was strong for the total summary score (.88). Test-retest reliability was not reported. In a recent paper, Kolk, Schipper, Hanewald, and Casari (2000) gave several examples of criterion validity. They noted that the measure correlated with a measure of quality of life among mothers of asthmatics and that the more severe the illness, the greater the impact on the family. Kolk et al. (2000) also cited several examples where the measure has been utilized in studies of a variety of chronic conditions.

Summary of Strengths and Limitations. The measure is notable for a number of reasons: its focus on children with chronic conditions, its focus on the impact on the family versus the individual, it applicability to all age groups, and its appropriateness for use with an urban, low SES population. Psychometric properties appear sound, but test-retest reliability is unclear. Applicability to other populations and to caregivers other than biological mothers also requires further study.

Additional Readings

Kolk, A. M., Schipper, J. L., Hanewald, G.J.F.P., & Casari, E. F. (2000). The Impact-On-Family Scale: A test of invariance across culture. *Journal of Pediatric Psychology, 5,* 323–329.

Stein, R. K., & Jessop, D. (1985). *Tables documenting the psychometric properties of a measure of impact of chronic illness on the family.* New York: Albert Einstein College of Medicine.

KIDCOPE

Source

Spirito, A., Stark, L. H., & Williams, C. (1988). Development of a brief coping checklist for use with pediatric populations. *Journal of Pediatric Psychology, 13,* 555–574.

Availability

From the first author. Anthony Spirito, Clinical Psychology Training Consortium, Potter Building, Box G-BH, Brown University, Providence, Rhode Island, 02912.

Purpose.   The Kidcope was designed to be a screening measure of coping in pediatric populations for use in clinical research. Coping is conceptualized as a process rather than as a stable personality trait, and thus is expected to change depending on the situation or time of assessment.

Description.   Children are asked to identify a hospital-related problem and one problem unrelated to being sick. Children with chronic illnesses may be asked to identify an illness-related problem. Children then rate the frequency they use 10 coping strategies on a 4-point scale and rate the effectiveness of the strategies on a 5-point scale. There are two versions available for children 7 to 12 years and 13 to 18 years. There are not summary scores or subscales.

Standardization and Norms.   The Kidcope has not been standardized. Although reliability and validity was assessed with six different samples ranging from healthy adolescents to pediatric patients, item means and standard deviations for the samples were not reported. The samples were predominantly Caucasian, middle-class families.

Reliability and Validity.   Test-retest reliability coefficients were adequate over 3 to 7 days for the frequency ratings, but the efficiency ratings were less reliable. As expected, test-retest reliability decreased for longer time periods. Internal consistency reliability could not be assessed since the measure does not yield summary scores. As evidence of criterion validity, the authors analyzed correlations between eight of the frequency items and eight scales on the coping strategies inventory (Tobin, Holroyd, & Reynolds, 1984). Five of these correlations were significant with a Bonferroni correction. When compared to an adolescent coping measure, 7 out of 10 correlations were significant.

Summary of Strengths and Limitations. As Spirito (1996) noted, the greatest strength of the Kidcope is its brevity. A major limitation for data analysis is the lack of summary scores resulting in item-by-item analyses. Spirito (1996) suggested that factor structures vary by situation and by sample. He suggests developing factors for each study if the sample size allows. It is unclear whether each single item truly represents a category of coping strategies since correlations with existing coping scales were not significant for all 10 items. The reliability and validity of the efficiency ratings require further study. Other limitations include the homogeneity of the validation samples, and the lack of published reliability and validity data with younger children.

Additional Readings

Spirito, A. (1996). Commentary: Pitfalls in the use of brief screening measures of coping. *Journal of Pediatric Psychology, 21,* 573–575.

Tobin, D. L., Holroyd, K. A., & Reynolds, R.V.C. (1984). *Manual for the Coping Strategies Inventory.* Unpublished manuscript. Athens: Ohio University.

SCHOOLAGERS' COPING STRATEGIES INVENTORY

Source

Ryan-Wenger, N. M. (1990). Development and psychometric properties of the Schoolagers' coping strategies inventory. *Nursing Research, 39,* 344–349.

Availability

From the author. Nancy Ryan-Wenger, PhD, RN, The Ohio State University, College of Nursing, Ohio State University, 1585 Neil Avenue, Columbus OH, 43210.

Purpose. The Schoolagers' Coping Strategies Inventory (SCSI) measures the frequency and effectiveness of behavioral and cognitive coping strategies in school-aged (8- to 12-year-old) children. The theoretical framework for the SCSI is Lazarus' stress-coping paradigm designed for adults (Lazarus & Folkman, 1984). Ryan-Wenger (1990) made a point of distinguishing coping strategies from coping styles. Coping strategies are learned, deliberate, specific, and personal cognitive and behavioral ways of dealing with stressors. Coping strategies can also vary with age and situations. Coping styles, on the other hand, are partially inherent, global responses that are stable over time. Because they are stable over time, coping styles are much less amenable to coping interventions that coping strategies.

Description. The 26-item scale taps several broad categories of behavioral and cognitive strategies children use to deal with stressors. The self-report scale takes about 10 minutes to complete. Children are asked to respond to the frequency of using and effectiveness of each strategy in response to a specific (i.e., pain, having diabetes, coming to the hospital for chemotherapy) or general (i.e., something that makes you feel bad, nervous, or worried) stressors. Frequency (never, once in a while, a lot, and most of the time) and effectiveness (never do it, does not help, helps a little, and helps a lot) are rated on a word-response format. A zero-to 3-point scale is used for scoring. Three scores can be calculated: Frequency Scale, Effectiveness Scale, and Total SCSI.

Standardization and Norms. Initial pilot work (item identification) was done with primarily Caucasian 8- to 12-year-old children from a midwestern college town. The samples represented a wide range of SES. Subsequently, coping strategies were investigated in African-American children (N = 59) of the same age range from a low-income census track in a large midwestern city. While the measure has not been standardized, subsequent to development, it has been used with well children, as well as children with acute and chronic conditions. Both Spanish and Korean versions are available.

Reliability and Validity. Internal consistency of the 30-item scale was .85. Other psychometric properties were investigated on the 26-item scale with a sample of 242 children, their parents, and their teachers. Internal consistency using Cronbach alpha was .76 for the frequency scale, .77 for the effectiveness scale, and .79 for the total SCSI. Test-retest reliability after a 2-week interval was $r = .73$ for the Frequency scale, $r = .82$ for the Effectiveness scale, and $r = .81$ for the total SCSI. Child development experts evaluated content validity, and the reading level was determined to be appropriate for 8- to 12-year-old children.

Construct validity was evaluated using the multitrait-multimethod technique. The SCSI demonstrated adequate discriminate validity. Convergent validity could not be established, most likely because of the lack of another reliable measure of coping strategies. However, the SCSI distinguished between a subsample of children with no reported health symptoms and a subsample of children with two or more reported health symptoms. Factor analysis was conducted on the Frequency scale, Effectiveness scale, and total SCSI. Eight factors were extracted in each solution. Explained variance ranged from moderate (59%) to minimal (10%). Cronbach alpha for Factor I was moderate (.79) but low for Factor II (.61) suggesting that the SCSI is unidimensional. Accordingly, it is recommended that only the total SCSI score be used in data analysis. As preliminary evidence of criterion-related validity for children with higher stress-related problems, as identified by teachers, had less effective coping strategies. Reliability and validity was similar for both the Caucasian and the African-American samples.

Summary of Strengths and Limitations. The SCSI has a clear theoretical and developmental foundation. Internal consistency is good, as is test-retest reliability. The measure has been used with diverse samples. Validity of the scale is promising, and the widespread use of the measure will likely show further evidence of criterion validity. Finally, a unique strength is that the measure includes children's ratings of the effectiveness of their coping, which may be more predictive of adaptation than the behaviors themselves.

Additional Readings

Huth, M. M. (1999). Measurement of children's coping. *Journal of Child and Family Nursing, 2,* 215–221.

Lazarus, R. S., & Folkman, S. (1984). Stress, appraisal, and coping. New York: Springer.

Ryan-Wenger, N. M., & Gresham Copeland, S. (1994). Coping strategies used by Black school-aged children from low income families. *Journal of Pediatric Nursing, 9,* 33–40.

7

Cognitions, Attributions, and Attitudes

Lilless McPherson Shilling
Ronald T. Brown
Medical University of South Carolina

INTRODUCTION

The field of social cognition attempts to explain how thoughts, emotions, and behaviors are affected by the "actual, imagined, or implied presence of others" (Allport, 1985, p. 3). It examines individuals within a social or cultural context and the means by which people process information (Sternberg, 1994). Experts in the area of social cognition include Bandura (1986) who studied learning within social contexts, Bem (1972) who was responsible for the developmental of self-perception theory; and Weiner (1986) who introduced attribution theory. Several important constructs that are relevant to child assessment in pediatric settings include health care beliefs and attitudes, attributions (e.g., locus of control), and motivation to engage in healthy behaviors.

The *Health Belief Model,* originally developed in the 1950s (Rosenstock, 1974) has been called the grandparent of all theories related to health behavior change (Fisher & Fisher, 2000). The health belief model proposes that health behavior (e.g., seeking care for an ailment) is a function of the extent to which one believes that she or he is vulnerable to a particular disease. For example, a child whose grandmother died of heart disease may believe that she is susceptible to cardiac problems and for this reason may exercise frequently. The model also emphasizes the importance of demographic variables (e.g., SES, gender, race, and age) and environmental factors that can influence beliefs and behavior.

Attribution theory focuses on how individuals make attributions about the cause of their own behavior and that of others (Heider, 1958; Weiner, 1986). Weiner (1986) and others (Pintrich & Schunk, 1996) noted that attributions are made regarding locus of causality (internal vs. external) and controllability (controllable vs. uncontrollable). Attributions can either be stable or unstable (Morrone & Pintrich, 1997). For example, an adolescent who develops an infection may either believe that she or he is susceptible to infections because of a weak immune system (attribution to internal cause) or that she or he caught the infection from a classmate (attribution to external cause). The adolescent might believe that frequent hand washing can prevent a future ailment (attribution of controllable cause) or that she or he cannot do anything to avoid becoming ill (attribution of uncontrollable cause). The degree to which these beliefs are incorporated into the adolescent's schema about health is an index of stability.

Locus of control has also been conceptualized as a stable individual trait, namely, the extent to which people consistently report a belief that they have control over events affecting them. Those who have a high internal locus of control (internals) hold the belief that their own actions or behaviors strongly influence the events in their lives. In contrast, people with a high external locus of control (externals) think that luck, chance, fate, or other people determine what happens to them (Hellriegel, Slocum, & Woodman, 2001). There is strong evidence to indicate that children become more internal in their locus of control as a function of age (Nowicki & Strickland, 1973). Locus of control is an important construct for clinicians and researchers interested in child health outcomes because it is related to children's beliefs and attitudes about the degree of control they have in the prevention, management, or recovery from an illness. Thus, children with an internal locus of control may believe that eating the right foods prevents illness. In contrast, children with an external locus of control may believe that their illness was the result of bad fortune or fate. This chapter includes two specific measures of children's health locus of control: Children's Health Locus of Control and the Multidimensional Health Locus of Control Scale adapted for pediatric populations.

Attitudes refer to enduring beliefs, feelings, and behaviors regarding specific groups, people, issues, ideas, or objects (Myers, 1993). Attitudes are learned through experiences with significant others including caregivers, peer groups, and acquaintances in social and work groups. There is also some recent evidence to suggest that attitudes may be shaped by genetic factors (Baumeister, 1999). Attitudes have three dimensions: affective (emotions), cognitive (beliefs, opinions, and knowledge), and behavioral (propensity to respond in a specific way; Breckler, 1984). This chapter includes two measures of attitudes: Children's Health Care Attitudes Questionnaire and Children's Attitudes Toward Illness Scale.

Motivation refers to those forces exerted on or within an individual that cause him or her to behave in a specific goal-directed way. Motivation is also an important factor in the prevention, management, and recovery from illness. Wearing seatbelts and avoiding second-hand cigarette smoke are examples of behavior based on the intrinsic motivation to prevent injury and illness. Complying with prescribed physical therapy and taking medication are examples of behaviors based upon motivation to manage and recover from juvenile rheumatoid arthritis. This chapter includes one measure, the Health Self-Determinism Index for Children, which assesses health motivation in pediatric populations.

While instruments measuring social cognitions in children and adolescents are useful in assessing attributions, beliefs, and attitudes about health and illness, there are limitations. Limited data about the reliability, validity, and generalizability of many such instruments are available. Methods to assess these constructs among children seen in health care settings are still being developed. All of the instruments described here use children or adolescents as the sole informants. However, the impact of age and developmental status upon a child's ability to formulate and express beliefs and attitudes is not clear. As with a variety of measures in the field of social psychology, these instruments are affected by demand characteristics or the tendency to provide a socially desirable response. Thus, in studies using these instruments, researchers may wish to control for social desirability. Finally, a growing body of literature demonstrates the impact of ethnicity and cultural background upon health beliefs and attitudes. Therefore, further development of normative data for these instruments when used with minority populations is warranted.

REFERENCES

Allport, A. (1985). The historical background of social psychology. In G. Lindzey & E. Aronson (Eds.), *Handbook of social psychology* (pp. 1–46). New York: Random House.

Bandura, A. (1986). *Social foundations of thought and action: A social-cognitive theory.* Englewood Cliffs, NJ: Prentice-Hall.

Baumeister, R. F. (1999). On the interface between personality and social psychology. In L. A. Pervin & O. P. John (Eds.), *Handbook of personality* (pp. 367–377). New York: Guilford.

Bem, D. (1972). Self-perception theory. In L. Berkowitz (Ed.), *Advances in Experimental Social Psychology* (Vol. 6, pp. 1–62). New York: Academic Press.

Breckler, S. J. (1984). Empirical validations of affect, behavior, and cognition as distinct components of attitude. *Journal of Personality and Social Psychology, 47,* 1191–1205.

Fisher, J. D., & Fisher, W. A. (2000). Theoretical approaches to individual level change in

HIV risk behavior. In J. L. Peterson & R. J. DeClemente (Eds.), *Handbook of HIV prevention* (pp. 3–55). New York: Kluwer Academic/Plenum.

Heider, F. (1958). *The psychology of interpersonal relations.* New York: Wiley.

Hellriegel, D., Slocum, J. W., Jr., & Woodman, R. W. (2001). *Organizational behavior* (9th ed.). Cincinnati, OH: South-Western College.

Morrone, A. S., & Pintrich, P. R. (1997). In G. G. Bear, K. M. Minke, & A. Thomas (Eds.), *Children's needs II: Development, problems, and alternatives* (pp. 387–395). Bethesda, MD: National Association of School Psychologists.

Myers, D. G. (1993). *Social psychology* (4th ed.). New York: McGraw-Hill.

Nowicki, S., & Strickland, B. (1973) A locus of control scale for children. *Journal of Consulting and Clinical Psychology, 40,* 148–154.

Pintrich, P. R., & Schunk, D. H. (1996). *Motivation in education: Theory, research, and applications.* Englewood Cliffs, NJ: Prentice Hall.

Rosenstock, I. M. (1974). Historical origins of the health belief model. *Health Education Monographs, 2,* 328–335.

Sternberg, R. (1994). *In search of the human mind.* New York: Harcourt Brace.

Weiner, B. (1986). *An attributional theory of achievement motivation and emotion.* New York: Springer-Verlag.

CHILD ATTITUDE TOWARD ILLNESS SCALE

Source

Austin, J. K., & Huberty, T. J. (1993). Development of the child attitude toward illness scale. *Journal of Psychology, 18,* 467–480.

Availability

Joan K. Austin, Indiana University School of Nursing, 1111 Middle Drive, Indianapolis, IN 46202.

Purpose. The Child Attitude Toward Illness Scale (CATIS) was designed to assess positive or negative children's attitudes are about having a chronic physical condition. Like the Children's Health Care Attitudes Questionnaire (CHCAQ) described, the measure is based on the framework that more positive attitudes promote adaptation to stressful medical events. Based on social psychology, the measure assesses attitudes as defined by the favorable or unfavorable evaluation of an event or entity.

Description. Children respond to 13 items on a five-point scale. Four items assess feelings, and the endpoints of the likert scale correspond to opposite adjectives, such as feeling "very bad," "a little bad," "not sure," a "little good," and "very good." For the remaining items, children endorse how often they feel a certain way from "never" to "very often," such as how often they feel like their condition keeps them from doing the things they want to do. The first item of the questionnaire is repeated but with a reversal of the direction of responses to assess for the consistency of responses. The 16 items are summed to form a single summary score. The CATIS requires a third-grade reading level and is designed for children ages 8–12.

Standardization and Norms. The measure was first piloted with a sample of 50 children ages 8–12, half with asthma and half with epilepsy. Demographic data were not reported. The second sample included 269 children (136 with epilepsy and 133 with asthma). The authors reported that a SES scale was utilized to obtain demographic data. They stated that the sample mean score of 59 reflects a mother with one year of college and a head of household who is in a midlevel management position. Ethnicity was not reported.

Reliability and Validity. The authors report adequate internal consistency reliability in three administrations of the CATIS with Cronbach's alphas ranging from .77 to .82. To demonstrate test-retest reliability, the authors report that the total score correlated .80 with a second administration 2 weeks after baseline. The authors report that items were identified based on review of the literature and previous literature of children with epilepsy and asthma. The authors do not report any additional procedures to ensure face validity. As evidence of construct validity, a factor analysis yielded a single factor solution supporting the single summary scale. As evidence of criterion validity, the measure was significant with a negative correlation with regard to measures of depression and behavior problems and significant with a positive correlation of self-esteem.

Summary of Strengths and Limitations. The CATIS appears to be an excellent tool to assess attitudes towards health in chronically ill children. Its brevity and strong psychometric properties are key strengths. The primary limitation is the reliance on a middle-class sample with no reported ethnicity data. The generalizability of findings to low-income families and to other chronic conditions requires further study.

Additional Readings

Austin, J. K., Dunn, D. W., Huster, G. A., & Rose, D. (1998). Development of scales to measure psychosocial care needs of children with seizures and their parents. *Journal of Neuroscience Nursing, 30,* 155–160.

Dunn, D. W., Austin, J. K., & Huster, G. A. (1999). Symptoms of depression in adolescents with epilepsy. *Journal of American Academy of Child and Adolescent Psychiatry, 38,* 1132–1138.

Heimlich, T. E., Westbrook, L. E., Austin, J. K., Cramer, J. A., & Devinsky, O. (2000). Brief report: Adolescents' attitudes toward epilepsy: Further validation of the child attitude toward illness scale (CATIS). *Journal of Pediatric Psychology, 25,* 339–345.

Developer's Comments

The developer provided several references but no additional comments.

CHILDREN'S HEALTH CARE ATTITUDES QUESTIONNAIRE

Source

Bush, J. P., & Holmbeck, G. N. (1987). Children's attitudes about health care: Initial development of a questionnaire. *Journal of Pediatric Psychology, 12,* 429–443.

Availability

Joseph P. Bush, Ph.D., Fielding Graduate Institute, 2112 Santa Barbara Street, Santa Barbara, CA, 93105.

Purpose. The CHCAQ was designed to measure attitudes, cognitions, and beliefs about their health care along three dimensions: Like–Dislike, Effectiveness–Ineffectiveness, and Approach–Avoidance. The measure is based on the hypothesis that more positive attitudes result in better adaptation to stressful medical events.

Description. Children respond to 24 items on a 5-point likert scale. Each dimension contains eight items targeting children's attitudes: doctors, nurses, hospitals, medicine, shots, blood tests, and surgery. The Like–Dislike dimension items are rated from "I really like them a lot" to "I really hate them." The Effectiveness-Ineffectiveness dimension items are rated from "It always helps them" to "They get worse." The Approach–Avoidance items are rated from "I would try not to ___ no matter what" and "I would want to ___." A visual analogue is provided along with the written options to assist younger children. The measure was developed using children ages 5 to 19, and the authors report that 95% of children over the age of 5 were able to complete the questionnaire, though younger children often needed the items read to them. The measure was not intended to yield a single summary score. The measure also includes pain ratings, which will not be discussed as this chapter focuses on cognitions.

Standardization and Norms. The measure was first piloted with a sample of primarily Caucasian, suburban children (N = 168). Another sample of 36 children from a Girl Scout troop and a private school was utilized to examine test-retest reliability after a 2-week interval, but no additional demographic information was presented about this sample. Of two additional studies reporting normative data on the CHCAQ, one (Hackworth and McMahon, 1991) utilized a similarly higher SES sample. However, Bachanas and Roberts (1995) utilized the CHCAQ with a lower SES, primarily minority population.

Reliability and Validity. The authors report adequate reliability with Cronbach's alphas ranging from .63 to .76 and test-retest reliability coefficients ranging from .70 to .76. The authors did not report any procedures to ensure face validity. Hackworth and McMahon (1991) provided further evidence of internal consistency with alphas ranging from .72 to .80. As evidence of construct validity, a factor analysis yielded 3 factors that were consistent with the three scales. However, one item related to liking surgery did not load on any factor. One of the Approach–Avoidance items fell on the factor with most of the Liking items, and two of the Liking items fell on the factor with most of the Approach–Avoidance items. The three factors accounted for 35% of the variance. Furthermore, Bachanas and Roberts (1995) and Hackworth and McMahon (1991) found that different factors were associated with different subscales suggesting that the subscales be treated as separate attitudinal constructs. As evidence of criterion validity, the authors investigated correlations between the three dimensions and children's expectations of the painfulness of medical procedures. As hypothesized, children who were higher on the Avoidance dimension were more likely to perceive procedures as more painful, but no other relationships were significant in the full sample. Contrary to hypotheses, females who were higher on the Effectiveness dimension were more likely to perceive procedures as more painful. In a follow-up study of criterion validity, children with higher scores on Liking and lower on Avoidance were more likely to demonstrate lower levels of distress and report less fear during local dental anesthesia. Finally, other researchers have found that subscales of the CHCAQ have been significantly associated with children's health locus of control and maternal health care attitudes (Bachanas & Roberts, 1995; Hackworth & McMahon, 1991). In fact, these authors have reported promising psychometric properties of a parent version of the CHCAQ.

Summary of Strengths and Limitations. The measure fulfills its intention as a preliminary step to developing a psychometrically sound measure of children's health care attitudes. The measure has satisfactory internal consistency and test-retest reliability. The three-factor structure appears to be a good foundation for future endeavors, but further research is necessary as the factors only accounted for 35% of the variance. The validity of the Liking scale is questionable. Two of the items fell on a separate factor, and another did not fall on any factor. It is unclear how children can respond that they like surgeries or other medical procedures. The measure shows excellent criterion validity. The measure must be tested with more diverse samples and with children with chronic conditions for full demonstration of psychometric properties.

Additional Readings

Bachanas, P. J., & Roberts, M. C. (1995). Factors affecting children's attitudes toward health care and responses to painful medical procedures. *Journal of Pediatric Psychology, 20,* 261–275.

Bush, J. P., Sullivan, T. N., & McGrath, M. L. (1998). Children's attitudes predict distress during local dental anesthesia. *Annals of Behavioral Medicine, 20,* s161.

Hackworth, S. R., & McMahon, R. J. (1991). Factors mediating children's health care attitudes. *Journal of Pediatric Psychology, 16,* 69–85.

Developer's Comments

The developer made minor editorial changes but had no additional comments.

CHILDREN'S HEALTH LOCUS OF CONTROL SCALE

Source

Parcel, G. S., & Meyer, M. P. (1978). Development of an instrument to measure children's health locus of control. *Health Education Monographs, 6,* 149–158.

Availability

From the first author. Guy S. Parcel, Ph.D., Professor, Center for Health Promotion and Prevention Research, University of Texas Health Science Center at Houston, 7000 Fannin Street, Houston, TX 77030.

Purpose.   The Children's Health Locus of Control Scale (CHLC) was developed to assess the potential of social learning theory, particularly the health belief model, to explain health behavior. This measure is intended to address the health motivation variable of the health belief model, and to move beyond general measures of locus of control as this cognition may vary based on the situation or context.

Description.   School-age children and adolescents answer "yes" or "no" to 20 statements about the sources of health. Items are classified as internal or external. Children receive 2 points for each internal item and 1 point for each external item. The points are summed, with higher total scores indicating a more internal locus of control.

Standardization and Norms.   Initial reliability and validity studies were conducted on a sample of 168 children from grades 3 through 5 at a single elementary school. The sample was 40% African American, 25% Caucasian, and 31% Mexican American. SES was not reported. The measure has been widely used in healthy children, and has also been used with several chronic illness populations (Goertzel & Goertzel, 1991).

Reliability and Validity.   The authors report good internal consistency (.75) and adequate test-retest reliability (.62). Factor analysis suggests three factors: (a) Powerful Others Control subscale; (b) Internal Control subscale; and (c) Chance Control subscale. Eight items did not fall on these three factors, and the authors suggested rewording and assignment of the items to one of the three subscales. Reliability of the subscales was not reported. As evidence of construct validity, the authors pointed to significant correlations between the CHLC and a general measure of locus of control. Evidence of criterion validity was not presented. Goertzel and Goertzel (1991) tested reliability and validity of the measure with 38 pediatric cancer patients, ages 8 to 18. They found adequate internal consistency reliability for the total scale (alpha = .71) and for the Powerful Others subscale (alpha = .73), but poor reliability for the Internal (.23) and Chance (.49) subscales. The authors reported that the measure had poor construct reliability because it did not correlate with self-concept or anxiety, but it is a conceptual leap to hypothesize that measures of self-concept and anxiety assess the same construct of locus of control. Evidence of criterion validity was not presented in the original paper, but Parcel (1988) noted that the measure has been used in over 30 studies. A literature search suggests that the measure has continued to be utilized in research studies over the last decade.

Summary of Strengths and Limitations.   The CHLC holds promise as a psychometrically sound measure of an important social learning construct that may potentially predict health behavior. However, reliability of the subscales has not been adequately demonstrated. The two-option response format limits internal consistency reliability. Second, criterion validity was not reported by the developers, though may be evidenced in research studies over the last two decades. Finally, the measure was developed with elementary school children, and reliability and validity of the measure with older children and adolescents requires further support. Olvera, Remy, Power, Bellamy, and Hays (2001) translated the measure into Spanish.

Additional Readings

Goertzel, L., & Goertzel, T. (1991). Health locus of control, self-concept, and anxiety in pediatric cancer patients. *Psychological Reports, 68,* 531–540.

Olvera, N., Remey, R., Power, T. G., Bellamy, C., & Hays, J. (2001). Observed maternal strategies and children's health locus of control in low-income Mexican American families. *Journal of Family Psychology, 15,* 451–463.

Parcel, G. S. (1988). CHLC scale developer comments on applicability. *Journal of School Health, 58,* 20.

THE HEALTH SELF-DETERMINISM INDEX FOR CHILDREN

Source

Cox, C. L., Cowell, J. M., Marion, L. N., & Miller, E. H. (1990). The Health Self-Determinism Index for Children. *Research in Nursing and Health, 13,* 267–271.

Availability

Available from Dr. Cheryl L. Cox, College of Health Professions, University of Lowell, One University Avenue, Lowell, MA 01854.

Purpose. The Health Self-Determination Index for Children (HSDI-C) is used to measure intrinsic motivation for health behavior in children.

Description. The HSDI-C is a 27-item scale adapted from the Health Self-Determinism Index developed for use with adults (Cox, 1985). The HSDI-C consists of four subscales: Behavior and goals, Competence,

Internal–external cue responsiveness, and Judgment. Responses are made on a structured alternative format. For example, subjects are presented with two sets of behavior: "Some kids do things for their health because they want to be healthier" but "Other kids do things for their health because someone makes them." Subjects first decide which kid they are most like and then decide if the statement is really true or sort of true for them. The format is based on the child and Adolescent Self-Perception Profile for Children developed by Harter (1985). According to Harter, the structured alternative format facilitates children to give accurate perceptions rather than socially desirable responses.

Scoring is on a 1 to 4 scale where 1 indicates the maximum extrinsic orientation and 4 indicates the maximum intrinsic orientation for the item. Items are summed to form subscale and total scores. Total scores have a possible range of 27 to 108.

The theoretical basis for the scale is Deci's cognitive evaluation theory (Deci, 1975, 1980; Deci & Ryan, 1985). Unlike more global and unidimensional views of motivation, such as locus of control, Deci viewed motivation as multidimensional and varying in strength along the intrinsic–extrinsic continuum. Deci characterized intrinsic motivation as active, self-satisfying, and competence building. For example, children who are intrinsically motivated respond to internal rewards for various behaviors, such as developing a sense of self-competency and determinism. In contrast, children who are extrinsically motivated need external and tangible rewards in order to sustain behaviors. Although motivation can be changed, the primary reason for knowing an individual's motivation is to provide interventions that match motivational orientation. The HSDI-C is intended as a diagnostic aid in the clinical setting.

Standards and Norms. The HSDI-C was tested with three convenience samples of children in grades 3–7. Cox et al. (1990) stated that the samples were heterogeneous in respect to SES and race but specific demographic characteristics were not given. The first sample consisted of 501 children and the second sample consisted of 50 children. The school nurse nominated the third sample (n = 21) children because she believed they demonstrated positive health behaviors.

Reliability and Validity. Internal consistency (alpha coefficient) was .92 and .90 for the behavior–goal subscale, .84 and .88 for the competency subscale, .84 and .88 for the internal–external subscale, and .63 and .77 for the judgment subscale. The total scale had an alpha coefficient of .87 and .88. Two-week test-retest reliability ranged from .63 to .88 for the subscales and total score.

Criterion-related reliability was addressed by comparing the original sample to another sample of similarly aged youngsters who were nominated by the school nurse as having exceptional positive health promotion behaviors. Total scores for the nominated subsample was 106.5 compared to 76.5 for the original study sample.

Experts in motivational theory and motivation in adults evaluated content validity when the adult version of the HSDI was first modified for children. Construct validity was addressed by administering the intrinsic versus extrinsic orientation in the classroom scale (Harter, 1981) at the same time as the HSDI-C. The moderate correlation of .36 indicated some commonality in the constructs. Factor analysis supported the existence of four factors thus supporting the multidimensional nature of motivation for health behavior. The moderately strong loadings supported the item content of the factors and the low to moderate correlation between the factors supported the distinctiveness of each. Together the four factors explained 38% of the variance in children's motivation for health behavior.

Summary of Strengths and Limitations.   Although the HSDI-C is directed toward motivation for health behavior, it has considerable potential for assisting children to make behavioral changes necessary to manage health problems, especially since illness management is often presented as necessary to stay healthy. It might also be useful to help parents provide the type of rewards that match the child's motivational style. The major limitation of the scale is that it is not in widespread use and there are very few published reports using the scale in the literature. According to Cox, the HSDI-C has been translated into Spanish, and several of the eastern Asian languages, including Vietnamese. The HSDI-C is currently in use by the developer, and nursing faculty at the University of Illinois is using the scale with Latino males. This should result in some very interesting cross-cultural comparisons, as well as many potentially interesting questions and answers about motivation and behavior in children under different circumstance and among different populations.

Additional Readings

Cox, C. L. (1985). The health self-determination index. *Nursing Research,* 34(3), 177–183.

Deci, E. L. (1975). *Intrinsic motivation.* New York: Plenum Press.

Deci, E. L. (1980). *The psychology of self-determinism.* Lexington, MA: Lexington Books.

Deci, E. L., & Ryan, R. M. (1985). *Intrinsic motivation and self-determination in human behavior.* New York: Plenum Press.

Farrand, L. L., Cox, C. L. (1993). Determinants of positive health behavior in middle childhood. *Nursing Research, 42,* 208–213.

Harter, S. (1981). A new self-report scale of intrinsic versus extrinsic orientation in the classroom: Motivational and informational components. *Developmental Psychology, 17,* 300–312.

Harter, S. (1985). *Manual for the self-perception profile for children.* Denver, CO: University of Denver.

TABLE 7.1
Disease-Specific Measures

Disease	Measure	Reference
Asthma	Child Asthma Self-Efficacy Scale	Bursch, Schwankovsky, Gilbert, & Zeiger (1999)
	Parent Asthma Self-Efficacy Scale	Bursch et al. (1999)
	Parent Treatment Efficacy Scale	Bursch et al. (1999)
Diabetes	Maternal Self-Efficacy for Diabetes	Leonard, Skay, & Rheinberger (1998)
	Personal Models of Diabetes	Skinner, John, & Hampson (2000)
Short Stature	Attitude to Growth Scale	Boulton, Dunn, Quigley, Taylor, & Thompson (1991)
	Silhouette Apperception Technique	Grew, Stabler, Williams, & Underwood (1983)

References

Boulton, T. J., Dunn, S. M., Quigley, C. A., Taylor, J. J., & Thompson, L. (1991). Perceptions of self and short stature: Effects of two years of growth hormone treatment. *Acta Paediatrica Scandinavica, 377,* 20–27.

Bursch, B., Schwankovsky, L., Gilbert, J., & Zeiger, R. (1999). Construction and validation of four childhood asthma self-management scales: Parent barriers, child and parent self-efficacy, and parent belief in treatment efficacy. *Journal of Asthma, 36,* 115–128.

Grew, R. S., Stabler, B., Williams, R. W., & Underwood, L. E. (1983). Facilitating patient understanding in the treatment of growth delay. *Journal of Pediatrics, 101,* 477–489.

Leonard, B. J., Skay, C. L., & Rheinberger, J. D. (1998). Self-management development in children and adolescents with diabetes: The role of maternal self-efficacy and conflict. *Journal of Pediatric Nursing, 13,* 224–233.

Skinner, T., John, M., & Hampson, S. (2000). Social support and personal models of diabetes as predictors of self-care and well-being: A longitudinal study of adolescents with diabetes. *Journal of Pediatric Psychology, 25*(4), 260.

8

Environment

Branlyn E. Werba
Sheila M. Eyberg
University of Florida

INTRODUCTION

Pediatric psychologists have long recognized the important role of environmental factors, specifically those related to the family, in their influence on a child's health and behavioral outcome (Kazak, 1997). The role of families in pediatric practice is exemplified by the attention devoted to family functioning in medical textbooks. A recent edition of a popular medical oncology text noted:

> The naturally worried parents through their vigilance tend to encourage dependency, to overindulge or overprotect their child, and they find it difficult to administer any discipline. (Hersh, Wiener, Figueroa, & Kunz, 1997, p. 1252).

These kinds of impressions of the parenting skills of the mothers and fathers of chronically ill children taught to medical students may influence current and future care of these families and require study. They are the subject matter of pediatric psychology. In fact, two studies by Noll and colleagues began to address the validity of such impressions. They found that child-rearing practices, assessed by maternal self-report ratings, did not differ between children with cancer or sickle cell disease and healthy classmate controls (Davies, Noll, DeStefano, Bukowski, & Kulkarni, 1991; Noll, McKellop, Vannatta, & Kalinyak, 1998). Is this finding more valid than clinical impression? It depends on the validity of the instrument used to measure child rearing.

The psychometric properties of the measures we use determine the validity of our scientific findings. Robinson and Eyberg (1984) described the application of generalizability theory to pediatric psychology as a coherent model for evaluating the psychometric properties of our instruments. Rather than considering reliability and validity as separate issues, individual aspects can be evaluated according to the degree to which scores generalize across more specific dimensions that are applicable to both traditional and behavioral instruments (Cone, 1977). To demonstrate confidence in our findings, data obtained from instruments should generalize between scorers, items, times, and settings (i.e., be reliable) in the same populations over the same length of time without significant change. Data measuring the same behavior should also be generalizable across methods, such as structured interview, behavioral observation, and self-report (i.e., convergent validity), and across dimensions of related behavior (i.e., concurrent validity). Generalizability theory provides a framework to determine whether data generalize not just to populations of acute and chronically ill children, their families, and hospital or clinic environments, but to pediatric populations of different genders, ages, ethnic groups, and perhaps specific illness groups as well.

In addition to evaluating an instrument's psychometric properties by considering the generalizability of its data, each construct should be conceptualized within a specific theoretical framework. The transactional model of development provides an overarching theory of how ill children relate to their environment (Eyberg, Schuhmann, & Rey, 1998; Fiese, 1997; Sameroff & Chandler, 1975). According to the transactional model, a child's developmental outcome results from complex, reciprocal interactions between factors within the child (e.g., cognitive, temperamental, and physical health) and factors outside the child (e.g., life-sustaining habits, environmental hazards, the family, peer group, and other social groups). The ways in which a child interacts with the environment are expected to differ with age and wider spheres of interacting reciprocal influences, from parents and family to the broader social network of neighborhood, school, peers, and teachers.

Due to the range of situations and people that serve as reciprocal influences on child and family outcome, it is important to use multiple measures, informants, and methods of measurement to understand these complex interactions (Campbell & Fiske, 1959; Eyberg, 1985; Kazdin, 1998). Different measures of the same construct do not necessarily measure the same thing. For example, a recent study found that depression scores on the Beck Depression Inventory versus the depression subscale of the Parenting Stress Index related quite differently to observed maternal behaviors with their children, despite high correlations between the two depression measures (Querido, Eyberg, Algina, & Boggs, 1999). Different informants using the same instrument may also provide different results as a function of differing perspectives of mothers, fathers, teachers, doctors, and others who interact with children. The limited information on fathers as informants, in particular, is a widely acknowledged weakness in pediatric psychology research (Chaney et al., 1997; Drotar, 1997; Kazak, 1997). Finally, it is important to use multiple methods of measurement to protect results from misinterpretations or errors due to shared method variance or idiosyncratic findings. For example, when maternal discipline strategies were assessed by multiple methods, differences between discipline strategies of mothers of children with cancer and healthy controls emerged when assessed by an interview, but not when assessed by self-report (Jelalian, Stark, & Miller, 1997).

The scope of an instrument must also be considered when evaluating a measure for use in pediatric psychology research and, specifically, whether an instrument captures general variables, illness-specific variables, or both, which may influence child and family outcome. Most studies have focused on general features of individual or family functioning, such as anxiety or adaptability, to the neglect of characteristics that may relate to the management of specific illnesses (Drotar, 1997). However, both general instruments (which allow comparison with healthy populations) and illness-specific instruments (which allow within-population comparisons) have an important role in helping us to understand the common and unique reciprocal influences in illness populations (Quittner & DiGirolamo, 1998).

The instruments we choose for clinical and research use have far-reaching implications for increasing our ability to understand and effectively treat pediatric populations. More accurate measures will lead to better detection of the environmental factors that place children at risk for mental and physical health problems and to a clearer delineation of the mechanisms of treatment that affect healthy transactions and positive outcomes. With the growing numbers of children living with chronic illness and the increasing role of their families in illness management (Quittner & DiGirolamo, 1998), psychometrically refined instruments to assess the reciprocal influences among the child, family, and larger environment allow greater opportunity to impact these families' quality of care and quality of life.

REFERENCES

Campbell, D. T., & Fiske, D. W. (1959). Convergent and discriminant validation by the multitrait-multimethod matrix. *Psychological Bulletin, 56,* 81–105.

Chaney, J. M., Mullins, L. L., Frank, R. G., Peterson, L., Mace, L. D., Kashani, J. H., & Goldstein, D. L. (1997). Transactional patterns of child, mother, and father adjustment in insulin-dependent diabetes mellitus: A prospective study. *Journal of Pediatric Psychology, 22,* 229–244.

Cone, J. D. (1977). The relevance of reliability and validity for behavioral assessment. *Behavior Therapy, 8*, 411–426.

Davies, W. H., Noll, R. B., DeStefano, L., Bukowski, W. M., & Kulkarni, R. (1991). Differences in the child-rearing practices of parents of children with cancer and controls: The perspectives of parents and professionals. *Journal of Pediatric Psychology, 16*, 295–306.

Drotar, D. (1997) Relating parent and family functioning to the psychological adjustment of children with chronic health conditions: What have we learned? What do we need to know? *Journal of Pediatric Psychology, 22*, 149–165.

Eyberg, S. M. (1985). Behavioral assessment: Advancing methodology in pediatric psychology. *Journal of Pediatric Psychology, 10*, 123–139.

Eyberg, S. M., Schuhmann, E. M., & Rey, J. (1998). Child and adolescent psychotherapy research: Developmental issues. *Journal of Abnormal Child Psychology, 26*, 71–82.

Fiese, B. H. (1997). Family context in pediatric psychology from a transactional perspective: Family rituals and stories as examples. *Journal of Pediatric Psychology, 22*, 183–196.

Hersh, S. P, Wiener, L. S., Figueroa, V., & Kunz, J. F. (1997). Psychiatric and psychosocial support for the child and family. In P. A. Pizzo & D. G. Poplac (Eds.), *Principles and practice of pediatric oncology* (3rd ed., pp. 1241–1266). Philadelphia: Lippincott.

Jelalian, E., Stark, L. J., & Miller, D. (1997). Maternal attitudes toward discipline: A comparison of children with cancer and non-chronically ill peers. *Children's Health Care, 26*, 169–182.

Kazak, A. E. (1997). A contextual family/systems approach to pediatric psychology: Introduction to the special issue. *Journal of Pediatric Psychology, 22*, 141–148.

Kazdin, A. (1998). *Research Design in Clinical Psychology (3rd ed.)*. Needham Heights, MA: Allyn & Bacon.

Noll, R. B., McKellop, J. M., Vannatta, K., & Kalinyak, K. (1998). Child-rearing practices of primary caregivers of children with sickle cell disease: The perspective of professionals and caregivers. *Journal of Pediatric Psychology, 23*, 131–140.

Querido, J., Eyberg, S., Algina, J., & Boggs, S. (1999, March). *Pathways linking maternal depressive symptomatology and child behavior problems*. Paper presented at the annual meeting of the Southeastern Psychological Association, Savannah, GA.

Quittner, A. L., & DiGirolamo, A. M. (1998). Family adaptation to childhood disability and illness. In R. T. Ammerman & J. V. Campo (Eds.), *Handbook of pediatric psychology and psychiatry* (Vol. II, pp. 70–102). Boston: Allyn & Bacon.

Robinson, E. A., & Eyberg, S. M. (1984). Behavioral assessment in pediatric settings: Theory, method, and application. In P. R. Magrab (Ed.), *Psychological and behavioral assessment: Impact on pediatric care* (pp. 91–140). New York: Plenum.

Sameroff, A. J., & Chandler, M. J. (1975). Reproductive risk and the continuum of caretaking casualty. In F. D. Horowitz, M. Hetherington, S. Scarr-Salapatek, & G. Siegel (Eds.), *Review of Child Development Research* (Vol. 4, pp, 187–244). Chicago: University of Chicago Press.

FAMILY ADAPTABILITY AND COHESION EVALUATION SCALE

Source

Olson, D. H., Bell, R., & Portner, J. (1985). *Family Adaptability and Cohesion Scales II (FACES II)*. Minneapolis, MN: Life Innovations.

Olson, D. H., Portner, J., & Lavee, Y. (1985). *Family Adaptability and Cohesion Scales III (FACES III)*. Minneapolis MN: Life Innovations.

Availability

From Life Innovations, PO Box 190, Minneapolis, MN 55440. E-mail: *CFIP@lifeinnovations.com* or by accessing the Life Innovations website at *www.lifeinnovations.com*. The Family Inventories manual contains FACES II, FACES III, and three other family instruments, overviews, and scoring procedures. The measures are copyrighted.

Purpose. The Family Adaptability & Cohesion Evaluation Scale (FACES) was designed to measure family adaptability (flexibility) and cohesion, two major concepts in Olson's Circumplex Model of Marital and Family Functioning.

Description. There are two versions currently in use. The FACES II is designed for use in research with families, while FACES III is designed for clinical work with families. The alpha reliability is higher for FACES II (see the following), and for that reason it is recommended for research. The FACES II consists of 30 items, while FACES III consists of 20 items. For each scale, half of the items measure adaptability (flexibility) and half measure cohesion. The scales are used to measure an individual's perception of their family. There is a couples version for families without children. Family members over the age of 12 can complete the scale. As many family members as possible should complete the scale. The FACES II and III are easy to administer and take approximately 10 minutes to complete. They can be administered face to face with individuals, couples, or groups and are also suitable for mail-out surveys. Reading level is approximately seventh grade.

Items on FACES II and III are answered on a 5-point scale (almost never, once in a while, sometimes, frequently, or almost always) to indicate how often the behavior occurs in a given family. Sample items include, "We ask each other for help" for Cohesion, and "Rules change in our family" for Adaptability. Items for each subscale are summed. When the FACES III is used to operationalize the Circumplex Model, total Cohesion scores are used to classify families into one of four levels: disengaged, separated, connected, or enmeshed. Total Adaptability (Flexibility) scores are used to classify families into one of four levels: rigid, structured, flexible, or chaotic. The level of cohesion and the level of adaptability are then used to place the family into one of 16 family types. Calculation of the *perceived family–ideal family* discrepancy score has been used as a measure of satisfaction with one's current family system. Options for handling scores from more than one family member are to use family mean scores or family member discrepancy scores. Instructions, formulas, and cutting points for these various scoring strategies are provided in the manual.

Initially, the scoring of FACES II and FACES III was based on the hypothesis that the relationship of cohesion and adaptability to family functioning was curvilinear. That is, families in the middle levels of adaptability and cohesion and the central four family types on the Circumplex Model were believed to function better than families at either extreme of cohesion, adaptability, or family type. In 1991, Olson presented a revised model and recommended linear scoring of the FACES II and III in response to the numerous studies that failed to support the curvilinear hypothesis. In view of these revisions and recommendations, high scores on the cohesion and adaptability subscales of FACES II and FACES III should be interpreted as indicating a more functional family type. Although the cutting points for classifying family types for FACES III did not change (Olson, 1991), the extremes of cohesion, adaptability, and family type have been renamed very connected, very flexible, and balanced, respectively.

Summary of Standardization and Norms.   Norms and cutting points for FACES II and III are available for three groups: adults across all family life stages (n = 2,453), families with adolescents (n = 1,315), and young couples (n = 242). Data were drawn from a cross-sectional, national survey of non-problem and intact families across the life span (Olson et al., 1989). Families from 31 states were represented. The sample of 1,140 couples (no single parents) and 412 adolescents was primarily middle to upper income and Lutheran. Race–ethnicity of the sample was not reported. The FACES II was administered along with a number of other established and newly developed family instruments.

Reliability and Validity.   Updated alpha reliabilities for FACES II were .89 for cohesion and .81 for adaptabililty. For FACES III, updated alpha reliabilities were .80 for cohesion and .76 for adaptability. Four- to 5-week test-retest reliability with FACES II was .83 for cohesion and .80 for adaptability.

Construct validity of the FACES scales was established by conducting factor analyses. Factor analysis with the FACES II resulted in the 20-item FACES III. Items were added, dropped, and replaced while maintaining the validity and independence of the factors. The 20-item scale was subsequently administered to a second sample. The factor structure was replicated and the correlation between adaptability and cohesion was reduced to r = .03. Additional evidence of validity is the high subscale item to total scale score correlation and a near zero order correlation between adaptability and social desirability.

Summary of Strengths and Limitations. FACES II and III are well-developed, conceptually sound, and extensively tested scales. The measures have been used in over 1,000 published studies on a wide variety of topics and with diverse populations. They may arguably be the most frequently used measures of family functioning and family system relationships. Although the instruments measure general dimensions of family functioning, they have been used extensively in health care research with families facing a wide variety of acute and chronic health problems. An early criticism of the scales was that the normative population consisted of two parent, Caucasian, primarily middle income families with over one-third living in rural areas. However, given the extensive use of the scale, research on diverse demographic, geographic, clinical, and community samples can be found in the literature. In addition, information about the scales and other available resources from the publisher make FACES III very user friendly for both research and clinical practice.

Additional Readings

Olson, D. H. (1991). Commentary: three-dimensional (3-D) Circumplex Model and revised scoring of FACES III. *Family Process, 30,* 74–79.
Olson, D. H. (2000). Circumplex Model of Marital and Family Systems. *Journal of Family Therapy, 22,* 144–167.
Olson, D.H., McCubbin, H. I., Barnes, H., Larsen, A., Muxen, M., & Wilson, M. (1989). Families what makes them work. Beverly Hills, CA: Sage Publications.

Developer's Comments

The author forwarded several editorial changes but made no additional comments.

FAMILY ENVIRONMENT SCALE

Source

Moos, R. H., & Moos, B. S. (1994). Family Environment Scale Manual: Development, applications, research (3rd ed.). Palo Alto, CA: Consulting Psychological Press, Inc.

Availability

From Consulting Psychological Press, Palo Alto, CA 94306, 1–800–624–1765 or by accessing the CPP web site at *www.cpp.db.com*. All forms of the FES are copyrighted.

Purpose.   The purpose of the Family Environmental Scale (FES) is to measure the actual, preferred, and expected social environment of the family system.

Description.   The FES is a self-report questionnaire that consists of 10 subscales: cohesion, expressiveness, conflict, independence, achievement orientation, intellectual-cultural orientation, active-recreational orientation, moral-religious emphasis, organization, and control. When combined, the subscales identify three underlying dimensions of family systems: relationships (cohesion, expressiveness, and conflict), personal growth or goal orientation (independence, achievement, intellectual-cultural, active recreational, and moral-religious), and system maintenance (organization and control). Each subscale has nine items, for a total of 90 items, answered with a true–false response scale. Scoring is aided by the use of a template that identifies which response (true or false) represents the more positive direction of a given family characteristic. There are many scoring options including individual subscales, family dimensions, and total FES scores.

There are several forms of the FES. The Real form is one's perception of his own family. The Ideal form is one's preference for how a family should be. The Expectation form is a description of how one expects a family to be. Differences in the forms are in the wording of the items. The forms are suitable for adults and adolescents as young as 11 years of age. The reading level is reported to be fifth grade. Although a picture format form is available for 5- to 11-year-old children, there are limited reports on its use in the literature. Expected time to complete the scale is 10 to 20 minutes. It is recommended that the questionnaires be read to children, younger adolescents, and others with limited reading ability or a short attention span.

Standardization and Norms.   Both individual and family level discrepancy scores and standard scores can be derived. Normative data (from 1979 and 1981 studies) is available for normal, distressed, single parent, African-American and Latino families, and children. In addition, the FES has been translated and used with Arabic, Asian, Chinese, Dutch, Estonian, French, Hebrew, Japanese, Portuguese, Russian, Spanish, and Swedish populations.

Reliability and Validity. Reliability and validity data for the FES are extensive, and a comprehensive review is beyond the scope of this chapter. In addition to the manual and user's guide, many other researchers have addressed reliability and validity for general, as well as minority populations, and information about reliability and validity is included in the over 200 published studies that used the FES. However, the initial pool of 200 items was identified through naturalistic interviews with different types of families and examination of data from Moos' other social climate scales. The scale was tested with over 1,000 diverse families including distressed or troubled families. Development of the final form was based on conceptual, empirical, psychometric criteria that supported the intent of scale developers to measure broad constructs or dimensions that differentiate family environments. Internal consistency based on Cronbach's alpha ranged from .61 to 78 and 1-year test-retest reliability ranged from .53 to .84 for subscales.

Summary of Strengths and Limitations. The strengths of the FES are its wide-ranging use, making it possible to compare family environments across samples and populations. The scale has been used extensively with families facing acute and chronic health problems. The numerous forms facilitate its use in a variety of circumstances ranging from premarital counseling (expectations form), family transitions (ideal form) to assessment of treatment outcomes (real form). Because the FES has been used with adolescents and young children, data can be collected on adolescent and child perceptions of the family.

The most frequently identified limitations of the FES relate to the modest reliability of some subscales, availability of normative data, more limited history of use with minority, and non-English speaking populations, and construct validity (Dashiff, 1994; Loveland-Cherry, Youngblut, & Leidy, 1989; Munet-Vilaro, & Egan, 1990; Wilk, 1991). Despite the questions raised about the FES, it is one of the most widely used, family-functioning measures in the social, health, and family sciences and is often used as the standard for establishing the criterion-related validity of newly developed family measures.

References

Brady, N. (1999). Instruments for research with families the Family Environment Scale (FES) and Feetham's Family Functioning Survey (FFFS). *Journal of Child and Family Nursing, 2,* 63–67.

Dashiff, C. J. (1994). Decision points in choosing family self-report scales in research. *Image Journal of Nursing Scholarship, 26,* 283–288.

Loveland-Cherry, C. J., Youngblut, J. M., & Leidy, N. J. (1989). A psychometric analysis of the family environment scale. *Nursing Research, 38,* 262–266.

Moos, R. J. (1994). *The social climate scales: A user's guide.* Palo Alto, CA: Consulting Psychological Press, Inc.

Munet-Vilaro, F., & Egan, M. (1990). Reliability issues of the family environment scale for cross-cultural research. *Nursing Research, 39,* 244–247.

Pino, C. J., Simons, N., & Slawinowski, M. J. (1984). *The children's version of the family environment scale manual.* East Aurra, NY: Slosson Educational Publications.

Wilk, J. (1991). Family instrument selection and study fit. *Western Journal of Nursing Research, 13,* 449–553.

FAMILY INVENTORY OF LIFE EVENTS

Source

McCubbin, H. I., & Patterson, J. M. (1991). FILE family inventory of life events and changes. In H. I. McCubbin & A.I. Thompson (Eds). *Family assessment inventories for research and practice* (pp. 81–98). Madison, WI: The University of Wisconsin–Madison.

Availability

From the Center for Excellence in Family Studies, Family Stress, Coping, and Health Project, University of Wisconsin–Madison, 1300 Linden Drive, Madison, WI 53706. The measure is copyrighted.

Purpose. The Family Inventory of Life Events (FILE) is an index of family stress. The construct of stress is measured by assessing the number of stressful life events experienced by the family in the recent past.

Description. The FILE consists of 71 statements of normative and non-normative life events and changes across nine content areas and several subcontent divisions (in parentheses): intra-family strains (conflict and parenting), marital strains, pregnancy and childbearing strains, finance and business strains (family finance and family business), work-family transitions and strains (work transitions, family transitions, and work stains), illness and family care strains (illness onset and child care, chronic illness strains, and dependency strains), losses, transitions in and out, and family legal violations. These content areas were identified from a review of individual life-change instruments, the family life-cycle literature, and family stress theory and research. Sample items are as follows: Increased disagreements about a member's friends or activities (intra-family strains–conflicts); increased strains on family money for food, clothing, energy, and home care (family finance); and child became seriously ill or injured (illness and family care strains). Respondents are instructed to read each item and indicate by checking yes or no whether it happened to anyone in their family in the past 12 months. The FILE can be completed by more than one family member and is suitable for use with any type of family structure (single parent, blended family, gay–lesbian, etc.).

There are five scoring options. Family life events or stress is calculated by coding yes items as 1 and no items as 0. Positive responses are summed for subscale and total scale scores. Higher scores represent higher levels of family stress in the past year. Family scores are derived by summing all positive responses that are endorsed by any family member. Family discrepancy scores can also be calculated and may indicate areas of miscommunication. The two other methods of scoring are based on the methodology of Holmes and Rahe (1967) that used weighted scores to reflect the magnitude and severity of various life events. Standardized family weights are available for each FILE item. However, the authors report that the unweighted summed score has been found to be just as useful as the weighting scoring method.

Standardization and Norms. Normative data are available for families across seven family life-cycle stages. Norms are based on a national sample of intact families (n = 1,140) across the life cycles (see FACES III for additional details of the survey). Normative scores (means) are provided for seven family developmental stages. In addition, there are cutting points to classify families as low, moderate, or high stress.

Reliability and Validity. Cronbach's alpha for the 71-item scale was .81. Internal consistency for the subscales ranged from .16 to .72. The low coefficients are most likely due to the wide variance in the frequency of occurrence of events, especially in the areas of marital strain, pregnancy, and childbearing. Accordingly, the authors recommend the use of the total scale score.

Test-retest reliability was conducted with a sample of 150 high school and college students. Four- to 5-week retest reliabilities resulted in alpha coefficients ranging from .66 to .84 for the subscales and .80 for the total FILE score.

Factor analysis generally replicated the structure of the FILE, but was most likely affected by the distribution and low occurrence of some of the events as noted previously. However, discriminate analysis between low and high conflict families and a large number of life changes and negative correlations between a larger number of life changes and family functioning provide evidence of construct validity. Negative correlations between the content areas of FILE, total life changes, and the health status of 100 children with cerebral palsy provide evidence of predictive validity. That is, as family stress increased, the health status of the child deteriorated.

Summary of Strengths and Limitations. The FILE is a conceptually sound, well-developed scale that can be used with virtually all families regardless of structure or size. Inclusion of items related to child health and illness status makes it especially useful for families in the health care setting. A limitation of the FILE is that the items tend to be directed more toward middle-income families than low income or otherwise disadvantaged families. Somewhat different stresses and strains may affect disadvantaged families, especially those living in poverty.

Additional Readings

Holmes, T. H., & Rahe, R. H. (1967). The social readjustment scale. *Journal of Psychosomatic Research, 11*, 213–218.

PARENTS OF CHILDREN
WITH DISABILITIES INVENTORY

Source

Noojin, A. B., & Wallander, J. L. (1996) Development and evaluation of a measure of concerns related to raising a child with a physical disability. *Journal of Pediatric Psychology, 21,* 483–498.

Availability

From the second author, Civitan International Research Center, University of Alabama at Birmingham, CIRC 235D, Birmingham, Alabama, 35294–0021.

Purpose. Traditional measures of parenting stress were not developed for use with parents of children with health problems. Therefore, instrument content often does not include the types of stressors faced by such parents and may not adequately predict their adjustment. The Parents of Children With Disabilities Inventory (PCDI) is a self-report questionnaire that was specifically designed to measures the amount and perception of stress experienced by parents of children with physical disabilities.

Description. The PCDI is a 40-item instrument that consists of a list of problems or stressors faced by parents. The respondent is asked to rate on a 6-point rating scale: (a) how often the problem occurs (concern score) and (b) how much the problem causes the respondent to worry (frequency score). The PCDI has four rationally derived subscales (Medical and Legal Concerns, Concerns for the Child, Concerns for the Family, and Concerns for the Self). Subscale scores are calculated by summing the items that load on each scale. A total score can also be obtained by adding all item scores.

Standardization and Norms. The instrument was developed in two outpatient clinics in the southern United States serving children with physical disabilities. Sixty-three mothers of children with spina bifida or cerebral palsy completed the instrument. Seventy-four percent were Caucasian. Thirty-five percent were not high school graduates, 35% had a high school education, and the remainder had various levels of post-high school education. Means and standard deviations on the PCDI are provided for the sample, but standard scores are not provided and would have to be derived.

Reliability and Validity. The psychometric data presented by the authors of the PCDI are for the concern scores. Two month test-retest reliability data was obtained for the PCDI from a subsample of 31 mothers chosen at random from the total sample. Stability of PCDI scores was moderate at best (.60 for the total score, and .41–.66 for the scale scores), which may reflect some inherent degree of variability in the occurrence of stressful events. Internal consistency for the PCDI was moderately strong. Cronbach's alpha for the total Score was .90 and ranged from .65 to .84 for the four subscales.

Content validity was established by generating an initial pool of 125 items for the measure from mothers of children with chronic physical disabilities who provided examples of specific problems they faced due to their child's disability. The item pool was reduced to the final 40-item scale through evaluation of item-response distribution, item-total correlation for each scale, and inter-item correlation. Criterion validity of the PCDI was assessed by comparing the PCDI total score and subscale scores to scores on a variety of other established measures, including measures of stress related to caring for a disabled family member, family functioning, maternal mental health, maternal physical health, and child behavior problems. The Medical and Legal Concerns scale was found to be moderately and strongly correlated with a measure of parent stress. The Concerns for Child Scale was found to be moderately and strongly correlated with a measure of child behavior problems, and the Concerns for Self Scale was found to be moderately strongly correlated with measures of maternal mental health and physical health.

Summary of Strengths and Limitations. The PCDI is one of the only instruments available that was specifically designed to measure stress experienced by parents of children with disabilities. Therefore, it has the advantage of including items not found on traditional measures of parenting stress that are highly salient for parents of ill children (i.e., sadness that child has a disability). Although the instrument was developed with a sample of mothers of children with physical disabilities such as cerebral palsy, instrument content appears appropriate for parents of children with a variety of health problems. Information regarding the psychometric properties of the instrument when used with fathers is not currently available. Additional information regarding the construct and predictive validity of the instrument, particularly the four subscales, is also needed to improve research utility. The lack of extensive standardization limits clinical utility at the present time.

PARENT-CHILD RELATIONSHIP INVENTORY

Source

Gerard, A. B. (1994). *Parent-Child Relationship Inventory Manual.* Los Angeles: Western Psychological Services.

Availability

From WPS, 12031 Wilshire Boulevard, Los Angeles, CA 90025–1251. The measure is copyrighted.

Purpose. The Parent-Child Relationship Inventory (PCRI) is designed to yield a quantitative assessment of parent-child relationships to complement other assessment methods, such as interview and observation. The measure assesses parents' attitudes toward their children and parenting.

Description. Parents rate 78 statements on a 4-point likert-type scale from strongly agree to strongly disagree. The questionnaire may be administered to an individual or a group. It takes about 15 minutes to complete and requires a fourth-grade reading level. Items are summed to create seven content scales with higher scores indicating more positive parenting. The scales should not be summed as the measure is not meant to yield a single summary scale. The content scales include: Parental Support (9 items), Satisfaction with Parenting (10 items), Involvement (14 items), Communication (9 items), Limit Setting (12 items), Autonomy (10 items), and Role Orientation (9 items). In addition, there are two validity indicators based on patterns of responses. The social desirability indicator includes the remaining five items, which are generally not endorsed positively. The inconsistency indicator is calculated by reviewing 10 pairs of highly correlated items. Raw scores are all converted to scale scores, T scores based on the normative sample described in the following. T scores less than 40 indicate concerns in the area of the particular scale.

Standardization and Norms. The PCRI was standardized using a normative sample of 1,100 mothers and fathers from schools and day-care centers across the United States. Children's ages ranged from less than 3 to greater than 13, and about half the children were female. Parents age ranged from 18 to greater than 55. The sample had a moderately higher SES and had fewer minorities than the U.S. population, as reflected by 1991 Census data. The majority of the sample was Caucasian (86%), and 63% attended college. The authors noted that ethnicity and education have a significant effect on scores. African-American parents reported less satisfaction with parenting and less promotion of child autonomy than Caucasian parents. Parents who completed college reported more social support than other parents, and parents who attended some college reported more promotion of autonomy than parents with high school or less than high school education.

Reliability and Validity. The manual described several studies demonstrating satisfactory internal consistency and test-retest reliability. To ensure content validity, items were drawn from a review of the parenting literature and were reviewed by a panel of experts. The manual reported data on confirmatory factor analysis and item-total correlations as evidence of construct validity. Studies of criterion validity have shown that families undergoing court-ordered custody mediation fall below T scores of 40 on several scales, and that the PCRI predicted child adjustment within this group of families. The PCRI also predicted discipline strategies in a sample of families living at or below the poverty line, and, as hypothesized, a number of scale scores for the PCRI fell below a T score of 40 in a sample of inner-city adolescent mothers.

Strengths and Limitations. The PCRI is a psychometrically sound measure of parenting, and computerized scoring and interpretative reports are available. Though the normative sample may not be adequately representative of lower SES and ethnically diverse populations, the measure has shown validity among diverse samples. Psychometric properties and normative data for chronic illness populations are unknown, and require further study.

PARENTING STRESS INDEX

Source

Abidin, R. R. (1995). *Parenting Stress Index.* Lutz, FL: Psychological Assessment Resources, Inc.

Availability

From Psychological Assessment Resources, Inc., P.O. Box 998, Odessa, FL 33556. The measure is copyrighted.

Purpose. The Parenting Stress Index (PSI) is designed to measure parents' perceptions of stress in the parent-child system.

Description. The PSI consists of 101 items representing 2 domains and 13 subscales. Items in the child domain tap the impact of the child's temperamental qualities on the parent. Subscales in the child domain are Adaptability (11 items), Acceptability (7 items), Demandingness (9 items), Mood (5 items), Distractibility–Hyperactivity (9 items), and Reinforces Parent (6 items). Items in the parent domain tap parent and family contextual characteristics that potentially impact on parenting ability or competence. Subscales in the parent domain are Depression (7 items), Attachment (7 items), Restrictions of Role (7 items), Sense of Competence (7 items), Social Isolation (7 items), Relationship with Spouse (7 items), and Parent Health (7 items). There is also an optional 19-item Life Stress Scale. Most items are presented as descriptors of behaviors or beliefs relative to each domain. For example: "My child does not seem to smile as much as most children" and "There are some things that my child does that really bother me a lot." In general, response options are on a 5-point scale ranging from "strongly agree" to "strongly disagree." However, several items have a unique response option, which is printed on the PSI form. Subscale, domain, and total scale scores may be calculated by summing the weighted item scores (provided in the manual). Higher scores represent higher stress in the parent-child system. Scoring options, norms, interpretation of scores, and recommendations for follow up are provided in the manual. English and Spanish versions are available.

A short form of the PSI (PSI–SF) was developed to facilitate clinical evaluation. The PSI–SF consists of 36 items from the longer form. Three subscales are represented: parental distress, parent-child dysfunctional interaction, and difficult child. These subscales subsume several subscales from the long form. For example, parent distress contains items from the depression, role restriction, isolation, and spouse subscales. In addition, the PSI–SF contains a defensive responding scale to rule out bias on the part of the respondent.

Any primary caretaker can complete the PSI. The standard PSI takes approximate 20 to 30 minutes to complete. The short form can be completed in 10 minutes or less. Reading level is approximately fifth grade. Percentile scores are presented for each scale item and by age of the target child.

Standardization and Norms. Abidin (1995) reported normative data for three groups: 2,633 mothers of 1 month to 12-year-old children and 200 fathers of children from 6 months to 6 years recruited from public and private clinics, day care centers, and public schools in Virginia, Massachusetts, New York City, North Carolina, and Georgia; and 223 Hispanic parents recruited from New York City. In the two original samples, 76% of the mothers and 95% of the fathers were Caucasian. Nearly one half of the sample reported vocational or some college education. Seventy-seven percent of the mothers were married, and 88% of the fathers were employed full time. The mean age of the target child was 4.2 years. Approximately 4% of the sample had a child referred for a behavioral or chronic health problem. The Hispanic normative sample was recruited from Puerto Rico, the Dominican Republic, various areas of the United States, Ecuador, and several Spanish-speaking countries. All completed the Spanish version of the PSI. Sixty-four percent of the sample was married and over 50% of the sample was classified as middle to low income. Mean age of the target child was 4.3 years.

The normative sample for the PSI–SF consisted of 800 subjects from the initial PSI development pool and an additional replication sample. Although demographics of the sample were provided, descriptive statistics for the scale were not. The sample was 98% married and 96% Caucasian. Approximately one third of the sample reported vocational or college education

Since the PSI has had such widespread use, reference group profiles are available for groups of children with attention deficit, hyperactivity, autism, cerebral palsy, and developmental delay, and children who have been abused or the result of an unplanned or unwanted pregnancy. Data from many other community and clinical samples can be found in the literature.

Reliability and Validity. Initial alpha coefficients ranged from .62 to .70 and .55 to .80 for the child and parent domain subscales, respectively. The child domain, parent domain, and total PSI score reliability coefficients were .89, .93, and .95, respectively. The alpha coefficients obtained by Hauenstein, Scarr, and Abidin (1986) from a multicultural sample (N = 435) yielded almost identical reliability estimates. Stability of the PSI was investigated with four additional samples. Three-week test-retest alpha coefficients were .82 and .71, 1- to 3-month alpha coefficients ranged from .63 to .77 and .69 to 91, and 1-year alpha coefficients were .55 and .70, for the child and parent domains, respectively. For the total PSI, 3-week retest alpha coefficient was .96, and 1-year alpha coefficient was .65.

Content validity for the PSI was established by completing a comprehensive review of the literature in the infant development, child abuse and neglect, parent-child interaction, child psychopathology, and stress, developing of a comprehensive list of parent stress domains, and identification of items to tap these domains. Pilot testing for readability, format, and administration time and rating of the items for content adequacy by a panel of experts followed. Finally, all items were evaluated to determine if research supported that the attribute measured was a stressor for parents of young children. Additional revisions were based on examination of item to subscale correlations, the logistics of scoring, administration, and scale length.

Abidin (1990) cited numerous studies to support the construct, concurrent, and predictive validity of the PSI in the areas of child development, parenting, behavior problems, and marital relationships with both normal and specialty populations. Numerous other studies using the PSI since 1990 can be identified in the child development, social science, and health care literature.

Internal consistency of the PSI–SF is .87, .80, .85, and .91 for the parental distress, parent-child dysfunctional behavior, difficult child, and total stress score, respectively. Test-retest reliability ranged from .68 to .85 for the subscales and total stress score. In addition to factor analysis, the validity is supported by a very high correlation (r = .94) between total stress scores on the long and short versions. Correlation between the short form subscales of parent distress and difficult child were strongly correlated with the long form subscales of parent domain and child domain, respectively. However correlations with the short form subscale of parent-child dysfunctional interaction and the child and parent domains were smaller because the short form subscale drew questions from both domains of the longer version.

Summary of Strengths and Limitations. The PSI has a strong empirical and theoretical basis, was carefully developed, and shows evidence of reliability and validity across many populations. The accompanying materials are extensive and facilitate administration, scoring, and interpretation for both research and clinical use. Length, the major limitation of the PSI, is addressed by the PSI–SF. The PSI–SF shows very strong initial psychometric properties. However, there is not yet a large body of independent research to support its validity and utility. Generalizability of norms and psychometric properties to chronic illness populations requires further study.

Additional Readings

Abidin, R. R. (1990). *Parenting Stress Index test manual (3rd ed.).* Charlottesville, VA: Pediatric Psychology Press.

Hauenstein, E., Scarr, S., & Abidin, R. R. Detecting children at-risk for developmental delay. Efficacy of the Parenting Stress Index in a non-American culture. Unpublished manuscript, University of Viginia, Charlottesville.

SYMPTOM CHECKLIST-90-R AND BRIEF SYMPTOM INVENTORY

Source

Derogatis, L. R. (1993). *SCL-90 (R) administration, scoring, and procedures manual* (3rd ed.). Minneapolis, MN: NCS Pearson, Inc.

Derogatis, L. R. (1993). Brief Symptom Inventory administration, scoring, and procedures manual (3rd ed.). Minneapolis, MN: NCS Pearson, Inc.

Availability

From National Computer Systems, Inc., P.O. Box 1416, Minneapolis, MN, 55440. 1–800–627–7271. The measure is copyrighted.

Purpose. The Symptom Checklist–90-R (SCL-90-R) and Brief Symptom Inventory (BSI) are self-report measures of psychological status. The instruments are self-report symptom inventories designed to reflect symptom patterns of community, medical, and psychiatric populations. The BSI is a shortened version of the SCL-90-R.

Description. The measures may be administered to adolescents and adults ages 13 and older. They each include a list of problems, and individuals rate how much the problem has bothered them in the last 7 days on a 5-point scale from "not at all" to "extremely." According to the author, assessment intervals of up to 14 days do not significantly affect ratings. The SCL-90-R contains 90 problems or items and takes 12 to 15 minutes to complete. The BSI contains 56 items and takes 8–10 minutes to complete. Both measures include the same subscales or dimensions: Somatization, Obsessive-Compulsive, Interpersonal Sensitivity, Depression, Anxiety, Hostility, Phobic Anxiety, Paranoid Ideation, and Psychoticism. Both measures yield three global indices: Global Severity Index, Positive Symptom Total, and the Positive Symptom Distress Index. Raw scores for each dimension are calculated by adding the appropriate items. The Global Severity Index is the mean of the total number of items in each measure. The Positive Symptom Total is a count of the number of items endorsed with a positive response (i.e., anything but not at all). The Positive Symptom Distress Index is the sum of all the items divided by the Positive Symptom Total. These raw scores are all converted to standardize T scores according to the norm group (see the following).

Standardization and Norms.   The SCL-90-R was standardized using four normative samples. The first sample included 1,002 psychiatric outpatients presenting with a range of psychiatric problems. This sample included 425 males and 588 females. The sample was 67% Caucasian, 33% African American, and less than 1% from other ethnicities. The sample was skewed toward the lower end of the socioeconomic scale. Mean age was 31.2 years. The second sample included 975 nonpatients of which about half were male. Eighty-five percent of the sample was Caucasian, and 11% were African American. SES was not reported for this sample. The sample was older than the other groups with a mean age of 46 years. The third sample of 423 inpatients was 44% African American and 56% Caucasian. The sample was 63% female and 37% male. Like the outpatient sample, this group was skewed toward the lower end of SES. The mean age was 33 years. Finally, the last sample of 806 adolescent nonpatients (mean age = 15.6) was 59% female and 41% male, almost exclusively Caucasian and predominantly middle to lower middle class. The BSI was standardized using the same first three samples. However, the adolescent nonpatient sample was much larger (N = 2408) and more diverse. Thirty percent were African American, and 12% were from other ethnicities. The sample included more males (66.5%) and was somewhat skewed to the lower SES groups.

Reliability and Validity.   The manual described several studies demonstrating satisfactory internal consistency and test-retest reliability for both the SCL-90-R and the BSI. Construct validity of the SCL-90 has been demonstrated in studies of internal structure (confirmatory factor analysis) and studies of factorial invariance (factors are constant across different populations). Finally, the widespread use of the measure has yielded an abundance of evidence of criterion validity, and a number of these studies are discussed in the manual.

Strengths and Limitations. The SCL-90 and BSI are psychometrically robust self-report measures of psychological symptoms. Computerized scoring and interpretative reports are available. The BSI may be more appropriate for adolescents due to its shorter administration time and the larger standardization sample of adolescent nonpatients. Use of the measures with ethnic groups other than African Americans and Caucasians may be more questionable due to the demographics of the standardization samples. When used by pediatric health care professionals, the measure is best viewed as a measure of parental psychopathology. However, use with chronically ill adolescents may be appropriate, though the Somatization dimension must be interpreted with caution.

Developer's Comments

The author forwarded several editorial changes but no additional comments.

TABLE 8.1
Disease-Specific Measures

Disease	Measure	Reference
Diabetes	Diabetes Family Behavior Checklist	Schafer, McCaul, & Glasgow (1986); Schafer, Glasgow, McCaul, & Preher (1983)
	Diabetes Responsibility and Conflict Scale	Rubin, Young-Hyman, & Peyrot (1989)

References

Rubin, R. R., Young-Hyman, D., & Peyrot, M. (1989). Parent responsibility and conflict in diabetes care. *Diabetes, 38,* 28A.

Schafer, L. C., McCaul, K. D, & Glasgow, R. E. (1986). Supportive and non-supportive family behaviors: Relationships to adherence and metabolic control in persons with Type I diabetes. *Diabetes Care, 9,* 179–185.

Schafer, L. C., Glasgow, R. E., McCaul, K. D., & Preher, M. (1983). Adherence to IDDM regimens: Relationship to psychosocial variables and metabolic control. *Diabetes Care 6,* 493–498.

Consumer Satisfaction

Patricia T. Siegel
Wayne State University

INTRODUCTION

There is an increased recognition within the health care industry that consumer opinions must be considered in order to satisfy patient's expectations and needs (Ryan, Collins, Dowd, & Pierce, 1995). By identifying the major elements of service delivery that underlie patient expectations and opinions, we can learn what is desired from the health care system. This information, in turn, can help direct decisions that make health services more effective and efficient (Krahn, Eisert, & Fifield, 1990). This is especially important when making decisions for children with special health needs. Such children will require services throughout their life span that address overall well-being as well as the impact of their condition on family functioning (King, King, & Rosenbaum, 1996).

Satisfaction with care is important because it influences whether a person seeks medical advice, complies with treatment and maintains a continuing relationship with a provider (Jones, Carnon, Wylie, & Hedley, 1993). Consumer satisfaction refers to a judgment about the quality of care and includes both the patient's reaction and provider's reaction to structure, process, and outcome (Donabedian, 1988; Naar-King, 2000). Structure refers to the attributes of the settings where care is provided (convenience and continuity), process refers to the personal interactions between providers and patients (professional competence and respectful–supportive care), and outcome refers to the medical and behavioral effects on the patient (health status and adherence).

Investigations of the structural aspects of care indicate that easy accessibility (Kelley, Alexander & Morris, 1991), continuity of providers and coordination of services (King, Cathers, King & Rosenbaum, 2001) are all associated with consumer satisfaction. When process elements are examined, the key predictor of consumer satisfaction is the quality of the patient–professional relationship (Williams & Calan, 1991). Specifically, satisfied consumers value respectful and supportive care, desire clear communication between themselves and providers and expect providers to be technically competent (Jones et al., 1993). Finally, satisfaction with care has been shown to impact outcomes, such as adherence to medical treatment and ultimate health status, while dissatisfaction leads to missed appointments and losses to follow-up (Jones et al., 1993).

Early research on consumer satisfaction reveals that the major problem in using satisfaction measures is the tendency for recipients to report high levels of satisfaction. If data are collected a long time after the patient enters care, this positive bias increases. On the other hand, if data is collected close to the point of entry, patients have not experienced the complete service package and dropouts will not be included. One suggestion to avoid sampling biases is to design investigations within the same service program that include comparisons over time (Nguyen, Attkisson, & Stegner, 1983).

Because there are many ways to measure consumer opinion, selecting a valid method of measurement is another concern in the process of investigating consumer satisfaction. Jones et al. (1993) suggested using a combination of methods, such as self-ratings (closed questions) along with either comment cards or specific open-ended questions to obtain the most balanced view of consumer opinions. Measurement of consumer satisfaction must also take into account that age, education, and race have all been identified as moderator variables. Specifically, younger, more educated Caucasian patients are the least satisfied with health care services. Older patients (> 50 years) in general and African-American patients specifically, report having higher mean satisfaction with health care, perhaps because they have lower expectations (Kelley et al., 1991).

Another problem in measuring consumer satisfaction is the general failure of investigators to examine the elements defining dissatisfaction (King et al., 2001). The few studies that have looked at dissatisfaction in parents of children with special health needs suggest that parents were dissatisfied when their worries were minimized or discounted, when services were either insufficient or inappropriate, and when their practical concerns were not addressed (McKay & Hensey, 1990). More recently, King et al. (2001) assessed elements of both satisfaction and dissatisfaction of parents of children receiving rehabilitative services by asking the parents what they liked best and least about the services provided. They found that parent satisfaction is strongly tied to respectful and supportive care, continuity and coordination of care, and clarity in the delivery of general information. Parent dissatisfaction, on the other hand, was linked to both structural and process factors. Specifically, lack of access to existing services along with perceived lack of respectful, supportive care led to parent dissatisfaction.

Children with special health conditions need a regular source of care and a designated provider who supplies families with information and support and also assumes responsibility in the management of the condition (Kelley et al., 1991). Early studies indicate that both structural and process aspects of service provision are important to satisfaction and dissatisfaction. Therefore, satisfaction measures need to encompass all of the major elements of both satisfaction and dissatisfaction (King et al, 2001). Finally, in the current managed care environment, it may be that the relationship between parents and other members of the primary health care team will become increasingly important and hence measurement of consumer opinion may need to focus upon health care teams rather than the physician alone (Williams & Calan, 1991).

REFERENCES

Donabedian, A. (1988). The quality of care: How can it be assessed? *Journal of the American Medical Association, 260,* 1743–1748.

Jones, R. B., Carnon, A. G., Wylie, H., & Hedley, A. J. (1993). How do we measure consumer opinions of outpatient clinics? *Public Health, 107,* 235–241.

Kelley, M. A., Alexander, C. S., & Morris, N. M. (1991). Maternal satisfaction with primary care for children with selected chronic conditions. *Journal of Community Health, 16,* 213–224.

King, G., King, S., & Rosenbaum, P. (1996). Interpersonal aspects of care-giving and client outcomes: A review of the literature. *Ambulatory Child Health, 2,* 151–160.

King, G., Cathers, T., King, S., & Rosenbaum, P. (2001). Major elements of parents' satisfaction and dissatisfaction with pediatric rehabilitation services. *Children's Health , 30,* 11–134.

Krahn, G. L. Eisert, D., & Fifield, B. (1990). Obtaining parental perceptions of the quality of services for children with special health needs. *Journal of Pediatric Psychology, 15,* 761–774.

McKay, M., & Hensey, O. (1990). From the other side: Parents' views of their early contacts with health professionals. *Child: Care, Health and Development, 16,* 373–381.

Naar-King, S. (2000). Tools for assessing consumer satisfaction with multidisciplinary pediatric care. *Journal of Child and Family Nursing, 4,* 217–222.

Nguyen, T. D., Attkisson, C. C., & Stegner, B. L. (1983). Assessment of patient satisfaction: development and refinement of a service evaluation questionnaire. *Evaluation and Program Planning , 6,* 299–314.

Ryan, M. E., Collins, F. J., Dowd, J. B., & Pierce, P. K. (1995). Measuring patient satisfaction: A case study. *Journal of Nursing Care Quality, 9,* 44–53.

Williams, S. J., & Calan, M. (1991). Convergence and divergence: assessing criteria of consumer satisfaction across general practice, dental and hospital care settings. *Social Science Medicine, 33,* 707–716.

ASSESSMENT OF PARENT SATISFACTION

Source

Krahn, G. L., Eisert, D., & Fifield, B. (1990). Obtaining parental perceptions of the quality of services for children with special health needs.
Journal of Pediatric Psychology, 15, 761–774.

Availability

From the first author. Gloria Krahn, Child Development and Rehabilitation Center, Oregon Health Sciences University, PO Box 574, Portland,
OR, 97207.

Purpose.   The measure was designed to assess parental perceptions
of quality of care with emphasis on the multidisciplinary care of children
with special health needs. The measure was designed to assess access to
care in addition to physician conduct. The measure was adapted from the
Client Services Questionnaire (CSQ; Larsen, Attkisson, Hargreaves, &
Nguyen, 1979), an assessment of client satisfaction with mental health
services.

Description.   Parents rate items on a 4-point scale. Ratings of 1 are
indicative of the most positive response and ratings of 4 are indicative of
the most negative response. The original measure as piloted included
the eight items from the CSQ and 14 additional items to address specific
concerns of the population. An initial principal components analysis
with varimax rotation suggested that four factors accounted for 53% of
the variance. The first factor included 14 items indicating general satisfaction and accounted for 34% of the total variance. The second factor
consisted of six items and reflected Clarity of Communication. The third
factor, Preappointment Wait and Information, included three items. The
last factor, Efficiency, included three items related to time involved and
quality of the services. From the results of these analyses, the authors
modified the questionnaire to include the mostly highly loaded items.
Ten items highly loaded on the general satisfaction factor, and five of
these were selected based on the authors' perceptions of content validity. Only two items from each of the remaining factors loaded highly on
that factor. Another principal components analysis was conducted on
the resulting 11-item questionnaire. The same four factors emerged and
now accounted for 72% of the variance. The factors should not be
regarded as subscales because of the small number of items on three of
the factors. The administrator calculates only a single summary score
that indicates overall satisfaction.

Standardization and Norms. Surveys were mailed to a convenience sample of 475 parents from clinics serving children of all ages with a variety of special health needs in Portland and Eugene, Oregon. Only families receiving evaluation services were included. The authors reported a 62% response rate with no significant demographic differences between responders and nonresponders. For the families that responded, the child's age ranged from birth to 16 years (M = 5.1 years). Other demographic data for responders were not provided.

Reliability and Validity. Based on the pilot data from the sample previously described, the internal consistency coefficient for the entire measure was .76. Again, scales were not computed due to the small number of items loading on three of the factors. No other reliability or validity data were reported.

Summary of Strengths and Limitations. The Assessment of Parent Satisfaction is an attempt to rectify the lack of measures available for children with special health needs. Strengths of the measure are the use of this population in its development and the short administration time. However, the items do not reflect the multidisciplinary nature of these services. Also, the multidimensional nature of parent satisfaction cannot be adequately assessed when using a single summary score. Test-retest reliability, validity, and most demographic data were not reported.

Additional Readings

Larsen, D. L., Attkisson, C. C., Hargreaves, W. A., & Nguyen, T. D. (1979). Assessment of client/patient satisfaction: Development of a general scale. *Evaluation and Program Planning, 2,* 197–207.

CHILD PERCEPTIONS OF SPECIALTY CARE

Source

Naar-King, S., Siegel, P. T., Smyth, M., & Simpson, P. (2000). Evaluating collaborative health care programs for children with special needs. *Children's Services, 3,* 233–245.

Availability

From the first author. Sylvie Naar-King, Ph.D., Children's Hospital of Michigan, Department of Psychiatry/Psychology, 3901 Beaubien Boulevard, Detroit, MI 48201. The measure is not copyrighted.

Purpose. The Child Perceptions of Specialty Care (CPSC) was intended to assess children's perceptions of multidisciplinary care. Existing measures of child satisfaction are generally only applicable to single provider settings.

Description. The CPSC is a single-scale instrument consisting of nine items. The items address communication with the team, perceived helpfulness of staff, and understanding of condition and are rated on a 5-point scale from "all of the time" to "none of the time," "very helpful" to "not at all helpful," or from understanding "very well" to "not well at all."

Standardization and Norms. The measure was piloted with 101 children (ages 8 to 18) from the same population described in the Parent Perception of Specialty Care (PPSC). Families were 41% African American, 46% Caucasian, and 13% biracial or other. Forty-nine percent of families reported an income of less than $20,000 per year.

Reliability and Validity. Reliability was satisfactory for the resulting single scale with an alpha of .78. The measure was correlated with measures of parent and staff satisfaction as evidence of criterion validity. A confirmatory factor analysis suggested that all items loaded on a single factor suggesting construct validity for a unitary construct.

Summary of Strengths and Limitations. The CPSC is a good first attempt at capturing the perspectives of children. However, further research is necessary to improve the psychometric properties. Child satisfaction is likely not a unitary construct, and further work to develop subscales for the dimensions included may help to improve internal consistency. In addition, further research is necessary to determine other dimensions of child perceptions (e.g., perceived provider empathy) not captured by this measure.

CHILD SATISFACTION QUESTIONNAIRE AND THE PHYSICIAN ATTRIBUTE CHECKLIST

Source

Rifkin, L., Wolf, M. H., Lewis, C. C., & Pantell, R. H. (1988). Children's perception of physician and medical care. *Journal of Pediatric Psychology, 13,* 247–254.

Availability

Catherine C. Lewis, University of California, San Francisco, 400 Parnassus Avenue, A-204, Box 0314, San Francisco, California, 94143.

Purpose. The instruments are designed to measure children's (6–14 years) perceptions of satisfaction with services and of physician characteristics. The measure was originally developed for primary care visits.

Description. The Child Satisfaction Questionnaire (CSQ) is a 12-item scale where children rate their agreement with statements about a medical visit on a 5-point scale—not at all true, very little, some, a lot, or really a lot. Thus, scores on the 12-item CSQ range from 1 to 60. A 19-item scale is available for children ages 12 and older, and scores range from 1 to 95. Fifty-three items were initially generated from adult satisfaction measures, children's attitudinal measures, interviews with pediatricians and child psychiatrists, and structured interviews with children in local schools. The items assessed perceptions of physician empathy, communication skills, and technical skills. A panel of two pediatricians and two psychologists chose 44 items for field testing. Half the items were negatively worded to avoid a response set. On the Physician Attribute Checklist (PAC), children respond "yes" or "no" to whether 32 attributes characterize their physician. Each positive attitude endorsed and each disagreement with a negative attitude received a score of one. Scores range from 0 to 32 with higher scores indicating a more positive perception. The list of one-word descriptors were adapted from the Personal Attribute Inventory for Children (Rifkin et al., 1988). The two questionnaires were administered to 75 children after an ambulatory pediatric appointment in a university hospital. Two-thirds of the children self-administered the CSQ, and items were read out loud to the remainder of the children. The measures require a fourth-grade reading level, and both can be self-administered in about 15 minutes.

Results suggested that 19 items on the CSQ had satisfactory item-total correlations and unrestricted ranges. Factor analysis with varimax rotation resulted in two factors indicating physician–child rapport (12 items) and physician communication skills (7 items). The authors considered this analysis to be exploratory because of the limited number of subjects per variable. Additionally, the factors may be an artifact because the first factor contained only positively worded items, and the second factor contained all negatively worded items. Children under age 12 tended to respond affirmatively to all negatively worded items suggesting comprehension difficulties. Thus, the authors consider the CSQ a 12-item measure with a 19-item version of the scale for older children. The data indicated that of the 32 original attributes, 25 were eliminated due to lack of variability, low item-total correlations, poor comprehension, or all of the above. The remaining seven attributes included happy, calm, boring, understanding, listens, special, and explains.

Standardization and Norms. There are no published norms. The instrument was developed with an urban sample of children ages 6 to 14 (M = 10.9, SD = 2.85). The sample was 43% Caucasian, 28% African American, 17% Hispanic, and 12% Asian. Median family income was between $10,000 and $20,000. Reasons for the medical visit were well-child checkups (43%), acute illness (33%), illness follow-up (15%), and injuries (8%). Ten percent of the sample had a chronic illness or disability with the most common chronic illness being asthma.

Reliability and Validity. The 12-item CSQ showed good internal consistency with a Cronbach's alpha of .89. The additional 7-item scale on the 19-item CSQ was also internally consistent with an alpha of .89. The 7-item PAC showed lower but adequate internal consistency with an alpha of .70. Test-retest reliability was not assessed. Factor analysis of the CSQ is a preliminary demonstration of construct validity, but the analysis was exploratory due to the limited number of subjects per variable. The item-generation procedures of the CSQ suggested good content validity. Finally, the authors reported a significant correlation (.53) between the CSQ and the PAC as preliminary evidence of criterion validity.

Summary of Strengths and Limitations. The CSQ and PAC appear to be commendable attempts at assessing child satisfaction with medical care and perceptions of physician characteristics. While the measure was developed for primary care visits, applicability to pediatric specialty services seems appropriate with one caveat. The instruments focus on satisfaction with physicians and do not ask about other clinic staff. Thus, the measure cannot be used for multidisciplinary care without changing item wording. Further research is necessary to confirm construct and criterion validity, to examine test-retest validity, and to assess the utility of the measures in medical settings other than primary care. A significant weakness of the measure is the use of all positively worded items in the 12-item CSQ. While the 19-item CSQ includes negatively worded items for older children, the two-factor solution of this measure is suspect. Further studies should evaluate the CSQ amending the valence of some of the items.

CLIENT SATISFACTION QUESTIONNAIRE AND THE SERVICE SATISFACTION SCALE

Source

Attkisson, C. C., & Greenfield, T. K. (1994). The Client Satisfaction Questionnaire–8 and the Service Satisfaction Questionnaire–30. In M. E. Maruish (Ed.), *The use of psychological testing for treatment planning and outcome assessment.* Hillsdale, NJ: Lawrence Erlbaum Associates.

Availability

CSQ—Dr. Attkisson, Fax: 415–476–9690. SSS-30—Dr. Greenfield, Fax: 510–642–7175. The measure is copyrighted.

Purpose. These self-administered surveys are designed to be direct measures of satisfaction and to be used with a wide range of clients and services. The Client Satisfaction Questionnaire (CSQ) family of instruments (CSQ-8, CSQ-18, CSQ-31) are self-report questionnaires developed over a decade ago to be used for scientific and evaluation research and program planning in a broad range of settings. The more recently developed Service Satisfaction Scale (SSS-30) uses more specific items with changed scaling to yield a strong multifactorial instrument to be used in primary care and mental health settings. Because the longer SSS-30 includes multiple dimensions of satisfaction, discussion of the CSQ will be limited to the CSQ-8, a brief assessment yielding a single general satisfaction score.

Description. For both measures, patients–parents rate their level of agreement with specific statements. On the CSQ-8, subjects rate the services on a 4-point likert scale. The wording of the anchors varies across the eight items. The measure was developed from a large pool of items covering a number of domains of satisfaction (Larsen et al., 1979). The eight-item, unidimensional measure resulted from item and factor analyses across a number of studies. Items are summed to yield a general satisfaction score ranging from 8 to 32 with higher scores indicating greater satisfaction. The SSS-30 consists of 30 characteristics of services that patients–parents rate on a 5-point scale from "delighted" to "terrible." The authors reported that the use of the more extreme anchors reduced the ceiling effect and negative skew associated with the CSQ. Factor analyses identified two stable subscales across primary care and mental health settings. Practitioner Manner and Skill (9 items) and Perceived Outcome (8 items), and both scales shared one item. Two other scales were identified but were not found consistently across settings— Office Procedures (5 items) and Accessibility (4 items). Two additional items address waiting time, which may be combined with Access. Three other items did not fall on any scale. Eight additional items assess demographic information. The 30 items may be summed for a global satisfaction score.

Standardization and Norms.   Norms for the CSQ across a variety of settings are available (Nguyen, Attkisson, & Stegner, 1983). Norms for the SSS-30 are available for a general population primary-care medical outpatient service, a student mental health service, an employee assistance program, and a mandated alcohol and driving treatment program.

Reliability and Validity.   The CSQ-8 has shown high levels of internal consistency across studies with Cronbach's alphas ranging from .83 to .93. The SSS-30 as a composite satisfaction measure has also show strong internal consistency ranging from .93 to .96. Adequate reliability has been reported for the subscales with the two main scales being strongest. The authors reported mean Cronbach's alphas across studies as .88 for Practitioner Manner and Skill, .83 for Perceived Outcome, .74 for Office Procedures, and .67 for the 4-item Access scale. The factor analyses demonstrate construct validity for the two main subscales. As evidence of construct validity for the composite score, the authors reported that the CSQ-8 and the SSS-30 composite score correlated .70 in a study of a drinking-driving treatment program. Test-retest reliability and criterion validity were not specifically reported in the summary previously referenced. Review of the numerous studies using the CSQ may illustrate its criterion validity. The authors reported that further examination of criterion validity will be their next generation of research studies.

Summary of Strengths and Limitations.   The CSQ and SSS-30 appear to be psychometrically sound measures of consumer satisfaction across a wide range of services. The measures allow for a multidimensional view of satisfaction while also yielding a global satisfaction score. The measures have been studied with numerous samples encompassing a wide range of demographic characteristics. Both measures have been used successfully in pediatric settings (see Krahn, Eisert, & Fifield, 1990; Naar-King & Siegel, in press). The availability of norms is a unique strength. Weaknesses include weaker construct validity of the Office Procedures and Access scales, and the need for further examination of criterion validity.

Additional Readings

Nguyen, T. D., Attkisson, C. C., & Stegner, B. L. (1983). Assessment of patient satisfaction: Development and refinement of a Service Evaluation Questionnaire. *Evaluation and Program Planning, 6,* 299–313.

MEASURE OF PROCESSES OF CARE

Reference

King, S., Rosenbaum, P., & King, G. (1995). *The Measure of Processes of Care (MPOC). A Means to Assess Family-Centered Behaviors of Health Care Providers. Neurodevelopmental Clinical Research Unit.* Hamilton, ON: McMaster University.

Availability

From the second author. Peter Rosenbaum, M.D., CanChild Centre for Childhood Disability Research, McMaster University, Building T-16, Room 126, 1280 Main Street West, Hamilton, Ontario L8S 4K1, Canada. The measure is copyrighted.

Purpose. The Measure of Processes of Care (MPOC-56) is designed to assess parents' perceptions of the services their children receive. The measure does not assess satisfaction in terms of an overall judgement, and it does not focus on the structure or content of services. Rather, parents are asked to rate the behavioral and interactional components of the care their children receive. As a measure based on dimensions of caregiving valued by parents, the MPOC taps the important features of family-centered care.

Description. Parents rate how often 56 actions or behaviors of health care professionals occur on a 7-point scale from "never" to "to a great extent." Factor analyses yielded five factors, and items with factor loadings of .50 or higher were retained. The five factors (or scales) are: enabling and partnership (16 items), providing general information (9 items), providing specific information about the child (5 items), coordinated and comprehensive care (17 items), and respectful and supportive care (9 items). The MPOC-56 is multidimensional, and the authors did not use a total MPOC score. Mean item scores for each scale are used in subsequent analyses with higher scores indicating greater extent of positive behaviors or interactions. The measure is self-administered and requires an eighth-grade reading level.

Standardization and Norms. A convenience sample of 1,002 families was recruited from rehabilitation centers in Ontario, Canada. The authors reported a response rate of 75%, and complete data from 537 mothers and 116 fathers were included in data analyses. Families were primarily from major or small urban settings (79%), and were primarily two-parent families (82%). The children were seen for chronic, mostly neurodevelopmental conditions, and their ages ranged from 7 months to 20 years with a median age of 6 years, 8 months. There are no norms for this measure.

Reliability and Validity. Based on the pilot data from the sample previously described, internal consistency coefficients for the scale scores were satisfactory and ranged from .81 to .96. In a separate reliability study, parents (N = 29) completed the MPOC-56 twice, an average of 27 days between administrations. Test-retest reliability coefficients for the five scales were also satisfactory, ranging from .78 to .88. Factor analyses are evidence of construct validity, and the items were generated from parents' rankings of important aspects of care and from focus groups to ensure content validity. As evidence of criterion validity, the authors reported that four of the five scales correlated significantly with the total score on a measure of client satisfaction, and the scales were also significantly negatively correlated with parental stress.

Summary of Strengths and Limitations. The MPOC-56 is a soundly developed, psychometrically strong assessment tool, and is particularly relevant to the family-centered care approach dominating pediatric settings. The measure moves beyond standard judgements of satisfaction to assess parents' perceptions of actual behaviors. It can be completed in 15 to 20 minutes, and is suitable for mailed surveys. Limitations result from the pilot sample, which included primarily middle-class families with children with stable neurodevelopmental conditions. While the measure is general enough to be used in a variety of settings, the use of the measure with American families, with inner city populations, and with other chronic conditions, such as diabetes or pediatric cancer requires further study. Finally, the length of the MPOC may inhibit its use in large outcome evaluations. Two of the factors have greater than 10 items, and such a large number of items may unnecessarily lengthen the measure without significantly contributing to its psychometric properties. Preliminary analyses of a shorter version of the scale (MPOC-20) provide good evidence of reliability and validity.

Additional Readings

King, S., Rosenbaum, P. L., & King, G. A. (1996). Parents' perceptions of caregiving: Development and validation of a measure of process. *Developmental Medicine and Child Neurology, 38,* 757–772.

Developers' Comments

The MPOC was developed as a means of measuring the extent to which parents of children with long-term medical conditions of health or development experience a variety of service provider behaviors that had previously been ascertained to be important to parents, and were felt to be examples of family-centered service. As such, MPOC is not a measure of parental satisfaction, although not surprisingly the scale scores correlate fairly highly with judgements of overall satisfaction. We believe that MPOC can be used both as a measure to assess the extent of family-centeredness of a program, and as an educational tool for service providers, in order to identify and characterize elements of service provider behavior that are important to families. Users of MPOC should consider purchasing the manual as it contains details of the creation, validation, scoring, and interpretation of the measure.

METRO ASSESSMENT OF CHILD SATISFACTION

Reference

Simonian, S. J., Tarnowski, K. J., Park, A., & Bekeny, P. (1993). Child, parent, and physician perceived satisfaction with pediatric outpatient visits. *Developmental and Behavioral Pediatrics, 14,* 8–12.

Availability

From the first author. Susan J. Simonian, Ph.D. Department of Pediatrics H-421, Case Western Reserve University, MetroHealth Medical Center, 2500 MetroHealth Drive, Cleveland, OH 44109.

Purpose. The Metro Assessment of Child Satisfaction (MACS) was designed as a measure of child satisfaction with outpatient medical care that can be used with diverse patient groups. By building on the work of Rifkin and colleagues (1988), the authors hoped to create a measure that is useful across pediatric settings, is easy to understand, includes both positively and negatively worded items, and can be compared to parent satisfaction and physician perceptions of satisfaction.

Description.   Children ages six years and older respond "yes" or "no" to questions about their doctor. The original item pool included 11 items generated from interviews with children, psychologists, and pediatricians along with four items from the CSQ reworded to improve readability. The measure was administered to 55 children ages 6 to 14 receiving routine pediatric care. The children were read each item and were told to place a token in either a box marked yes or a box marked no. Results suggested significant item-total correlations with one exception, and the item was dropped from the measure. Six items did not show variability and were also dropped. Scores on the final eight-item measure ranged from 1 to 8 with higher scores indicating greater satisfaction. These items were subject to a principal components analysis. Four factors accounted for 77% of the variance reflecting patient acceptance–trust, patient understanding, physician empathy, and physician acceptance.

Standardization and Norms.   The measure was developed with an urban sample of lower SES (Mean Hollingshead = 27.91). Mothers were Caucasian (62%) and African American (38%). The majority of mothers (67%) completed high school. Children's ages ranged from 6 to 14 years (M = 8.46, SD = 1.87). SES and age were significantly positively correlated with total MACS scores. The authors reported that the average score on the MACS was 6.69, and they considered scores greater than or equal to 6.0 as indicative of satisfaction with care.

Reliability and Validity.   Although the remaining items on the MACS showed significant item-total correlations, a Cronbach's alpha indicating internal consistency was not reported. Test-retest reliability was not evaluated. Although the factor analysis suggested four factors, these cannot be used as subscales because of the small number of items on each factor. Construct validity requires further study. As preliminary evidence of criterion validity, the MACS showed fair to moderate concordance with a rating of maternal satisfaction and with physician perception of satisfaction.

Summary of Strengths and Limitations.   The MCAS is a brief, easily administered measure of child satisfaction with medical care. However, further research is necessary to determine reliability and validity. Cronbach's alphas were not reported, and validity requires further demonstration. The use of a yes–no format greatly reduces the variability of scores thereby reducing the utility of the measure for research purposes. Also, the lack of reliable and valid subscales hinders a multidimensional view of child satisfaction. Like the Child Satisfaction Scale, the measure focuses on perceptions of the doctor to the exclusion of other clinic staff or a multidisciplinary team. The generalizability of the measure to non-urban settings and higher SES groups requires further study.

PARENT PERCEPTIONS OF SPECIALTY CARE

Source

Naar-King, S., Siegel, P. T., Smyth, M., & Simpson, P. (2000). Evaluating collaborative health care programs for children with special needs. *Children's Services: Social Policy, Resesarch, and Practice, 3*, 233–245.

Availability

From the first author. Sylvie Naar-King, Ph.D., Children's Hospital of Michigan, Department of Psychiatry/Psychology, 3901 Beaubien Boulevard, Detroit, MI 48201.

Purpose. The instrument is designed to measure parents perceptions of specialty care including those aspects addressed by satisfaction questionnaires with additional items added to address multidisciplinary pediatric care.

Description. The Parent Perceptions of Specialty Care (PPSC) includes the first six items of the Perception of Procedures Questionnaire (PPQ; Kazak, Penati, Waibel, & Blackall, 1996), and six items from the SSS-30 addressing access to services. Eleven items were added to address integrated pediatric health care programs. The measure requires less than a sixth-grade reading skill. A principal components analysis with a varimax rotation was conducted to determine the salient dimensions underlying the item responses. Three of the factors contained only one or two items and were dropped from the questionnaire. Of the remaining items, 10 items fell on one factor reflecting general satisfaction. These included the six items from the PPQ, two of the Access scale items from the SSS-30, and two added items addressing the treatment plan. These 10 items make up the General Satisfaction subscale. The four added items assessing the worth of the time involved fell on the second factor, the worth subscale. The four remaining items on the third factor originated from the access and wait subscales of the SSS-30. Items on the general satisfaction and access subscales are rated on a 5-point scale from delighted to terrible as in the SSS-30 to increase variability. The four items of the worth subscale are rated on a 5-point scale from "very worthwhile" to "not at all worthwhile." Thus, the final scale included 18 likert scale items, 13 items assessing services received, and additional demographic items.

Standardization and Norms. The measure was developed using 324 parents attending one of 16 collaborative pediatric specialty clinics. The sample was 49% African American, 40% Caucasian, 4% Asian–Pacific, 3% Latino, 1% Native American, and 1% other. The sample represented a wide range of educational backgrounds: 22% did not finish high school, 46% completed high school only, 16% had some college education, and 14% were college graduates. Income was consistent with an urban population with 36% reporting less than $10,000 per year, 15% between $10,000 and $20,000, 28% between $20,000 and $40,000, 12% between $40,000 and $60,000, and 9% greater than $60,000. Normative data have not been published, but descriptive data from the pilot sample are available from the first author.

Reliability and Validity. As a measure of internal consistency, Cronbach's alphas were calculated for items on each of the three remaining factors and on all the items combined. Reliability was satisfactory with an alpha of .92 for the 10-item General Satisfaction scale, .84 for the four-item Worth scale, and .83 for the four-item Access scale. Cronbach's alpha for the global satisfaction scale (all items) was .94. To enhance content validity, the 11 additional items were generated by the multidisciplinary team previously described. The confirmatory factor analysis suggested adequate construct validity. Criterion validity was demonstrated by correlations between the PPSC and measures of child and staff satisfaction with the same program.

Summary of Strengths and Limitations. The PPSC has good psychometric properties, and focuses on areas critical to pediatric specialty programs including multidisciplinary care, access to services, and the length of time spent in clinic. Another key strength is the use of a diverse sample for instrument development. Limitations include the focus on judgements versus behaviors and the lack of focus on family centered care. Because the scale is newly developed, further studies are necessary to determine its utility and generalizability of psychometric properties to other populations.

Additional Readings

Kazak, A. E., Penati, P., Waibel, M. K., & Blackall, G. F. (1996). The Perception of Procedures Questionnaire. *Journal of Pediatric Psychology, 21,* 195–207.

Naar-King, S., Siegel, P. T., & Smyth, M. (2002). Consumer satisfaction with a collaborative, interdisciplinary health care program for children with special needs. *Children's Services: Social Policy, Resesarch, and Practice, 5,* 189–200.

PATIENT SATISFACTION QUESTIONNAIRE

Source

Ware, J. E., Snyder, M. K., Wright, W. R., & Davies, A. R. (1983). Defining and measuring patient satisfaction with medical care. *Evaluation and Program Planning, 6,* 247–263.

Availability

From the first author. John E. Ware, Jr., QualityMetric, Inc., 640 George Washington Hwy, Lincoln, RI, 02865. The measure is copyrighted.

Purpose. This self-administered survey was designed to obtain subjective ratings of satisfaction with medical care. The authors attempted to create a taxonomy of characteristics of patient care with the hypothesis that satisfaction is a multidimensional construct. Satisfaction may vary across different facets of medical care. The survey focuses on characteristics of physicians and medical care services.

Description. Patients–parents rate their level of agreement with specific statements on a 5-point scale from strongly agree to strongly disagree. Development of the measure began in the 1970s and included 12 studies over a 4-year period. The result of this effort was the Parent Satisfaction Questionnaire (PSQ) Form II, a shorter and easily self-administered version. This resulting measure was tested in four sites, and consisted of 68 items. A number of subscales were constructed using correlation matrices, factor analyses, and multitrait scaling techniques. The Non-financial Access scale consists of seven items related to emergency care, convenience of services, and access. The Financial Access scale includes 11 items related to cost of care, insurance coverage, and payment mechanisms. The Availability scale consists of six items assessing availability of physicians, hospitals, and specialists. The Continuity scale includes four items assessing continuity of providers for adult patients and their families and does not appear to be appropriate for assessing parent satisfaction with their child's care. Humaneness (eight items) assesses the physician's consideration and explanations. The Technical Quality scale (13 items) measures satisfaction with facilities, expenses, and competence. A General Satisfaction scale included four items. Two summary scales may be computed. Access total is a sum of the two access scales, and Doctor Conduct total is a sum of the humaneness and technical quality scales. Form II takes approximately 10 minutes to complete. Reading level was not reported. A 43-item PSQ short form is available and takes 8–9 minutes to complete. The developers note that questions about interpersonal manner are underrepresented in this version.

Standardization and Norms. Studies of Form II were completed in four sites, three general population household sites, and one family practice center. Subjects came from a wide range of socioeconomic, educational, and racial backgrounds. Sample sizes ranged from 323 to 640 at each site. Norms have not been published. In a study of 140 mothers of children with special health needs rating primary care services (Kelley, Alexander, & Morris, 1991), scores on the General Satisfaction scale ranged from 4 to 20 with a mean of 13.76 (S.D. = 3.32). Scores on the Access scale ranged from 12 to 35 with a mean of 26.09 (S.D. = 4.15), and scores on the Doctor Conduct scale ranged from 26 to 75 with a mean of 54.29 (S.D. = 9.28).

Reliability and Validity. The authors reported adequate internal consistency and test-retest reliability. Internal consistency for the global scales exceeded .60 across sites for all scales except Continuity of Care. Test-retest reliability exceeded .60 for the global scales across sites. The authors noted that the scales tended to be less reliable among St. Louis subjects who reported lower income and education. Correlations between scale scores administered 2 years apart ranged from .34 for Availability to .61 for Doctor Conduct. The authors reported a number of approaches to demonstrate validity. Good content validity is demonstrated by matching PSQ items with a taxonomy of characteristics of medical providers and services (Ware, Kane, Davies, & Brooks, 1978). As evidence of construct validity, persons who voiced complaints in open-ended questions generally scored lower on the specific scale reflecting the content of the complaint. Factor analyses are also evidence of construct validity. Finally, PSQ scales correlated significantly with objective questions about the services. For example, Access to Care was significantly negatively correlated with travel time. Test-retest reliability coefficients for the five scales were also satisfactory, ranging from .78 to .88. The authors reported that the scales are consistently good predictors of satisfaction with care in general, satisfaction with continuity of care, and satisfaction with a wide range of criterion variables (see Ware & Davies, 1983). The measure has been used with parents. One study asked parents of children with chronic illness to rate their primary care arrangements using three of the global scales of the PSQ (Kelly et al., 1991). The scales were significantly associated with receiving anticipatory guidance, access to care in the evening, and their child's health status. In a study of bereaved parents, satisfaction on the PSQ was associated with the physician's availability and provision of medical information and grief counseling (Harper & Wisian, 1994).

Summary of Strengths and Limitations. The PSQ is an extremely well-developed, psychometrically sound assessment tool. It allows for a multidimensional view of satisfaction while remaining easy to administer in a timely fashion. The measure has been studied with numerous samples encompassing a wide range of demographic characteristics. While initially developed for adult patients, certain global scales of the measure have been used to study parent satisfaction with pediatric care. However, other scales are not appropriate for pediatric care (e.g., continuity). The focus on the care of physicians precludes the use of the measure to assess satisfaction with multidisciplinary care or even nursing care. Studies of the measure substituting team for physician or repeating certain subscales for each discipline may demonstrate its usefulness for the multidisciplinary care prevalent in the pediatric specialties arena. Finally, the length of the measure may be prohibitive in certain settings.

Additional Readings

Harper, M. B., & Wisian, N. B. (1994). Care of bereaved parents: A study of patient satisfaction. *Journal of Reproductive Medicine, 39,* 80–86.

Kelley, M. A., Alexander, C. S., Morris, N. M. (1991). Maternal satisfaction with primary care for children with selected chronic conditions. *Journal of Community Health, 16,* 213–224.

Ware, J. E. & Davies, A. R. (1983). Behavioral consequences of consumer dissatisfaction with medical care. *Evaluation and Program Planning, 6,* 291–297.

Ware, J. E., Kane, R., Davies, A. R., & Brooks, R. (1978). *Medical Care Services Reivew, 1,* 1–15.

APPENDIX

Functional Disability Inventory

Functional Disability Inventory
Child and Adolescent Form

When people are sick or not feeling well it is sometimes difficult for them to do their regular activities. In the past two weeks, would you have had **any physical trouble or difficulty doing these activities?**

	No Trouble	A Little Trouble	Some Trouble	A Lot of Trouble	Impossible
1. Walking to the bathroom.	0	1	2	3	4
2. Walking up stairs.	0	1	2	3	4
3. Doing something with a friend. (For example, playing a game.)	0	1	2	3	4
4. Doing chores at home.	0	1	2	3	4
5. Eating regular meals.	0	1	2	3	4
6. Being up all day without a nap or rest.	0	1	2	3	4
7. Riding the school bus or traveling in the car.	0	1	2	3	4

Remember, you are being asked about difficulty due to physical health.

	No Trouble	A Little Trouble	Some Trouble	A Lot of Trouble	Impossible
8. Being at school all day.	0	1	2	3	4
9. Doing the activities in gym class (or playing sports).	0	1	2	3	4
10. Reading or doing homework.	0	1	2	3	4
11. Watching TV.	0	1	2	3	4
12. Walking the length of a football field.	0	1	2	3	4
13. Running the length of a football field.	0	1	2	3	4
14. Going shopping.	0	1	2	3	4
15. Getting to sleep at night and staying asleep.	0	1	2	3	4

Functional Disability Inventory
Parent Form

When people are sick or not feeling well it is sometimes difficult for them to do their regular activities. In the past two weeks, would your child have had **any physical trouble or difficulty doing these activities?**

	No Trouble	A Little Trouble	Some Trouble	A Lot of Trouble	Impossible
1. Walking to the bathroom.	0	1	2	3	4
2. Walking up stairs.	0	1	2	3	4
3. Doing something with a friend. (For example, playing a game.)	0	1	2	3	4
4. Doing chores at home.	0	1	2	3	4
5. Eating regular meals.	0	1	2	3	4
6. Being up all day without a nap or rest.	0	1	2	3	4
7. Riding the school bus or traveling in the car.	0	1	2	3	4

Remember, you are being asked about difficulty due to physical health.

	No Trouble	A Little Trouble	Some Trouble	A Lot of Trouble	Impossible
8. Being at school all day.	0	1	2	3	4
9. Doing the activities in gym class (or playing sports).	0	1	2	3	4
10. Reading or doing homework.	0	1	2	3	4
11. Watching TV.	0	1	2	3	4
12. Walking the length of a football field.	0	1	2	3	4
13. Running the length of a football field.	0	1	2	3	4
14. Going shopping.	0	1	2	3	4
15. Getting to sleep at night and staying asleep.	0	1	2	3	4

Functional Status Questionnaire

How Well Has Your Child Been?

Here are some statements that mothers have made to describe their
children.
Please answer them thinking about <u>this</u> child during the last 2 weeks.

Please answer only those Part
2 items for which you chose an
asterisked answer in Part 1.

Part 1: During the <u>last 2 weeks</u>, how often did this child:

Part 2: Was this due to illness?

				Part 2		
1. Eat well	*Never or rarely	*Some of the time	Almost always	Yes	Sometimes	No
2. Sleep well	*Never or rarely	*Some of the time	Almost always	Yes	Sometimes	No
3. Seem contended and cheerful	*Never or rarely	*Some of the time	Almost always	Yes	Sometimes	No
4. Act moody	Never or rarely	*Some of the time	*Almost always	Yes	Sometimes	No
5. Communicate what he/she wanted	*Never or rarely	*Some of the time	Almost always	Yes	Sometimes	No
6. Seem to feel sick and tired	Never or rarely	*Some of the time	*Almost always	Yes	Sometimes	No
7. Occupy him/ herself	*Never or rarely	*Some of the time	Almost always	Yes	Sometimes	No
8. Seem lively and energetic	*Never or rarely	*Some of the time	Almost always	Yes	Sometimes	No
9. Seem unusually irritable	Never or rarely	*Some of the time	*Almost always	Yes	Sometimes	No
10. Sleep through the night	*Never or rarely	*Some of the time	Almost always	Yes	Sometimes	No
11. Respond to your attention	*Never or rarely	*Some of the time	Almost always	Yes	Sometimes	No
12. Seem unusually difficult	Never or rarely	*Some of the time	*Almost always	Yes	Sometimes	No
13. Seem interested in what was going on around him/her	*Never or rarely	*Some of the time	Almost always	Yes	Sometimes	No
14. React to things by crying	Never or rarely	*Some of the time	*Almost always	Yes	Sometimes	No

PedsQL

| ID# _____ |
| Date: _____ |

TM

PedsQL
Pediatric Quality of Life
Inventory

Version 4.0

CHILD REPORT (ages **8-12**)

DIRECTIONS

On the following page is a list of things that might be a problem for you.
Please tell us **how much of a problem** each one has been for you
during the **past ONE month** by circling:

> **0** if it is **never** a problem
> **1** if it is **almost never** a problem
> **2** if it is **sometimes** a problem
> **3** if it is **often** a problem
> **4** if it is **almost always** a problem

There are no right or wrong answers.
If you do not understand a question, please ask for help.

PedsQL 2

*In the past **ONE month**, how much of a **problem** has this been for you ...*

ABOUT MY HEALTH AND ACTIVITIES (problems with...)	Never	Almost Never	Some-times	Often	Almost Always
1. It is hard for me to walk more than one block	0	1	2	3	4
2. It is hard for me to run	0	1	2	3	4
3. It is hard for me to do sports activity or exercise	0	1	2	3	4
4. It is hard for me to lift something heavy	0	1	2	3	4
5. It is hard for me to take a bath or shower by myself	0	1	2	3	4
6. It is hard for me to do chores around the house	0	1	2	3	4
7. I hurt or ache	0	1	2	3	4
8. I have low energy	0	1	2	3	4

ABOUT MY FEELINGS (problems with...)	Never	Almost Never	Some-times	Often	Almost Always
1. I feel afraid or scared	0	1	2	3	4
2. I feel sad or blue	0	1	2	3	4
3. I feel angry	0	1	2	3	4
4. I have trouble sleeping	0	1	2	3	4
5. I worry about what will happen to me	0	1	2	3	4

HOW I GET ALONG WITH OTHERS (problems with...)	Never	Almost Never	Some-times	Often	Almost Always
1. I have trouble getting along with other kids	0	1	2	3	4
2. Other kids do not want to be my friend	0	1	2	3	4
3. Other kids tease me	0	1	2	3	4
4. I cannot do things that other kids my age can do	0	1	2	3	4
5. It is hard to keep up when I play with other kids	0	1	2	3	4

ABOUT SCHOOL (problems with...)	Never	Almost Never	Some-times	Often	Almost Always
1. It is hard to pay attention in class	0	1	2	3	4
2. I forget things	0	1	2	3	4
3. I have trouble keeping up with my schoolwork	0	1	2	3	4
4. I miss school because of not feeling well	0	1	2	3	4
5. I miss school to go to the doctor or hospital	0	1	2	3	4

ID#	
Date:	

TM

PedsQL
Pediatric Quality of Life
Inventory

Version 4.0

PARENT REPORT for **CHILDREN** (ages **8-12**)

DIRECTIONS

On the following page is a list of things that might be a problem for **your child**. Please tell us **how much of a problem** each one has been for **your child** during the **past ONE month** by circling:

> **0** if it is **never** a problem
> **1** if it is **almost never** a problem
> **2** if it is **sometimes** a problem
> **3** if it is **often** a problem
> **4** if it is **almost always** a problem

There are no right or wrong answers.
If you do not understand a question, please ask for help.

PedsQL 2

In the past ONE month, how much of a problem has your child had with …

PHYSICAL FUNCTIONING (problems with…)	Never	Almost Never	Some-times	Often	Almost Always
1. Walking more than one block	0	1	2	3	4
2. Running	0	1	2	3	4
3. Participating in sports activity or exercise	0	1	2	3	4
4. Lifting something heavy	0	1	2	3	4
5. Taking a bath or shower by him or herself	0	1	2	3	4
6. Doing chores around the house	0	1	2	3	4
7. Having hurts or aches	0	1	2	3	4
8. Low energy level	0	1	2	3	4

EMOTIONAL FUNCTIONING (problems with…)	Never	Almost Never	Some-times	Often	Almost Always
1. Feeling afraid or scared	0	1	2	3	4
2. Feeling sad or blue	0	1	2	3	4
3. Feeling angry	0	1	2	3	4
4. Trouble sleeping	0	1	2	3	4
5. Worrying about what will happen to him or her	0	1	2	3	4

SOCIAL FUNCTIONING (problems with…)	Never	Almost Never	Some-times	Often	Almost Always
1. Getting along with other children	0	1	2	3	4
2. Other kids not wanting to be his or her friend	0	1	2	3	4
3. Getting teased by other children	0	1	2	3	4
4. Not able to do things that other children his or her age can do	0	1	2	3	4
5. Keeping up when playing with other children	0	1	2	3	4

SCHOOL FUNCTIONING (problems with…)	Never	Almost Never	Some-times	Often	Almost Always
1. Paying attention in class	0	1	2	3	4
2. Forgetting things	0	1	2	3	4
3. Keeping up with schoolwork	0	1	2	3	4
4. Missing school because of not feeling well	0	1	2	3	4
5. Missing school to go to the doctor or hospital	0	1	2	3	4

WeeFIM

WeeFIM® instrument

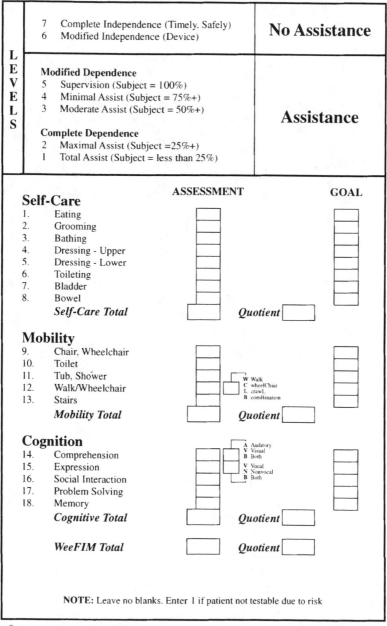

L E V E L S	7 Complete Independence (Timely. Safely) 6 Modified Independence (Device)	**No Assistance**
	Modified Dependence 5 Supervision (Subject = 100%) 4 Minimal Assist (Subject = 75%+) 3 Moderate Assist (Subject = 50%+) **Complete Dependence** 2 Maximal Assist (Subject =25%+) 1 Total Assist (Subject = less than 25%)	**Assistance**

ASSESSMENT   GOAL

Self-Care
1. Eating
2. Grooming
3. Bathing
4. Dressing - Upper
5. Dressing - Lower
6. Toileting
7. Bladder
8. Bowel
   Self-Care Total   *Quotient*

Mobility
9. Chair, Wheelchair
10. Toilet
11. Tub, Shower
12. Walk/Wheelchair
13. Stairs
    Mobility Total   *Quotient*

W Walk
C wheelChair
L crawL
B comBination

Cognition
14. Comprehension
15. Expression
16. Social Interaction
17. Problem Solving
18. Memory
    Cognitive Total   *Quotient*

A Auditory
V Visual
B Both

V Vocal
N Nonvocal
B Both

WeeFIM Total   *Quotient*

NOTE: Leave no blanks. Enter 1 if patient not testable due to risk

Family Responsibility Questionnaire

Who Does What?

Below are different tasks or situations about taking care of diabetes. Choose the one that best describes how each task is done in your family. Write the number (1- 5) in the box for each one.

1 = Caregiver takes or initiates responsibility for this almost all of the time.
2 = Caregiver and child share responsibility for this equally.
3 = Child takes or initiates responsibility for this almost all of the time.
4 = Someone else takes responsibility. Please write in who - for example, aunt, grandmother, brother, sister, etc.
5 = No one is really responsible.

Things or Tasks:

_____ 1. Remembering the day and time of clinic appointment.

_____ 2. Telling teachers about diabetes

_____ 3. Remembering to take insulin on time.

_____ 4. Making appointments with the dentist, eye doctor and other specialists.

_____ 5. Telling relatives about diabetes.

_____ 6. Taking more or less insulin according to the results of your blood glucose or urine

     tests.

_____ 7. Noticing differences in health, such as weight changes or signs of infection.

_____ 8. Telling friends about diabetes.

_____ 9. Noticing the early signs of an insulin reaction or low blood sugar?

_____10. Giving insulin injections.

_____ 11. Deciding what should or should not be eaten when meals are eaten away from home

     (in a restaurant or other family member's house).

_____ 12. Examining feet and making sure shoes fit properly.

_____ 13. Carrying some kind of sugar in case of an insulin reaction.

1 = Caregiver takes or initiates responsibility for this almost all of the time.
2 = Caregiver and child share responsibility for this equally.
3 = Child takes or initiates responsibility for this almost all of the time.
4 = Someone else takes responsibility. Please write in who - for example, aunt,
   grandmother, brother, sister, etc.
5 = No one is really responsible.

_____ 14. Explaining absences from school to teachers or other school personnel.

_____ 15. Rotating insulin injection sites.

_____ 16. Checking expiration dates on medical supplies.

_____ 17. Making sure there are enough test strips, insulin, syringes, etc.

_____ 18. Remembering times when blood sugar or urine should be tested.

_____ 19. Knowing that blood sugar is too high.

_____ 20. Deciding what to do when the blood sugar is too high.

Medical Compliance Incomplete Stories Test

MCIST Manual
1990 Revision

The Medical Compliance Incomplete Stories for Children and Adolescents

Story 1:

Bill went to the doctor for a checkup and was surprised when the doctor said, "You haven't had a booster shot in quite some time. I think I should give you one today." What do you think happened next?

Story 2:

Helen had been sick for two days. She had a headache, a stomach ache, and felt as though she might have to vomit. Her mother took her to the doctor. What do you think happened next?

Story 3:

The doctor came into Mike's hospital room and told him that he needed to have a serious operation. His right foot was diseased and it would have to be taken off, or else he might die. Mike knew that his foot was sore, but had not realized just how serious it was. What do you think happened next?

Story 4:

Jill had been sick for a long time, almost two years. Sometimes she felt better for a couple of months, and then got sick again for a time. Her doctor called her up one morning to tell her about a new treatment. It was so new that they did not know whether it would work for her or not. Sometimes it seemed to help some people with the same problem as Jill, but at other times it did not help or even seemed to make things worse. What do you think happened next?

Story 5:

Henry was born with a disease that he will have for his whole life. A lot of the time he feels perfectly well and not sick at all. Sometimes he even forgets he has a medical problem. The doctors told him that he would have to do special exercises and take ten pills every day to try and stay well. What do you think happened next?

MCIST Manual
1990 Revision

The Medical Compliance Incomplete Stories
Parent Form (MCIST-PF)

Story 1:

Mr. and Mrs. Jones took their son. Bill to the doctor for a checkup and were surprised when the doctor said "Bill hasn't had a booster shot in quite some time. I think I should give him one today." How do you think Bill's parents responded to this?

Story 2:

Mr. and Mrs. Black's daughter Helen had been sick for two days. On the third day she told her parents that she had a headache, a stomach ache, and felt as though she might have to vomit. How do you think Helen's parents responded to this?

Story 3:

The doctor came into the hospital waiting room and told Mr. and Mrs. Woods that their son Mike needed to have a serious operation. His right foot was diseased and it would have to be taken off, or else he might die. Mike's parents know that his foot was sore, but they had not realized just how serious it was. How do you think Mike's parents responded to this?

Story 4:

Mr. and Mrs. Brown's daughter Jill had been sick for a long time, almost two years. Sometimes their daughter feels better for a couple of months, and then gets sick again for a time. Her doctor called Mr. and Mrs. Brown up one morning to tell them about a new treatment. It was so new that the doctor did not know whether it would work for Jill or not. Sometimes it seemed to help some people with the same problem as Jill, but at other times it did not help or even seemed to make things worse. How do you think Jill's parents responded to this?

Story 5:

Mr. and Mrs. Smith's son Henry was born with a disease that he will have for his whole life. A lot of the time their son feels perfectly well and not sick at all. Sometimes they even forget he has a medical problem. The doctors told Mr. and Mrs. Smith that Henry would have to do special exercises and take ten pills every day to try and stay well. How do you think Henry's parents responded to this?

Oucher

OUCHER!™

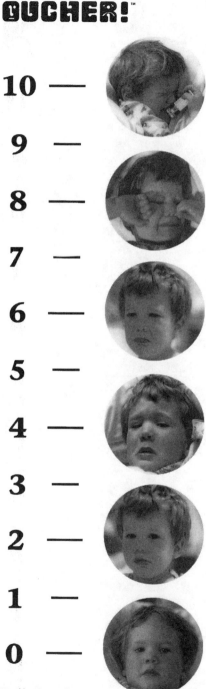

10 —

9 —

8 —

7 —

6 —

5 —

4 —

3 —

2 —

1 —

0 —

http://www.oucher.org

THE OUCHER: A SUMMARY

What is the OUCHER?

The OUCHER is a poster developed for children to help them communicate how much pain or hurt they feel. There are two scales on the OUCHER: A number scale for older children and a picture scale for younger children.

Which scale should be used?

Children who are able to count to 100 by ones or tens and who understand, for example, that 71 is greater than 43, can use the numerical scale. Children who do not understand numbers should use the picture scale. Some children who are able to use the number scale might prefer to use the picture scale. Ask the child which scale he or she would prefer.

How do I use the OUCHER?

Picture scale: The following is an example of how to explain the picture scale to a younger child. The words can be changed when using the picture scale with an older child.

This is a poster called the OUCHER. It helps children tell others how much hurt they have. (For younger children, it might be useful to ask: Do you know what I mean by hurt? If the child is not sure, then an explanation should be provided.) Here's how this works. This picture shows not hurt (point to the bottom picture), this picture shows just a little bit of hurt (point to the 2nd picture), this picture shows a little more hurt (point to the 3rd picture), this picture shows even more hurt (point to the 4th picture), this picture shows a lot of hurt (point to the 5th picture), and this picture shows the biggest hurt you could ever have (point to the 6th picture). Can you point to the picture that shows how much hurt you are having right now?

Once a children selects a picture, their picture selection is changed to a number score from 0-10.

    10 – Picture at the top of the scale
    8 – Second picture from the top
    6 – Third picture from the top
    4 – Fourth picture from the top
    2 – Fifth picture from the top
    0 – Picture at the bottom of the scale

Number scale: The following is an example of how to explain the number scale.

This is a poster called the OUCHER. It helps children tell others how much hurt they have. Here's how it works. 0 means no hurt. Here (point to the lower third of the scale, about 1 to 3), this means you have little hurts; here (point to the middle third of the scale, about 3 to 6) it means you have middle hurts. If your hurt is about here (point to the upper third of the scale, about 6 to 9), it means you have big hurts. But if you point to 10, it means you have the biggest hurt you could ever have. Can you point to the number (or tell me which number) that is like the hurt you are having right now?

The pain score for the number scale is the exact number from 0 to 10 that the child gives you.

What does the score mean? How should it be used?

The person who has pain is the expert or the one who knows best how the pain feels. The OUCHER score gives parents, teachers, nurses, and doctors some idea of how much pain the child is feeling. OUCHER scores can be used as a means to see if certain actions used to relieve pain, such as rest, applying heat or cold, eating or drinking, and medicine make a difference in how much pain the child feels. OUCHER scores can be recorded over a period of hours or days and would be useful information to share with nurses and doctors.

Remember, OUCHER scores only communicate how much pain the child is feeling. Other observations, such as changes in activity, location of the pain, what it feels like, and how long it lasts, are important. If you, as a parent or teacher, are concerned about the child's pain, you should contact your health care provider.

For information about the Oucher, write to: Dr. Judith E. Beyer, P.O. Box 411714, Kansas City, MO 64141 or go to the www.OUCHER.com website.

http://www.oucher.org

Pediatric Behavior Scale

Pediatric Behavior Scale
(Ages 6-16)

Child's Name:	Date: _____
Sex: ☐ Male ☐ Female	Birth Date: _____
	Age: _____

This form was completed by:

☐ Mother   ☐ Father   ☐ Other_____

Parents' Education (please list highest grade or degree completed):

Mother's education_____   Father's education_____

Parents' Occupation (please list the specific type of job):

Mother's work_____   Father's work_____

Child's Grade in School:_____   Has your child ever repeated a grade?

Type of School Program:
☐ No
☐ Yes (which one?) _____

☐ Regular classes

☐ Regular classes plus special services (such as resource room, speech therapy, or remedial reading)

(please describe):_____

☐ Self-contained special education class with integration into regular classes

(please describe):_____

☐ Self-contained special education class or special school

(please describe):_____

☐ Home tutor

☐ Other (please describe):_____

Compared to other children of the same age, how would you describe your child's:	Far Below Average	Below Average	Average	Above Average	Far Above Average
Ability and intelligence	☐	☐	☐	☐	☐
School achievement overall	☐	☐	☐	☐	☐
Academic achievement in:					
a. Reading/English	☐	☐	☐	☐	☐
b. Math/Arithmetic	☐	☐	☐	☐	☐
Effort in school	☐	☐	☐	☐	☐
School attendance	☐	☐	☐	☐	☐

Has your child been evaluated or treated for a medical, behavioral, emotional, or learning disorder?

☐ No   ☐ Yes (please explain)_____

Please list any drugs or medicines taken by your child on a regular basis:

	Name of Drug	Reason for Taking Drug	Dose (how much each day)
1.	_____	_____	_____
2.	_____	_____	_____
3.	_____	_____	_____
4.	_____	_____	_____

This checklist asks you to provide some information about your child's behavior. Below is a list of items that describe common behavior problems in children. Some of the items may be true of your child and some may not. Similar items are listed together. Please read each statement and decide how well it describes your child **during the past two months.** Then circle the number that best indicates how true each item is of your child.

0 = Almost never or not at all   2 = Often or pretty much
1 = Sometimes or just a little   3 = Very often or very much

1. Disobedient; won't mind or follow rules	0 1 2 3
2. Argues or quarrels	0 1 2 3
3. Uncooperative; won't help or work together with others	0 1 2 3
4. Defies authority or talks back	0 1 2 3
5. Mean or cruel to others	0 1 2 3
6. Threatens, bullies, or picks on other children	0 1 2 3
7. Starts fights	0 1 2 3
8. Hits, bites, or throws things at people	0 1 2 3
9. Destructive; breaks or smashes things on purpose	0 1 2 3
10. Lies or cheats	0 1 2 3
11. Steals	0 1 2 3
12. Hangs around with "bad" friends who often get into trouble	0 1 2 3
13. Explosive, unpredictable, or violent outbursts	0 1 2 3
14. Irritable; gets angry or annoyed easily	0 1 2 3
15. Overreacts to minor problems; "flies off the handle"	0 1 2 3
16. Loses temper; has temper tantrums	0 1 2 3
17. Shouts or screams a lot	0 1 2 3
18. Excitable; gets "wound up" easily	0 1 2 3
19. Can't concentrate or pay attention for long; short attention span	0 1 2 3
20. Easily distracted	0 1 2 3
21. Shifts frequently from one activity to another	0 1 2 3
22. Doesn't listen to directions	0 1 2 3
23. Fails to finish things he or she starts	0 1 2 3
24. Impulsive; acts without stopping to think	0 1 2 3
25. Can't stand waiting; wants things right away	0 1 2 3
26. Interrupts, talks out of turn, or blurts things out	0 1 2 3
27. Grabs for things; gets "into" everything	0 1 2 3
28. Rushes into danger without thinking about getting hurt	0 1 2 3
29. Hyperactive; always "on the go"	0 1 2 3
30. Restless; can't sit still	0 1 2 3
31. Squirms or fidgets	0 1 2 3
32. Constantly in motion; rarely slows down	0 1 2 3
33. Always running about or climbing on things	0 1 2 3
34. Tense, can't seem to relax	0 1 2 3
35. Nervous, "jumpy," or jittery; seems "on edge"	0 1 2 3
36. Nervous movements, shaking, or twitching	0 1 2 3
37. Picks at things (such as skin, clothes, or hair)	0 1 2 3
38. Fearful, anxious, or worried	0 1 2 3
39. Shy or timid	0 1 2 3
40. Self-conscious or easily embarrassed	0 1 2 3
41. Afraid to try new things for fear of making mistakes	0 1 2 3
42. Makes self "sick" with worry	0 1 2 3
43. Clings to adults or is too dependent on others	0 1 2 3
44. Panic attacks; gets so worried or upset that he/she can't be easily comforted	0 1 2 3
45. Feelings are easily hurt; sensitive to criticism	0 1 2 3
46. Lacks self-confidence; has low self-esteem	0 1 2 3
47. Feels worthless or inferior	0 1 2 3
48. Blames self for problems; feels guilty	0 1 2 3
49. Feels lonely, unwanted, or unloved; complains that no one loves him/her	0 1 2 3
50. Lacks motivation; gives up easily or doesn't try	0 1 2 3

PLEASE CONTINUE ON THE NEXT PAGE

51. Sad, unhappy, or depressed. 0 1 2 3
52. Cries a lot; cries easily for no good reason 0 1 2 3
53. Shows little interest or pleasure in activities; apathetic, doesn't seem to care about anything. 0 1 2 3
54. Thinks too much about death or dying; preoccupied with death 0 1 2 3
55. Talks about harming or killing self 0 1 2 3
56. Deliberately harms self or attempts suicide 0 1 2 3

57. Doesn't get along with other children 0 1 2 3
58. Has a hard time making friends 0 1 2 3
59. Ignored or rejected by others 0 1 2 3
60. Gets teased or picked on by other children 0 1 2 3
61. Withdrawn, doesn't get involved with others; spends a lot of time alone 0 1 2 3
62. Doesn't take part in normal social activities 0 1 2 3

63. Acts too young for his or her age; "childish" or immature. 0 1 2 3
64. Acts silly or giggles too much 0 1 2 3
65. Pesters or nags, is demanding; won't take "no" for an answer. 0 1 2 3
66. Asks personal or embarrassing questions 0 1 2 3
67. Loud 0 1 2 3
68. Talks too much 0 1 2 3
69. Hums or makes odd noises in public 0 1 2 3
70. Poor social judgment; not sensitive to other people's feelings or reactions 0 1 2 3
71. Careless about how he/she looks or dresses 0 1 2 3
72. Talks or thinks about sex too much 0 1 2 3
73. Plays with own sex parts too much 0 1 2 3
74. Bites or hits self, bangs head, or repeats other acts causing self-injury. 0 1 2 3
75. Odd movements or unusual posturing (such as hand-flapping or toe-walking). 0 1 2 3
76. Needs close or constant supervision 0 1 2 3

77. Talks or thinks about the same things over and over 0 1 2 3
78. Repeats certain actions over and over (please explain)_____ 0 1 2 3
79. Once he/she gets an idea, it's hard to get it out of his/her mind. 0 1 2 3
80. Repeats or "echoes" words or phrases said by others 0 1 2 3
81. Upset by changes in routine; insists on doing things the same way every time. 0 1 2 3

82. Sudden changes in mood or feelings; moody 0 1 2 3
83. Rapid shifts between sadness and excitement 0 1 2 3
84. Inconsistent; behavior or learning varies greatly from day to day 0 1 2 3
85. Shows changes in personality; is not always his/her "same old self". 0 1 2 3

86. Sees or hears things that aren't really there 0 1 2 3
87. Confuses reality and fantasy; unable to tell the difference between real and imaginary things 0 1 2 3
88. Says strange things that don't make sense; has odd or peculiar ideas
    (please explain)_____ 0 1 2 3
89. Strange, unusual, or bizarre behavior (please explain)____
    _____ 0 1 2 3
90. Very suspicious of others; thinks people are out to get him or her. 0 1 2 3

91. Drowsy or sleepy; not alert or wide awake 0 1 2 3
92. Sluggish or slow-moving; lacks energy 0 1 2 3
93. Stares into space; seems preoccupied or "in a world of his/her own" 0 1 2 3
94. Confused or disoriented; seems to be in a fog 0 1 2 3
95. Unresponsive; doesn't show feelings or emotions 0 1 2 3

96. Clumsy, awkward, or poorly coordinated 0 1 2 3
97. Bumps into things or falls a lot. 0 1 2 3
98. Speech is slurred or hard to understand 0 1 2 3
99. Shaky movements or tremor; hands tremble or shake 0 1 2 3
100. Draws or writes poorly 0 1 2 3
101. Has trouble hitting, kicking, or throwing a ball 0 1 2 3

102. Eats too much. 0 1 2 3
103. Overweight or gains too much weight 0 1 2 3
104. Poor appetite; doesn't eat much. 0 1 2 3
105. Underweight or loses too much weight 0 1 2 3
106. Eats things that are not food (please explain)_____ 0 1 2 3
107. Goes on eating binges; eats large amounts of food all at once 0 1 2 3
108. Vomits after eating (not due to illness or medication) 0 1 2 3

PLEASE CONTINUE ON THE NEXT PAGE

109.	Sleeps more than most other children	0	1	2	3
110.	Sleeps less than most other children	0	1	2	3
111.	Has trouble falling asleep	0	1	2	3
112.	Sleep is restless or disturbed; often tosses and turns in sleep	0	1	2	3
113.	Wakes up often in the night	0	1	2	3
114.	Has nightmares or bad dreams	0	1	2	3
115.	Talks, walks, or cries out in sleep	0	1	2	3
116.	Wakes up too early in the morning	0	1	2	3
117.	Headaches	0	1	2	3
118.	Stomach aches	0	1	2	3
119.	Aches or pains in muscles, limbs, chest, or back	0	1	2	3
120.	Complains of feeling "sick"	0	1	2	3
121.	Complains of dizziness or feeling faint	0	1	2	3
122.	Nausea or vomiting when nervous or emotionally upset	0	1	2	3
123.	Nausea or vomiting due to illness or medication	0	1	2	3
124.	Diarrhea or loose bowels	0	1	2	3
125.	Fever or high temperatures	0	1	2	3
126.	Complains of hot or cold spells (without having a fever)	0	1	2	3
127.	Hearing problems (please explain) ___ ___	0	1	2	3
128.	Problems with eyes or vision (other than needing eyeglasses) (please explain) ___ ___	0	1	2	3
129.	Rashes or other skin problems	0	1	2	3
130.	Asthma, wheezing, or trouble breathing	0	1	2	3
131.	Seizures that cause falling and loss of consciousness	0	1	2	3
132.	Seizures that are brief and do not cause complete loss of consciousness	0	1	2	3
133.	Tires easily; lacks stamina or physical endurance	0	1	2	3
134.	Constipated; doesn't have regular bowel movements	0	1	2	3
135.	Has bowel movements outside of the toilet; soils pants	0	1	2	3
136.	Wets the bed at night	0	1	2	3
137.	Wets self during the day	0	1	2	3
138.	Accident-prone; gets frequent cuts, scrapes, or bruises	0	1	2	3
139.	Illness requiring emergency room treatment or a stay in the hospital (please explain) ___ ___	0	1	2	3
140.	Other physical problems (please explain) ___ ___	0	1	2	3
141.	Doesn't follow doctor's orders for health problems	0	1	2	3
142.	Refuses or "forgets" to take pills or medicine he/she is supposed to take	0	1	2	3
143.	Refuses or "forgets" to complete special exercises or physical activities he/she is supposed to do	0	1	2	3
144.	If on a restricted diet, he/she sneaks food or eats foods he/she is not supposed to eat	0	1	2	3
145.	Worries about or is fearful of medical procedures (shots, blood tests, etc.)	0	1	2	3
146.	Physically resists or combats medical procedures (shots, blood tests, etc.)	0	1	2	3
147.	Careless or irresponsible about his/her health	0	1	2	3
148.	Has trouble expressing self; "can't get the words out"	0	1	2	3
149.	Quiet; doesn't talk very much	0	1	2	3
150.	Speech or articulation problems (please explain)___	0	1	2	3
151.	Gets mixed up when telling a story or explaining how something happened	0	1	2	3
152.	Has trouble remembering names for things or thinking of the right words to say	0	1	2	3
153.	Makes up words or substitutes words with similar meanings (such as "door" for "window")	0	1	2	3
154.	Thinks and works slowly	0	1	2	3
155.	Unable to think clearly and logically; has trouble figuring out how to solve problems	0	1	2	3
156.	Comprehension problems; difficulty in understanding directions or discussions	0	1	2	3
157.	Has trouble remembering things; forgets easily	0	1	2	3
158.	Thoughts are rambling or disorganized	0	1	2	3
159.	Has difficulty learning, even when he or she tries hard	0	1	2	3
160.	Underachieving; not working up to potential	0	1	2	3
161.	Has trouble with reading, writing, or arithmetic	0	1	2	3
162.	Fails to complete schoolwork or homework	0	1	2	3
163.	Schoolwork is sloppy, careless, or disorganized	0	1	2	3
164.	Gets low grades on school papers or tests	0	1	2	3
165.	Does not like school; doesn't want to go to school	0	1	2	3

PLEASE CHECK TO BE SURE YOU HAVE COMPLETED ALL ITEMS

Pediatric Symptom Checklist

Pediatric Symptom Checklist (PSC)

Emotional and physical health go together in children. Because parents are often the first to notice a problem with their child's behavior, emotions or learning, you may help your child get the best care possible by answering these questions. Please indicate which statement best describes your child.

Please mark under the heading that best describes your child:

		NEVER	SOMETIMES	OFTEN
1. Complains of aches and pains	1	_____	_____	_____
2. Spends more time alone	2	_____	_____	_____
3. Tires easily, has little energy	3	_____	_____	_____
4. Fidgety, unable to sit still	4	_____	_____	_____
5. Has trouble with teacher	5	_____	_____	_____
6. Less interested in school	6	_____	_____	_____
7. Acts as if driven by a motor	7	_____	_____	_____
8. Daydreams too much	8	_____	_____	_____
9. Distracted easily	9	_____	_____	_____
10. Is afraid of new situations	10	_____	_____	_____
11. Feels sad, unhappy	11	_____	_____	_____
12. Is irritable, angry	12	_____	_____	_____
13. Feels hopeless	13	_____	_____	_____
14. Has trouble concentrating	14	_____	_____	_____
15. Less interested in friends	15	_____	_____	_____
16. Fights with other children	16	_____	_____	_____
17. Absent from school	17	_____	_____	_____
18. School grades dropping	18	_____	_____	_____
19. Is down on him or herself	19	_____	_____	_____
20. Visits the doctor with doctor finding nothing wrong	20	_____	_____	_____
21. Has trouble sleeping	21	_____	_____	_____
22. Worries a lot	22	_____	_____	_____
23. Wants to be with you more than before	23	_____	_____	_____
24. Feels he or she is bad	24	_____	_____	_____
25. Takes unnecessary risks	25	_____	_____	_____
26. Gets hurt frequently	26	_____	_____	_____
27. Seems to be having less fun	27	_____	_____	_____
28. Acts younger than children his or her age	28	_____	_____	_____
29. Does not listen to rules	29	_____	_____	_____
30. Does not show feelings	30	_____	_____	_____
31. Does not understand other people's feelings	31	_____	_____	_____
32. Teases others	32	_____	_____	_____
33. Blames others for his or her troubles	33	_____	_____	_____
34. Takes things that do not belong to him or her	34	_____	_____	_____
35. Refuses to share	35	_____	_____	_____

Total score _____

Does your child have any emotional or behavioral problems for which she/he needs help? ( ) N   ( ) Y
Are there any services that you would like your child to receive for these problems?   ( ) N   ( ) Y

If yes, what
services?_____

Pediatric Symptom Checklist - Youth Report (Y-PSC)

Please mark under the heading that best fits you:

	Never	Sometimes	Often
1. Complain of aches or pains............................	___	___	___
2. Spend more time alone.................................	___	___	___
3. Tire easily, little energy.............................	___	___	___
4. Fidgety, unable to sit still.........................	___	___	___
5. Have trouble with teacher.................	___	___	___
6. Less interested in school..............	___	___	___
7. Act as if driven by motor............................	___	___	___
8. Daydream too much.....................................	___	___	___
9. Distract easily..	___	___	___
10. Are afraid of new situations..........................	___	___	___
11. Feel sad, unhappy......................................	___	___	___
12. Are irritable, angry...................................	___	___	___
13. Feel hopeless...	___	___	___
14. Have trouble concentrating............................	___	___	___
15. Less interested in friends...........................	___	___	___
16. Fight with other children............................	___	___	___
17. Absent from school.	___	___	___
18. School grades dropping.	___	___	___
19. Down on yourself......................................	___	___	___
20. Visit doctor with doctor finding nothing wrong........	___	___	___
21. Have trouble sleeping................................	___	___	___
22. Worry a lot...	___	___	___
23. Want to be with parent more than before...............	___	___	___
24. Feel that you are bad.................................	___	___	___
25. Take unnecessary risks................................	___	___	___
26. Get hurt frequently...................................	___	___	___
27. Seem to be having less fun............................	___	___	___
28. Act younger than children your age....................	___	___	___
29. Do not listen to rules................................	___	___	___
30. Do not show feelings..................................	___	___	___
31. Do not understand other people's feelings.............	___	___	___
32. Tease others..	___	___	___
33. Blame others for your troubles........................	___	___	___
34. Take things that do not belong to you.................	___	___	___
35. Refuse to share......................................	___	___	___

Estudio Sobre Adaptacion Social Y Emocional de los Ninos

La salud física y emocional son importantes para cada niño. Los padres son los primeros que notan un problema de la conducta emocional o de aprendizaje. Ud puede ayudar a su hijo a obtener el mejor cuidado del doctor por medio de contestar estas preguntas. Favor de indicar cual frase describe a su niño/a.

Indique cual síntoma mejor describe a su niño/a:

		NUNCA	ALGUNAS	SEGUIDO VECES
1. Se queja de dolores y malestares	1	_____	_____	_____
2. Pasa mucho tiempo solo(a	2	_____	_____	_____
3. Se cansa fácilmente, tiene poca energiá	3	_____	_____	_____
4. Nervioso, incapaz de estarse quieto	4	_____	_____	_____
5. Tiene problemas con un maestro	5	_____	_____	_____
6. Menos interesado en la escuela	6	_____	_____	_____
7. Es incansable	7	_____	_____	_____
8. Esta muy un sonador	8	_____	_____	_____
9. Se distrae facilmente	9	_____	_____	_____
10. Temeroso/a a nuevas situaciónes	10	_____	_____	_____
11. Se siete triste, infelix	11	_____	_____	_____
12. Es irritable, enojon	12	_____	_____	_____
13. Se siente sin esperanzas	13	_____	_____	_____
14. Tiene problemas para concentrarse	14	_____	_____	_____
15. Menos interesado en amistades	15	_____	_____	_____
16. Pelea con otros niños	16	_____	_____	_____
17. Se ausenta de la escuela a menudo	17	_____	_____	_____
18. Estan empeorando sus calificaciones	18	_____	_____	_____
19. Se critica a si mismo/a	19	_____	_____	_____
20. Visita al doctor sin que le encuentren nada	20	_____	_____	_____
21. Tiene problemas para dormir	21	_____	_____	_____
22. Se preocupa mucho	22	_____	_____	_____
23. Quiere estar con usted mas que antes	23	_____	_____	_____
24. Cree que el/ella es malo/a	24	_____	_____	_____
25. Toma riezgos innecesarios	25	_____	_____	_____
26. Se lastima frecuentemente	26	_____	_____	_____
27. Parece divertirse menos	27	_____	_____	_____
28. Actua mas chico que niños de su propia edad	28	_____	_____	_____
29. No obedece las reglas	29	_____	_____	_____
30. No demuestra sus sentimientos	30	_____	_____	_____
31. No comprende los sentimientos de otros	31	_____	_____	_____
32. Molesta o se burla de otros	32	_____	_____	_____
33. Culpa a otros por sus problemas	33	_____	_____	_____
34. Toma cosas que no le pertenecen	34	_____	_____	_____
35. Se rehusa a compartir	35	_____	_____	_____

Total _____

Necesita su nino(a) ayuda con problemas en el comportamiento con problemas emocionales?____ Si ____ No

M.S. Jellinek and J.M. Murphy, Massachusetts General Hospital

CUESTIONARIO (PSC-Y)

La salud física y emocional van juntas. Usted pueda ayudar al doctor/a a obtener el mejor servicio posible, contestando unas pocas preguntas acerca de usted. La informacion que nos de es parte de la visita de hov.

Indique cual síntoma mejor describe a su niño/a:

			NUNCA	ALGUNAS	SEGUIDO
1.	Se queja de dolores y malestares	1	_____	_____	_____
2.	Pasa mucho tiempo solo(a)	2	_____	_____	_____
3.	Se cansa fácilmente, poca energiá	3	_____	_____	_____
4.	Es inquieto(a)	4	_____	_____	_____
5.	Problemas con un maestro(a)	5	_____	_____	_____
6.	Menos interesado en la escuela	6	_____	_____	_____
7.	Es incansable	7	_____	_____	_____
8.	Es muy sonador	8	_____	_____	_____
9.	Se distrae facilmente	9	_____	_____	_____
10.	Temeroso(a) a nuevas situaciónes	10	_____	_____	_____
11.	Se siete triste, infeliz	11	_____	_____	_____
12.	Es irritable, enojon	12	_____	_____	_____
13.	Se siente sin esperanzas	13	_____	_____	_____
14.	Tiene problemas para concentrandose	14	_____	_____	_____
15.	Menos interesado(a) en amigos(as	15	_____	_____	_____
16.	Pelea con otros niños(as)	16	_____	_____	_____
17.	Falta a la escuela a menudo	17	_____	_____	_____
18.	Estan bejando sus calificaciones	18	_____	_____	_____
19.	Se critica a si mismo(a)	19	_____	_____	_____
20.	Va al doctor y no encuentren nada	20	_____	_____	_____
21.	Tiene problemas para dormir	21	_____	_____	_____
22.	Se preocupa mucho	22	_____	_____	_____
23.	Extranas a tus padres	23	_____	_____	_____
24.	Cree que eres malo(a)	24	_____	_____	_____
25.	Se pone en peligro sin necesidad	25	_____	_____	_____
26.	Se lastima facilmente	26	_____	_____	_____
27.	Parece divertise menos	27	_____	_____	_____
28.	Actua como un nino a su edad	28	_____	_____	_____
29.	No obedece reglas	29	_____	_____	_____
30.	No demuestra sus sentimientos	30	_____	_____	_____
31.	No comprende el sentir de otros	31	_____	_____	_____
32.	Molesta a otros	32	_____	_____	_____
33.	Culpa a otros de sus problemas	33	_____	_____	_____
34.	Toma cosas que no le pertenecen	34	_____	_____	_____
35.	Se rehusa a compartir	35	_____	_____	_____

Total _____

Necesita usted ayuda con problemas de comportamiento, emocionales o aprendizaje? _____ Si   _____ No

M.S. Jellinek and J.M. Murphy, Massachusetts General Hospital

Coping Health Inventory for Children

Date:_____/_____/_____   Interviewer's Initials:_____

Family No:_____   Family Member:_____ (M, F)   Visit:_____ (B, 12, 24)

COPING HEALTH INVENTORY FOR CHILDREN
(CHIC)

For the following 45 items, please choose the response that best describes how often your child does the described behavior in response to stress from the medical condition and associated problems. Please answer **ALL** items carefully. For each statement, there are 5 possible responses. Please respond with one of the following:

1 = Never
2 = Almost Never
3 = Sometimes
4 = Often
5 = Almost Always

(* Omit if your child has no brothers / sisters.)

My child . . .

1.
   Becomes more dependent on parents after illness episodes (e.g., stays with parents more)._____

2.
   Cries or acts sad and mopey after illness episodes._____

3.
   Assumes as much responsibility as possible in medical care (e.g., takes own medicine)._____

4.
   Complains about not being able to do things he / she wants to because of health problems._____

5.
   Uses illness to avoid social activities (e.g., says cannot participate when really can)._____

6.
   Says health problem is his / her fault._____

7.
   Acts out problems and bad feelings through activities._____

8.
   Maintains cheerful outlook on life (e.g., smiles, is happy). _____

9.
   After illness episode, ignores or does not follow usual rules and restrictions._____

10.
   Acts younger than his / her age after illness episodes._____

Austin, J.K., Patterson, J.M., & Huberty, T.J. (1991). Development of the coping health inventory for children. Journal of Pediatric Nursing, 8(3), 166-174.

11.

Takes risks that could lead to his / her getting hurt or sick._____

        1 = Never
        2 = Almost Never
        3 = Sometimes
        4 = Often
        5 = Almost Always

12.

Tries to learn about and understand his / her health problems._____

13.

Spends more time alone or away from family after illness episodes._____

14.

Says others are the cause or at fault for his / her health problems._____

15.

Spends time with others who have similar health problems._____

16.

Says is worried about having a health problem._____

17.

Seeks help from others in managing his / her health problems._____

18.

Talks to parents about feelings._____

19.

Resists going to school because of health problems even if he / she could go._____

20.

Denies or ignores health problems._____

21.

Tries to be independent and not let health problems interfere with activities._____

22.

Thinks about good things in his / her life (e.g., makes positive statements)._____

23.

Resists medical treatment (e.g., does not want to go to doctor)._____

24.

Works hard on school work and activities (e.g., completes homework, participates in class)._____

25.

Talks to friends about feelings._____

26.

Prays for help with health problems._____

Austin, J.K., Patterson, J.M., & Huberty, T.J. (1991). Development of the coping health inventory for children. Journal of Pediatric Nursing, 8(3), 166-174.

*27.

Talks to brothers / sisters about health problems.____

28.

Has a give up" attitude toward the health problem (e.g., says that he / she will always be sick).____

29.

Tries to develop a sense of competence (e.g., shows initiative to do new things).____

*30.

Argues and fights with brothers / sisters more after illness episodes.____

31.

Talks with doctors or nurses about health problems.____

1 = Never
2 = Almost Never
3 = Sometimes
4 = Often
5 = Almost Always

32.

Realizes that there are others with worse health problems (e.g., makes statements about others being sicker).____

33.

Becomes irritable after illness episodes.____

34.

Follows advice made by doctors and nurses.____

35.

Tries to avoid spending time with friends after illness episodes.____

*36.

Talks with brothers / sisters about feelings.____

37.

Accepts activity limitations caused by health problems.____

38.

Sees self as different than others because of health problems (e.g., makes statements about feeling different).____

39.

Talks with parents about how to cope with the health problem.____

40.

After illness episodes, does negative things just to get attention from family.____

41.

Sees self basically like others even though he / she has a health problem.____

Austin, J.K., Patterson, J.M., & Huberty, T.J. (1991). Development of the coping health inventory for children. Journal of Pediatric Nursing, 8(3), 166-174.

42.

    After illness episodes, tries to please family to get attention.____

43.

    Talks with friends about health problems.____

44.

    Picks on others after illness episodes.____

45.

    Develops a plan to handle health problems as they occur.____

chic.scl   9/13/96   jc

Austin, J.K., Patterson, J.M., & Huberty, T.J. (1991). Development of the coping health inventory for children. Journal of Pediatric Nursing, 8(3), 166-174.

Children's Coping Strategies Checklist

and

How I Coped Under Pressure Scale

CHILDREN'S COPING STRATEGIES CHECKLIST-Revision 1 (CCSC-R1)

Instructional Set:

Sometimes kids have problems or feel upset about things. When this happens, they may do different things to solve the problem or to make themselves feel better. For each item below, choose the answer that BEST describes how often you usually did this to solve your problems or make yourself feel better during the past month. There are no right or wrong answers, just indicate how often YOU USUALLY did each thing in order to solve your problems or make yourself feel better during the past month (or since [marker event]).[1]

The following tag was inserted every five items: *When you had problems in the past month,*

Response Set:

Never	Sometimes	Often	Most of the time
1	2	3	4

HOW I COPED UNDER PRESSURE SCALE-Revision 1 (HICUPS-R1)

Instructional Set:

Sometimes things happen that make you feel bad or upset. These could be things that happen in your family, at school, or with your friends. {**INSERT HERE THE PROBLEM YOU ARE ASKING THE CHILD TO REPORT ON THEIR COPING.** e.g. "Please describe one thing that happened between you and your brother or sister that made you feel bad or upset."}

When events like this happen, people think or do many different things to help make their situation better, or to make themselves feel better.

Below is a list of things kids may do when an event like this happens. Please tell us how much you thought or did *each* of the different things listed below to try and make things better, or to make yourself feel better when *{this event}* happened. There are no right or wrong answers, just mark how often *you* did each of these things during the event you just described.

The following tag was inserted every five items: *When {this event} happened...*

Response Set:

Never	Sometimes	Often	Most of the time
1	2	3	4

Program for Prevention Research (1999). Manual for the Children's Coping Strategies Checklist and the How I Coped Under Pressure Scale. (Available from Arizona State University, P.O. Box 876005, Tempe, AZ 85287–6005). Reprinted with permission.

ITEM SET FOR BOTH CCSC-R1 & HICUPS-R1[2]

Sub-scale	Item No.	Question
CDM	1.	You thought about what you could do before you did something.
POS	2.	You tried to notice or think about only the good things in your life.
REP	3.	You tried to ignore it.
SUPF	4.	You told people how you felt about the problem.
AVA	5.	You tried to stay away from the problem.
DPS	6.	You did something to make things better.
SUPA	7.	You talked to someone who could help you figure out what to do.
OPT	8.	You told yourself that things would get better.
DA	9.	You listened to music.
POS	10.	You reminded yourself that you are better off than a lot of other kids.
WISH	11.	You daydreamed that everything was okay.
PRE	12.	You went bicycle riding.
SUPF	13.	You talked about your feelings to someone who really understood.
SUPA	14.	You told other people what you wanted them to do.
REP	15.	You tried to put it out of your mind.
CDM	16.	You thought about what would happen before you decided what to do.
OPT	17.	You told yourself that it would be OK.
SUPF	18.	You told other people what made you feel the way you did.
CON	19.	You told yourself that you could handle this problem.

DA	20.	You went for a walk.
AVA	21.	You tried to stay away from things that made you feel upset.
SUPA	22.	You told others how you would like to solve the problem.
DPS	23.	You tried to make things better by changing what you did.
CON	24.	You told yourself you have taken care of things like this before.
PRE	25.	You played sports.
SU	26.	You thought about why it happened.
REP	27.	You didn't think about it.
SUPF	28.	You let other people know how you felt.
CON	29.	You told yourself you could handle what ever happens.
SUPA	30.	You told other people what you would like to happen.
OPT	31.	You told yourself that in the long run, things would work out for the best.
DA	32.	You read a book or magazine.
WISH	33.	You imagined how you'd like things to be.
CON	34.	You reminded yourself that you knew what to do.
CDM	35.	You thought about which things are best to do to handle the problem.
REP	36.	You just forgot about it.
OPT	37.	You told yourself that it would work itself out.
SUPA	38.	You talked to someone who could help you solve the problem.
PRE	39.	You went skateboard riding or roller skating.
AVA	40.	You avoided the people who made you feel bad.

POS   41.   You reminded yourself that overall things are pretty good for you.

DA   42.   You did something like video games or a hobby.

DPS   43.   You did something to solve the problem.

SU   44.   You tried to understand it better by thinking more about it.

POS   45.   You reminded yourself about all the things you have going for you.

WISH   46.   You wished that bad things wouldn't happen.

CDM   47.   You thought about what you needed to know so you could solve the problem.

AVA   48.   You avoided it by going to your room.

DPS   49.   You did something in order to get the most you could out of the situation.

SU   50.   You thought about what you could learn from the problem.

WISH   51.   You wished that things were better.

DA   52.   You watched TV.

PRE   53.   You did some exercise.

SU   54.   You tried to figure out why things like this happen.

[1] Since this version of the coping checklist was administered as part of a preventive intervention that was being evaluated in a randomized trial, children were asked to use a one month time frame in their reports of their coping strategies. The timeframe could be adjusted depending on the needs of the project. Of course the italicized prompts or tags that appear between every 5 items would also need to be adjusted.

[2] Newer versions of the instruments (i.e., CCSC-R2 and HICUPS-R2) are currently under development. Please contact the authors for the latest version.

DEFINITIONS FOR THE SUBSCALES ON THE CHILDREN'S COPING STRATEGIES
CHECKLIST-REVISION 1 (CCSC-R1) & THE HOW I COPED UNDER PRESSURE
SCALE-REVISION 1 (HICUPS-R1)

Subscale	Acronym	Description

ACTIVE COPING STRATEGIES

Problem focused Coping

Cognitive Decision Making	(CDM)	Planning or thinking about ways to solve the problem
Direct Problem Solving	(DPS)	Efforts to improve the problem situation
Seeking Understanding	(SU)	Efforts to find meaning in a problem situation or try to understand it better

Positive Reframing Coping

Positive Thinking	(POS)	Thinking about the good things that happened.
Optimistic Thinking	(OPT)	Thinking about things in the future with a optimistic manner
Control	(CON)	Thinking that you can handle or deal with the whatever happens

DISTRACTION STRATEGIES

Physical Release of emotions	(PRE)	Efforts to physically work off feelings with physical exercise, play or efforts to physically relax

Subscale	Acronym	Description
Distracting Actions	(DA)	Efforts to avoid thinking about the problem situation by using distracting stimuli, entertainment or some distracting activity

AVOIDANCE STRATEGIES

Subscale	Acronym	Description
Avoidant Actions	(AVA)	Efforts of avoiding the problem by staying away from it or leaving it
Repression	(REP)	Repressing thoughts of the problems
Wishful Thinking	(WISH)	Using wishful thinking or imaging the problem was better

SUPPORT SEEKING COPING STRATEGIES

Subscale	Acronym	Description
Support for Actions	(SUPA)	The use of other people as resources to assist in seeking solutions to the problem situation. This includes seeking advice or information or direct task assistance
Support for Feelings	(SUPF)	The involvement of other people in listening to feelings or providing understanding to help the person be less upset

Note. For a complete description of the inclusion and exclusion criteria for some of these categories that were used in a content analyses of children's coping responses, please see the categorization manual developed in earlier work. [Ayers, T. S., Sandler, I. N., Bernzweig, J. A., Harrison, R. J., Wampler, T. W., & Lustig, J. L. (1989). Handbook for the content analyses of children's coping responses. Tempe, AZ: Program for Prevention Research, Arizona State University.]

KIDCOPE

KIDCOPE
Older Version

INSTRUCTIONS: Please read each item and circle which phrase applies (if any). Then answer both questions to the right of each item, circling the best answer.	How often did you do this?				How much did it help?				
	Not at all	Some-times	A lot of the time	Almost all the time	Not at all	A little	Some-what	Pretty much	Very much
1. I thought about something else; tried to forget it; and/or went and did something like watch TV or play a game to get it off my mind.	0	1	2	3	0	1	2	3	4
2. I stayed away from people; kept my feelings to myself; and just handled the situation on my own.	0	1	2	3	0	1	2	3	4
3. I tried to see the good side of things and/or concentrated on something good that could come out of the situation.	0	1	2	3	0	1	2	3	4
4. I realized I brought the problem on myself and blamed myself for causing it.	0	1	2	3	0	1	2	3	4
5. I realized that someone else caused the problem and blamed them for making me go through this.	0	1	2	3	0	1	2	3	4
6. I thought of ways to solve the problem; talked to others to get more facts and information about the problem and/or tried to actually solve the problem.	0	1	2	3	0	1	2	3	4
7a. I talked about how I was feeling; yelled, screamed, or hit something.	0	1	2	3	0	1	2	3	4
b. Tried to calm myself by talking to myself, praying, taking a walk, or just trying to relax	0	1	2	3	0	1	2	3	4
8. I kept thinking and wishing this had never happened; and/or that I could change what had happened.	0	1	2	3	0	1	2	3	4
9. Turned to my family, friends, or other adults to help me feel better.	0	1	2	3	0	1	2	3	4
10. I just accepted the problem because I knew I couldn't do anything about it.	0	1	2	3	0	1	2	3	4

KIDCOPE
Younger Version

		Did you do this?		How much did it help?		
1.	I just tried to forget it	yes	no	Not at all	A little	A lot
2.	I did something like watch TV or played a game to forget it.	yes	no	Not at all	A little	A lot
3.	I stayed by myself.	yes	no	Not at all	A little	A lot
4.	I kept quiet about the problem.	yes	no	Not at all	A little	A lot
5.	I tried to see the good side of things.	yes	no	Not at all	A little	A lot
6.	I blamed myself for causing the problem.	yes	no	Not at all	A little	A lot
7.	I blamed someone else for causing the problem.	yes	no	Not at all	A little	A lot
8.	I tried to fix the problem by thinking of answers.	yes	no	Not at all	A little	A lot
9.	I tried to fix the problem by doing something or talking to someone.	yes	no	Not at all	A little	A lot
10.	I yelled, screamed, or got mad.	yes	no	Not at all	A little	A lot
11.	I tried to calm myself down.	yes	no	Not at all	A little	A lot
12.	I wished the problem had never happened.	yes	no	Not at all	A little	A lot
13.	I wished I could make things different.	yes	no	Not at all	A little	A lot
14.	I tried to feel better by spending time with others like family, grownups, or friends.	yes	no	Not at all	A little	A lot
15.	I didn't do anything because the problem couldn't be fixed.	yes	no	Not at all	A little	A lot

Schoolagers' Coping Strategies Inventory

ID NUMBER SCHOOLAGER'S COPING STRATEGIES INVENTORY

DIRECTIONS: This is not a test! Do not put your name on this paper.

When some children feel stressed, nervous, or worried about something, they do some of the things listed below. Think about when YOU feel stressed, nervous or worried. Circle HOW OFTEN you do each of these things either <u>before</u> the stressful thing happens, <u>while</u> you feel stressed, or <u>after</u> the stressful thing is over. Then tell me HOW MUCH each thing helps you feel better when you feel stressed, nervous or worried.

Stressful Thing

	HOW OFTEN DO YOU DO THIS?					HOW MUCH DOES IT HELP?		
1. Be by myself; be alone.	Never	Once in a while	A lot	Most of the time	Never do it	Does not help	Helps a little	Helps a lot
2. Bite my nails or crack my knuckles.	Never	Once in a while	A lot	Most of the time	Never do it	Does not help	Helps a little	Helps a lot
3. Cuddle my pet or stuffed animal.	Never	Once in a while	A lot	Most of the time	Never do it	Does not help	Helps a little	Helps a lot
4. Cry or feel sad.	Never	Once in a while	A lot	Most of the time	Never do it	Does not help	Helps a little	Helps a lot
5. Daydream.	Never	Once in a while	A lot	Most of the time	Never do it	Does not help	Helps a little	Helps a lot
6. Do something about it.	Never	Once in a while	A lot	Most of the time	Never do it	Does not help	Helps a little	Helps a lot
7. Do work around the house.	Never	Once in a while	A lot	Most of the time	Never do it	Does not help	Helps a little	Helps a lot
8. Draw, write, or read something.	Never	Once in a while	A lot	Most of the time	Never do it	Does not help	Helps a little	Helps a lot
9. Eat or drink.	Never	Once in a while	A lot	Most of the time	Never do it	Does not help	Helps a little	Helps a lot
10. Fight with someone.	Never	Once in a while	A lot	Most of the time	Never do it	Does not help	Helps a little	Helps a lot
11. Get mad.	Never	Once in a while	A lot	Most of the time	Never do it	Does not help	Helps a little	Helps a lot

	Never	Once in a while	A lot	Most of the time	Never do it	Does not help	Helps a little	Helps a lot
12. Hit, throw or break things.	Never	Once in a while	A lot	Most of the time	Never do it	Does not help	Helps a little	Helps a lot
13. Pick on someone.	Never	Once in a while	A lot	Most of the time	Never do it	Does not help	Helps a little	Helps a lot
14. Play a game or something.	Never	Once in a while	A lot	Most of the time	Never do it	Does not help	Helps a little	Helps a lot
15. Pray.	Never	Once in a while	A lot	Most of the time	Never do it	Does not help	Helps a little	Helps a lot
16. Run or walk away.	Never	Once in a while	A lot	Most of the time	Never do it	Does not help	Helps a little	Helps a lot
17. Say I'm sorry or tell the truth.	Never	Once in a while	A lot	Most of the time	Never do it	Does not help	Helps a little	Helps a lot
18. Sleep, take a nap.	Never	Once in a while	A lot	Most of the time	Never do it	Does not help	Helps a little	Helps a lot
19. Talk to myself.	Never	Once in a while	A lot	Most of the time	Never do it	Does not help	Helps a little	Helps a lot
20. Talk to someone.	Never	Once in a while	A lot	Most of the time	Never do it	Does not help	Helps a little	Helps a lot
21. Think about it.	Never	Once in a while	A lot	Most of the time	Never do it	Does not help	Helps a little	Helps a lot
22. Try to forget about it.	Never	Once in a while	A lot	Most of the time	Never do it	Does not help	Helps a little	Helps a lot
23. Try to relax, stay calm.	Never	Once in a while	A lot	Most of the time	Never do it	Does not help	Helps a little	Helps a lot
24. Walk, run or ride my bike.	Never	Once in a while	A lot	Most of the time	Never do it	Does not help	Helps a little	Helps a lot
25. Watch TV or listen to music.	Never	Once in a while	A lot	Most of the time	Never do it	Does not help	Helps a little	Helps a lot
26. Yell or scream.	Never	Once in a while	A lot	Most of the time	Never do it	Does not help	Helps a little	Helps a lot

**DIRECTIONS FOR USE OF THE SCHOOLAGERS' COPING STRATEGIES
INVENTORY (SCSI)**

Thank you for your request for information about the Schoolagers' Coping Strategies Inventory (SCSI). I have enclosed a copy of the instrument and directions for its use. Publications pertaining to the development and testing of the instrument are as follows:

Ryan, N.M. (1989). Stress-coping strategies identified from school age children's perspective. Research in Nursing & Health, 12, 111-122.

Ryan-Wenger, N.M. (1990). Development and psychometric properties of the Schoolagers' Coping Strategies Inventory. Nursing Research, 39, 344-349.

Sharrer, V.W., & Ryan-Wenger, N.M. (1991). Measurements of stress and coping among school-aged children with and without recurrent abdominal pain. Journal of School Health, 61, 86-91.

Ryan-Wenger, N.M., & Copeland, S.G. (1994). Coping strategies used by Black school-age children from low-income families. Journal of Pediatric Nursing, 9, 33-40.

Walsh, M., & Ryan-Wenger, N.M. (1994). Coping strategies used by school-age children with asthma. Pediatric Nursing, 9(3), 183-195.

Sharrer, V.W. & Ryan-Wenger, N.M. (1995). A longitudinal study of age and gender differences in school-age children's stressors and coping strategies. Journal of Pediatric Health Care, 9, 123-130.

Note: The original SCSI, as described in the Nursing Research manuscript (1990), included 25 items, and psychometric testing was done on these 25 items. Based on suggestions from the children and nurses who work with children, an additional item has recently been added. This item is #6, "Do something about it", and was considered important for children whose coping strategies include an attempt to change the stressor itself.

ADMINISTRATION

This instrument was developed for use by children ages 8 to 12. The directions to the children are provided on the instrument. If a specific stressor (e.g. divorce, chronic illness, school failure) is of primary interest to the researcher, the introductory statement can be modified to reflect that stressor. Children can be asked to identify the "stressful thing" they are thinking about at the top of the first page.

It seems to help if the investigator emphasizes that the first column lists things that **other** children have said that they do when they feel stressed, nervous or worried, and that the second column asks **how often** they do each of those things, and the third column asks how much it **helps**. Earlier editions of the SCSI used a number response format (0-3) in the columns next to each coping strategy, with the meaning of numbers at the top of the column, but trials have shown that repeating the **words** (e.g. never do it) after each item is less confusing to the children and therefore probably more reliable and valid than numbers. The SCSI you have received includes the word response format.

Data collection can be done in a classroom situation, or individually. Eight and nine year olds often do better if they use a ruler or straight-edge to keep their responses in the correct row. It is also helpful if the investigator reads each item to the eight and nine year olds if data collection is done in a large group. Older children catch on quickly and like to work at their own pace. It is important to scan the forms before collecting them to make sure that children did not leave items blank, or mark more than one answer for an item. Also, if "never" is circled in the "how often" column, indicating the child never uses this strategy, make sure that they also circled a "Never do it" in the "how much does it help" column.

SCORING

A. To score the SCSI, these numbers correspond to the following word responses:

FREQUENCY SCALE: "How often do you do this?"   0 = Never
                                                  1 = Once in a while
                                                  2 = A lot
                                                  3 = Most of the time

EFFECTIVENESS SCALE: "How much does it help?"   0 = Never do it
                                                    1 = Does not help
                                                    2 = Helps a little
                                                    3 = Helps a lot

B. The **FREQUENCY SCALE** yields two types of frequency scores:

1) Frequency Scale score: sum of children's responses on all 26 items in the "How often do you do this?" column. Scores can range from 0 to 78.

2) Number of different coping strategies used, regardless of frequency (total number of items, n=26, minus the number of items with a response of 0 (never). Scores can range from 0 to 26.

C. The **EFFECTIVENESS SCALE** indicates how helpful children perceive their coping strategies to be, and is the sum of the children's responses on all 26 items in the "How much does it help" column. Scores can range from 0 to 78.

D. My early manuscripts describe the calculation of a **TOTAL COPING SCORE** (sum of the Frequency and Effectiveness Scale Scores). This score was intended to reflect the theoretical construct of "coping" which should encompass not only the frequency with which coping strategies are used, but how effective they are perceived to be. I no longer recommend calculation of Total Coping Scores because the empirical meaning of this score has been difficult to explain and apply to practice. Further, statistical manipulation of the score is contraindicated because the two scales that make up total scores are necessarily highly correlated and not independent.

E. Frequency and Effectiveness Scale scores may mask important differences in specific strategies that children use. Therefore, **ITEM ANALYSIS** techniques may be informative when the investigator desires to determine if a particular group of children uses different strategies, or finds specific strategies to be more effective than another group. There is no assumption that one type of strategy is more adaptive or effective than another; scores simply reflect children's perceptions about their own coping resources and abilities to cope with stressors.

If the SCSI appears to meet your needs in the clinical or research setting, please feel free to duplicate the enclosed sample as needed. Other than revising directions to address a specific stressor, please do not alter the format or items without permission. I would appreciate hearing about your findings, particularly information about the sample and psychometric characteristics of the SCSI with that sample.

Note: If you would like to add additional coping strategies, please do so on a separate form, perhaps with a similar format. I would be interested in the results of a separate and combined analysis, since my goal is to improve the psychometric properties of the SCSI.

Please address any questions about the SCSI to:

Nancy Ryan-Wenger, PhD, RN, CPNP
Professor and Chair
Dept. of Community, Parent-Child and Psychiatric Nursing
College of Nursing
The Ohio State University
1585 Neil Avenue
Columbus, Ohio 43210

(614) 292-4078
E-mail address: ryan-wenger.10@osu.edu

SUMMARY OF SCSI SCORES WITH DIFFERENT SAMPLES
(Coefficient Alphas given when available)

TYPE OF SAMPLE	N	MEAN FREQUENCY SCORE & SD	MEAN EFFECTIVENESS SCORE & SD	FREQUENCY SCALE ALPHA	EFFECTIVE-NESS SCALE ALPHA
School[1]	242	30.7 (8.9)	35.1 (10.0)	0.76	0.77
RAP[2]	25	28.7 (9.0)	34.0 (9.3)		
Blacks[3]	59	38.8 (11.4)	42.9 (10.7)	0.80	0.73
Asthma[4]	78	29.5 (12.3)	31.8 (14.2)	0.85	0.89
School[5]	298	34.1 (8.67)	38.7 (8.9)		
Black	209	36.0 (8.6)	40.3 (9.8)		
White	85	33.4 (8.6)	38.1 (8.4)		
Catholic[6]	84	34.01 (10.7)	40.13 (10.8)	0.70	0.79
Military and Civilian[7]	91	24.5 (8.62)	32.4 (10.03)	0.74	0.78

[1]Ryan-Wenger, 1990

[2]Sharrer & Ryan-Wenger, 1991; RAP=Recurrent Abdominal Pain; this was a sub-sample of the 242 school-children in the above study.

[3]Ryan-Wenger & Copeland, 1994

[4]Walsh & Ryan-Wenger, 1994; the children with asthma were asked to respond to the coping items with respect to when they have problems with asthma. Having children respond to the same stressor is probably the reason for the larger alpha coefficients. In all other studies, each child selected his/her own stressor from which to respond.

[5]Dishion, T. J., 1992; unpublished masters thesis, University of Tennessee, Memphis.

[6]Sharrer & Ryan-Wenger (1995).

[7]Ryan-Wenger, 1998; unpublished manuscript: "the impact of the threat of war on military children"

NRW/mc Ryan-Wenger doc. SCSI.NRW (rev. 7/16/98)

Child Attitude Toward Illness Scale

Date:_____/_____/_____   Interviewer=s Initials:_____

Family No:_____   Family Member:___C___   Visit:_____ (B, 12, 24)

CHILD ATTITUDE TOWARD ILLNESS SCALE

I would now like to ask you how you feel about your seizure condition. If there is anything you do not understand, please ask me about it. For each question, tell me which best describes your feelings. I want you to answer EVERY question, even if some are hard to decide. There are no right or wrong answers. Only YOU can tell me how you REALLY feel.

1.   How often do you feel that your seizures are your fault? _____

   1 = Never
   2 = Not Often
   3 = Sometimes
   4 = Often
   5 = Very Often

2.   How often do you feel that your seizures keep you from doing things you like to do? _____

   1 = Never
   2 = Not Often
   3 = Sometimes
   4 = Often
   5 = Very Often

3.   How often do you feel that you will always be sick? _____

   1 = Never
   2 = Not Often
   3 = Sometimes
   4 = Often
   5 = Very Often

4.   How often do you feel happy even though you have seizures?_____

   1 = Never
   2 = Not Often
   3 = Sometimes
   4 = Often
   5 = Very Often

5.   How often do you feel different from others because of your seizures? _____

   1 = Never
   2 = Not Often
   3 = Sometimes

Austin, J.K., & Huberty, T.J. (1993). Development of the child attitude toward illness scale. Journal of Psychology, 18, 467-480.

Reprinted with permission by Joan K. Austin.

4 = Often
5 = Very Often

6.   How often do you feel bad because you have seizures? _____
         1 = Never
         2 = Not Often
         3 = Sometimes
         4 = Often
         5 = Very Often

7.   How often do you feel sad about being sick? _____
         1 = Never
         2 = Not Often
         3 = Sometimes
         4 = Often
         5 = Very Often

8.   How often do you feel that your seizures keep you from starting new things? _____
         1 = Never
         2 = Not Often
         3 = Sometimes
         4 = Often
         5 = Very Often

9.   How often do you feel just as good as other kids your age even though you have seizures? _____
         1 = Never
         2 = Not Often
         3 = Sometimes
         4 = Often
         5 = Very Often

10.   How good or bad do you feel it is that you have seizures? _____
         1 = Very Good
         2 = A Little Good
         3 = Not Sure
         4 = A Little Bad
         5 = Very Bad

Austin, J.K., & Huberty, T.J. (1993). Development of the child attitude toward illness scale. Journal of Psychology, 18, 467-480.

11.   How fair or unfair is it that you have seizures? _____
                                    1 = Very Fair
                                    2 = A Little Fair
                                    3 = Not Sure
                                    4 = A Little Unfair
                                    5 = Very Unfair

12.   How sad or happy is it for you to have seizures? _____
                                    1 = Very Sad
                                    2 = A Little Sad
                                    3 = Not Sure
                                    4 = A Little Happy
                                    5 = Very Happy

13.   How bad or good do you feel it is to have seizures? _____
                                    1 = Very Bad
                                    2 = A Little Bad
                                    3 = Not Sure
                                    4 = A Little Good
                                    5 = Very Good

catis.scl   9/13/96   jc

Austin, J.K., & Huberty, T.J. (1993). Development of the child attitude toward illness scale. Journal of Psychology, 18, 467-480.

Children's Health Care Attitudes Questionnaire

CHILDREN
Joseph P. Bush, Ph.D.
School of Psychology
Fielding Graduate Institute

Children's Health Care Attitudes Questionnaire

Boy: Girl:

Age:

Have you ever had an operation?   yes   no

Have you ever had to stay
overnight in a hospital?   yes   no

We want to know how you feel about hospitals, doctors, and dentists. This is not a test so there are
no right or wrong answers. Answer all of the questions as carefully as you can.

DO NOT WRITE BELOW THIS LINE

SR   RWH   RT

Problems and/or comments
1)   How do you like hospitals?

A)   I really hate them.
B)   I don't like them.
C)   I don't like them or hate them.
D)   I like them.
E)   I really like them a lot.

2)   How do you like doctors?

A)   I really hate them.
B)   I don't like them.
C)   I don't like them or hate them.
D)   I like them.
E)   I really like them a lot.

3)   How do you like taking medicine?

A)   I really hate it.
B)   I don't like it.
C)   I don't like it or hate it.
D)   I like it.
E)   I really like it a lot.

4)   How do you like dentists?

A)   I really hate them.
B)   I don't like them.
C)   I don't like them or hate them.
D)   I like them.
E)   I really like them a lot.

5)   How do you like shots?

A)   I really hate them.
B)   I don't like them.

Page 1

CHILDREN

C)   I don't like them or hate them.
D)   I like them.
E)   I really like them a lot.

6)   How do you like nurses?

A)   I really hate them.
B)   I don't like them.
C)   I don't like them or hate them.
D)   I like them.
E)   I really like them a lot.

7)   How do you like it when you get your finger pricked to get a drop of blood for a blood test?

A)   I really hate it.
B)   I don't like it.
C)   I don't like it or hate it.
D)   I like it.
E)   I really like it a lot.

8)   How would you like an operation?

A)   I would hate it.
B)   I wouldn't like it.
C)   I don't know if I would like it.
D)   I would like it.
E)   I would really like it a lot.

9)   When people go to the hospital, what happens?

A)   It always helps them.
B)   It usually helps them.
C)   It might help them or it might not.
D)   It usually makes them worse.
E)   They get worse.

10)   When people are sick and they go to see a doctor, what happens?

A)   It always helps them.
B)   It usually helps them.
C)   It might help them or it might not.
D)   It usually makes them worse.
E)   They get worse.

11)   When people are sick and the doctor gives them some medicine, what happens?

A)   It always helps them.
B)   It usually helps them.
C)   It might help them or it might not.
D)   It usually makes them worse.
E)   They get worse.

12)   When people have problems with their teeth and they go to see a dentist, what happens?

A)   It always helps them.
B)   It usually helps them.
C)   It might help them or it might not.
D)   It usually makes them worse.
E)   They get worse.

CHILDREN

13) When people are sick and the doctor gives them a shot, what happens?

A) It always helps them.
B) It usually helps them.
C) It might help them or it might not.
D) It usually makes them worse.
E) They get worse.

14) When people are sick and they go to see a nurse, what happens?

A) It always helps them.
B) It usually helps them.
C) It might help them or it might not.
D) It usually makes them worse.
E) They get worse.

15) When people are sick and the doctor pricks their finger to get a drop of blood for a blood test, what
happens?

A) It always helps them.
B) It usually helps them.
C) It might help them or it might not.
D) It usually makes them worse.
E) They get worse.

16) When people are sick and they have an operation, what happens?

A) It always helps them.
B) It usually helps them.
C) It might help them or it might not.
D) It usually makes them worse.
E) They get worse.

17) Let's say you were told that you might have to go to the hospital.

A) I would try not to go to the hospital no matter what.
B) I would go even though I would not want to.
C) I'm not sure what I would do.
D) I would want to go but only if I was very sick.
E) I would want to go to the hospital.

18) Let's say you were told that you might have to go see a doctor.

A) I would try not to go see a doctor no matter what.
B) I would go even though I would not want to.
C) I'm not sure what I would do.
D) I would want to go, but only if I was very sick.
E) I would want to go see a doctor.

19) Let's say you were told that you should take some medicine.

A) I would try not to take the medicine no matter what.
B) I would take the medicine even though I would not want to.
C) I'm not sure if I would take it.
D) I would want to take the medicine, only if I was very sick.
E) I would want to take the medicine.

20) Let's say you were told that you might have to go see a dentist.

A) I would try not to go see a dentist no matter what.
B) I would go even though I would not want to.
C) I'm not sure what I would do.

CHILDREN

D)   I would want to go, but only if I had a problem with my teeth.
E)   I would want to go see a dentist.

21) Let's say you were told that you should have a shot.

A)   I would try not to have the shot no matter what.
B)   I would have the shot even though I would not want to.
C)   I'm not sure what I would do.
D)   I would want to have a shot, but only if I was very sick.
E)   I would want to have a shot.

22) Let's say you were told that you might have to go see a nurse.

A)   I would try not to go see a nurse no matter what.
B)   I would go even though I would not want to.
C)   I'm not sure what I would do.
D)   I would want to go, but only if I was very sick.
E)   I would want to go see a nurse.

23) Let's say you were told that you should get your finger pricked to get a drop of blood for a blood
test.

A)   I would try not to have a blood test no matter what.
B)   I would have a blood test even though I would not want to.
C)   I'm not sure what I would do.
D)   I would want to have a blood test, but only if I was very sick.
E)   I would want to have a blood test.

24) Let's say you were told that you might have an operation.

A)   I would try not to have the operation no matter what.
B)   I would have the operation even though I would not want to.
C)   I'm not sure what I would do.
D)   I would want to have the operation, but only if I was very sick.
E)   I would want to have the operation.

You're doing great so far!   You have just a little more to do.

DIRECTIONS:
We would now like you to look at the thermometers on the last page. See how the liquid is higher
in some than in others. Let's pretend that these thermometers measure how much things hurt. That's
why they are called "pain thermometers." The higher the liquid, the higher the pain you feel. The
thermometer with the least amount of liquid means that you feel no pain at all and the thermometer
that is full means that you feel the worst pain you've ever felt. Write the number (1, 2, 3, 4, or 5)
of the thermometer that you feel goes with each sentence below. If you haven't had one of these
things happen to you before, imagine what it would feel like.

Getting a shot in your arm.
The worst headache you ever had.
When the doctor or nurse looks in your eyes.
Burning your hand on the stove.
When the dentist drills your tooth to put in a filling.
Getting weighed.
Getting stitches put in.

CHILDREN

Getting your throat checked, when they hold down your tongue with a wooden stick.
Hitting your thumb with a hammer.
When the doctor puts the cuff on your arm to get your blood pressure.
The worst stomach-ache you ever had.
Sticking your finger with a pin.
The kind of shot the dentist gives you to make your mouth numb.
Putting medicine on a cut on your hand.
Getting your temperature taken (in your mouth).
when the nurse pricks your finger to get a drop of blood.
when you wake up after an operation.

Thanks a lot! You've been a lot of help to us!

Scale Membership of Pain Stimuli

Pain Stimulus
Scale Membership

Getting a shot in your arm.
The worst headache you ever had.
When the doctor or nurse looks in your eyes.
Burning your hand on the stove.
When the dentist drills your tooth to put in a filling.
Getting weighed.
Getting stitches put in.
Getting your throat checked, when they hold down your tongue with a wooden stick.
Hitting your thumb with a hammer.
When the doctor puts the cuff on your arm to get your blood pressure.
The worst stomach ache you ever had.
Sticking your finger with a pin.
The kind of shot the dentist gives you to make your mouth numb.
Putting medicine on a cut on your hand.
Getting your temperature taken (in your mouth).
when the nurse pricks your finger to get a drop of blood.
when you wake up after an operation.
MP, TM, PS, TP
MI, TM, PS, TP
MP, TM, NPS, TP
NMS, PS, TP
MP, TM, PS, TP
MP, TM, NPS, TP
MP, TM, PS, TP
MP, TM, NPS, TP

NMS, PS, TP
MP, TM, NPS, TP

MI, TM, PS, TP
NMS, NPS, TP
MP, TM, PS, TP
MP, TM, NPS, TP
MP, TM, NPS, TP
MP, TM, NPS, TP
MP, TM, PS, TP

Note. MP-Medical Procedures, MI-Medical Illnesses, NMS-Nonmedical Stimuli, TM-Total
Page 5

Medical (includes Medical Procedures and Medical Illnesses), PS-Painful Stimuli, NPS-
Nonpainful Stimuli, TP-Total Pain (includes all pain stimuli).

The Children's Health Care Attitudes Questionnaire
CHCAQ
Joseph P. Bush, Ph.D.

INSTRUCTIONS

The following suggestions may be helpful in scoring. First of all, you are welcome to prepare
(retype and redraw) a neater copy for your own use. When I administer it to children, I read the
items to the child and use some posters I have prepared with the visual icons drawn in large size and
bold colors. Second, the clusters of letters on the first page refer to "Self-Read," "Read with Help,"
and "Read To." Next, as is made clear in the Bush & Holmbeck article, the attitude items are scored
into three scales. This is quite straightforward. The "Liking" items are on pages 2 & 3; score this
scale by summing across items where A=1, B=2, C=3, D=4, and E=5. The same scoring procedure
should be followed for the "Attributed Ineffectiveness" scale (pages 4 & 5), and for the "Approach"
scale (pages 6 & 7). Prorate if a small number of items are omitted or spoiled.

The attached sheet lists, for each of the Pain Scale items, the subscales into which it is scored.
Scores for each subscale, and for the total scale, are simply averaged across constituent items
(prorating for omissions or spoiled items). Of course, prorating on either the attitudes or pain scales
should be reflected in your placing less confidence in the resulting scores. I hope you will find these
materials useful. Please let me know about any research or clinical applications in which you
employ them.

Children's Health Locus of Control Scale

CHILDREN'S HEALTH LOCUS OF CONTROL

We would like to learn about different ways children look at their health. Here are some statements about health or illness (sickness). Some of them you will think are true and so you will circle the YES. Some you will think are not true and so you will circle the NO. Even if it is very hard to decide, be sure to circle YES or NO for every statement. Never circle both YES and NO for one statement. There are no right or wrong answers. Be sure to answer the way you really feel and not the way other people might feel.

PRACTICE: Try the statements below.

            a.   Children can get sick.

                      If you think this is true, circle.. YES

                      If you think this is not true, circle..   NO

            b.   Children never get sick.

                      If you think this is true, circle.. YES

                      If you think this is not true, circle ....   NO

            Try one more statement for practice.

            c.   When I am not sick, I am healthy... YES   NO

NOW DO THE REST OF THE STATEMENTS THE SAME WAY YOU PRACTICED.

    1.   Good health comes from being lucky.. YES   NO

    2.   I can do things to keep from getting sick... YES   NO

    3.   Bad luck makes people get sick.. YES   NO

    4.   I can only do what the doctor tells me to do... YES   NO

    5.   If I get sick, it is because getting sick just happens................................ YES   NO

    6.   People who never get sick are just plain lucky...................................... YES   NO

    7.   My mother must tell me how to keep from getting sick........................... YES   NO

    8.   Only a doctor or a nurse keeps me from getting sick............................. YES   NO

    9.   When I am sick, I can do things to get better....................................... YES   NO

    10.   If I get hurt is is because accidents just happen.................................... YES   NO

    11.   I can do many things to fight illness... YES   NO

    12.   Only the dentist can take care of my teeth... YES   NO

    13.   Other people must tell me how to stay healthy..................................... YES   NO

    14.   I always go to the nurse right away if I get hurt at school...................... YES   NO

    15.   The teacher must tell me how to keep from having accidents at school....... YES   NO

    16.   I can make many choices about my health.. YES   NO

    17.   Other people must tell me what to do when I feel sick........................... YES   NO

    18.   Whenever I feel sick I go to see the school nurse right away.................... YES   NO

    19.   There are things I can do to have healthy teeth.................................... YES   NO

    20.   I can do many things to prevent accidents.. YES   NO

Health Self-Determinism Index for Children

HEALTH QUESTIONS

IN THE CLASSROOM

Pupil's Form

Name: _____ **Age:** _____ **Birthday: (Month)** _____ **(Day)**____

Grade: _____ **Teacher:** _____

Sample Questions

Really True for Me	Sort of True for Me					Really True for Me	Sort of True for Me
(a)			Some kids would rather play out-doors in their spare time	BUT	Other kids would rather watch T.V.		
(b)			Some kids like hamburgers better than hot dogs	BUT	Other kids like hot dogs better. than hamburgers		
(1)			Some kids like to do things that are good for their health even though they may be hard	BUT	Other kids like to do easy things even though they may not be good for their health		
(2)			When some kids don't understand something about their health, they want someone else to tell them	BUT	Other kids would rather try and figure it by themselves		
(3)			Some kids like the doctor their parents to help them plan what to do for their health	BUT	Other kids like to make their own plans for their health		

Really   Sort of   Really   Sort of
True   True   True   True
for Me   for Me   for Me   for Me

(4)

☐   ☐   Some kids would   BUT   Other kids would   ☐   ☐
                   rather learn as   rather learn just
                   much as they can   what they have to
                   about their health   about their health

(5)

☐   ☐   Some kids think   BUT   Other kids almost   ☐   ☐
                   that their own   always think that
                   ideas about their   what the doctor
                   health are better   or nurse says is
                   than doctor's or   O.K.
                   nurse's ideas

(6)

☐   ☐   Some kids know if BUT   Other kids need   ☐   ☐
                   they are in good   to have the doctor
                   health without   or nurse tell them
                   someone else telling   if they are in
                   them   good health

(7)

☐   ☐   Some kids learn   BUT   Other kids learn   ☐   ☐
                   about their health   about their
                   because there are   health because
                   a lot of things   their teacher
                   they want to know   tells them to

(8)

☐   ☐   Some kids need to BUT   Other kids know   ☐   ☐
                   have someone else   when they are
                   tell them that   doing the right
                   they are doing the   things for their
                   right things for   health
                   their health

(9)

☐   ☐   Some kids work   BUT   Other kids only   ☐   ☐
                   really hard to be   do what their
                   healthy because   parents or
                   they like to   teachers make
                                             them do for
                                             their health

(10)

☐   ☐   Some kids feel that BUT   Other kids feel   ☐   ☐
                   the teacher's ideas   that their own
                   about health are   ideas about
                   often better than   health are
                   their own ideas   better

	Really True for Me	Sort of True for Me				Really True for Me	Sort of True for Me

(11) Some kids know whether or not they do a good job of taking caring of their health **BUT** Other kids aren't really sure if they're doing a good job of taking care of their health unless they check with others

(12) Some kids almost always think that what the teacher or doctor says about their health is O.K. **BUT** Other kids sometimes think their. own ideas about their health are better

(13) Some kids like doing things for their health even though they may be hard **BUT** Other kids like doing only those things for their health which are pretty easy

(14) Some kids want their teacher or parents to help them plan what to do for their health **BUT** Other kids want to make their own plans for what they do about their health

(15) Some kids do things for their health because they want to be healthier **BUT** Other kids do things for their health because someone makes them

(16) Some kids don't know if they're doing the right things for their health unless someone tells them **BUT** Other kids know by themselves when they are doing the right things for their health

(17) Some kids like to do the right things for their health even though they may be hard **BUT** Other kids don't like doing hard things even if it is good for their health

	Really True for Me	Sort of True for Me				Really True for Me	Sort of True for Me

(18)   ☐   ☐   Some kids would rather ask someone what to do when they make a mistake about their health   **BUT**   Other kids would rather figure out what to do by themselves   ☐   ☐

(19)   ☐   ☐   Some kids know whether or not they are doing well at taking care of their health without going to the doctor or nurse   **BUT**   Other kids need to check with the doctor or nurse to know if they're doing well at taking care of their health   ☐   ☐

(20)   ☐   ☐   Some kids agree with the teacher or doctor about their health because the teacher or doctor are right about most things   **BUT**   Other kids don't agree with the. teacher or doctor sometimes and stick to their own opinion   ☐   ☐

(21)   ☐   ☐   Some kids need to see a doctor or nurse to tell them if they are healthy   **BUT**   Other kids know for themselves if they are healthy without seeing a doctor or nurse   ☐   ☐

(22)   ☐   ☐   Some kids read things about their health because they are interested   **BUT**   Other kids read things about health because the teacher wants them to   ☐   ☐

(23)   ☐   ☐   If some kids don't know what to do about their health they ask the teacher or their parents for help   **BUT**   Other kids try to figure out what to do on their own   ☐   ☐

(24)   ☐   ☐   Some kids like to learn about new things that may make them healthier   **BUT**   Other kids would rather stick to. things that they already know to make them healthier   ☐   ☐

Really True for Me | Sort of True for Me | | | Really True for Me | Sort of True for Me

(25) Some kids will only do things for their health if it is pretty easy — BUT — Other kids will do things for their health even if they have to work hard' or give up things

(26) Some kids ask questions about their health because they want to learn — BUT — Other kids ask questions about their health because they want the teacher to notice them

(27) Some kids like to try to figure out how to do things on their own to help their health — BUT — Other kids would rather ask someone. how to do things for their health

(28) Some kids don't like to do healthy things because they think they don't matter — BUT — Other kids like to do healthy things because they make them healthier

(29) Some kids like to do things for their health without any help — BUT — Other kids like to have someone help them do things for their health

Assessment of Parent Satisfaction

Assessment of Parent Satisfaction

Please help us improve our program by answering some questions about the services you have received. We are interested in your honest opinions, whether they are positive or negative. *Please answer all of the questions.* We welcome your comments and suggestions, and we appreciate your help.

1. How long did you wait to get an appointment after your initial request?

   1_____ 0 - 4 weeks
   2_____ 4 - 6 weeks
   3_____ 6 – 8 weeks
   4_____ more than 8 weeks
   5_____ don't know

2. Did this waiting time seem

   1_____ short
   2_____ acceptable
   3_____ somewhat long
   4_____ very long

3. What did you think about the total length of the visit?

   4_____ too short
   1_____ all right
   4_____ too long

4. The staff was

   a) 1_____ very helpful   b) 4_____ late   C) 1_____ very easy to understand

      2_____ somewhat helpful   3_____ somewhat late   2_____ somewhat easy to understand

      3_____ not very helpful   2_____ Mostly on time   3_____ somewhat hard to understand

      4_____ not helpful at all   1_____ on time   4_____ very hard to understand

Parental Perceptions of Quality

5. The information you received was

   4_____ confusing
   3_____ not very clear
   2_____ somewhat clear
   1_____ clear

6. The recommendations you received were

   1_____ useful
   2_____ somewhat useful
   3_____ not very useful
   4_____ useless

7. To what extent has our program met you needs?

   4_____ none met
   3_____ only a few met
   2_____ most met
   1_____ almost all met

Page 2
Parental Perception of Quality

8. In an overall sense, how satisfied are you with the service you received?

    1 _____ very satisfied
    2 _____ mostly satisfied
    3 _____ indifferent/mildly dissatisfied
    4 _____ quite dissatisfied

9. If you were to seek help again, would you return to our program?

    4 _____ no, definitely not
    3 _____ no, I think not
    2 _____ yes, I think so
    1 _____ yes, definitely

10. a. What did you like best about the clinic?

_____

_____

_____

_____

    b. What would you like us to change about the clinic?

_____

_____

_____

_____

Child Perceptions of Specialty Care

ID#_____Clinic Name #_____
CHILD PERCEPTIONS OF SPECIALTY CARE

How old are you : _____ **Male___ Female___ (check one)**
How many years have you been coming to this clinic (if less than 1 year, write months)? _____

Please check your response.

1. Does the treatment team listen to you?

    All the time   Most of the Time   Some of the Time   Less than ½ the Time   Not at all

2. Does the staff help you when you are afraid or in pain?

    All the time   Most of the Time   Some of the Time Less than ½ the Time   Not at all

3. How helpful is talking to the doctor?

    Very helpful   Helpful   Mixed   Not Very Helpful   Not helpful at all

4. How helpful is talking to the nurse?

    Very helpful   Helpful   Mixed   Not Very Helpful   Not helpful at all

5. How well do you understand the symptoms of your illness/condition (How it makes you feel, the kinds of problems you have)?

    Very well   Somewhat well   Neutral   Not very well   Not well at all

6. How well do you understand the causes of your illness/condition?

    Very well   Somewhat well   Neutral   Not very well   Not well at all

7. How well do you understand the treatment of your condition (what you do at home, why you have to come to the hospital)?

    Very well   Somewhat well   Neutral   Not very well   Not well at all

8. How well do you understand the medications you take for your illness/condition (what they do, how to take it, side effects)?

    Very well   Somewhat well   Neutral   Not very well   Not well at all

9. Are included decisions about your treatment? Does anyone on the team ask you how you feel about the way your illness/condition is taken care of/treated?

    All the time   Most of the Time   Some of the Time Less than ½ the Time   Not at all

PLEASE WRITE ANY COMMENTS YOU HAVE ON THE BACK OF THIS PAGE

Naar-King, Siegel, Smyth, & Simpson, (2000)

Parent Perceptions of Specialty Care

I
D#_____Clinic Name #_____

PARENT PERCEPTIONS OF SPECIALTY CARE

Completed by: Mother_____ Father _____ Grandmother _____Other (specify)_____
How old is your child (if less than 1 year, indicate months) : _____ Male___ Female___ (check one)
How old was your child when he/she was first diagnosed (if less than 1 year indicate months)?
_____

How many years have you been coming to this clinic (if less than one year, indicate months)?
_____

Please check your response.

1. How satisfied are you with the services in this clinic?

   Delighted   Mostly Satisfied   Mixed   Mostly Dissatisfied   Terrible

2. How satisfied are you with each of the following parts of your child's treatment in the clinic:

   a. Communication with the medical treatment team

   Delighted   Mostly Satisfied   Mixed   Mostly Dissatisfied   Terrible

   b. The team's attention to your concerns about treatment and side effects

   Delighted   Mostly Satisfied   Mixed   Mostly Dissatisfied   Terrible

   c. The team's attention to giving complete and comprehensive care

   Delighted   Mostly Satisfied   Mixed   Mostly Dissatisfied   Terrible

   d. The team's ability to help pain, fear, and discomfort of treatment

   Delighted   Mostly Satisfied   Mixed   Mostly Dissatisfied   Terrible

   e. Emotional support provided by the team

   Delighted   Mostly Satisfied   Mixed   Mostly Dissatisfied   Terrible

3. How worthwhile is time involved in this type of team clinic?

   Very worthwhile   Worthwhile   Mixed   Not very Worthwhile
   Not at all worthwhile

4. How worthwhile is spending time talking to the:
   a. **Physician**

   Very worthwhile   Worthwhile   Mixed   Not very Worthwhile
   Not at all worthwhile

   b. **Nurse**

   Very worthwhile   Worthwhile   Mixed   Not very Worthwhile
   Not at all worthwhile

   c. **Other Team Members**

   Very worthwhile   Worthwhile   Mixed   Not very Worthwhile

Not at all worthwhile

5. Are you satisfied with your level of involvement in the treatment plan?

Delighted   Mostly Satisfied   Mixed   Mostly Dissatisfied   Terrible

6. **The staff in clinic assisted with:**

General health concerns (e.g. dental, colds)	Yes	No	Not needed
Financial concerns	Yes	No	Not needed
Transportation concerns	Yes	No	Not needed
Behavior concerns (e.g. fighting in school, not listening)	Yes	No	Not needed
Emotional concerns (e.g. sadness, fears)	Yes	No	Not needed
Social concerns (e.g making friends, teasing)	Yes	No	Not needed
Learning problems (e.g. development, school programming)	Yes	No	Not needed
Equipment concerns	Yes	No	Not needed
Pain management (e.g. chronic pain, needles)	Yes	No	Not needed
Medical compliance (e.g. not taking medicine)	Yes	No	Not needed
Helping me (parent) cope	Yes	No	Not needed
Preparation for procedures (e.g. surgery, hospitalization)	Yes	No	Not needed

Dietary ConcernsYesNoNot needed

What is your overall feeling about the...........

12. Location and accessibility of the services (distance, parking, public transportation, etc.)

Delighted   Mostly Satisfied   Mixed   Mostly Dissatisfied   Terrible

13. Waiting time between asking to be seen and the appointment date and time given

Delighted   Mostly Satisfied   Mixed   Mostly Dissatisfied   Terrible

14. Waiting time when you come to clinic

Delighted   Mostly Satisfied   Mixed   Mostly Dissatisfied   Terrible

15. Availability of appointment times that fit your schedule

Delighted   Mostly Satisfied   Mixed   Mostly Dissatisfied   Terrible

16. Response to crises or urgent needs during office hours

Delighted   Mostly Satisfied   Mixed   Mostly Dissatisfied   Terrible

17. Arrangements made for after hours emergencies or urgent help

    Delighted   Mostly Satisfied   Mixed   Mostly Dissatisfied   Terrible

18.   How many miles (one way) from the facility do you live?

    5 or less   6-10   11-15   16-20   20-25   26 or more

19.   Your sex:
    MALE
    FEMALE

20.   Your Age:

                under 20   21-25 26-35   36-45 46-55 56-65 66-75
    76-85   86+

21.   Yearly Family Income:
    Under $10,000 $10,000-$20,000

    $20,001-$40,000 $40,001-$60,000

    $60,001-$80,000   Over $80,000

22.   Your Education:
    Grade 8 or less   Some high school

    High school graduate   Some college

    College graduate   Some post graduate training.

    Masters   Ph.D., M.D., etc.

23.   Ethnic Background:
    Caucasian/White   Asian/Pacific American
    Native American/Indian   Hispanic/Latino
    African American/Black   Other (Specify)   Prefer not to answer

PLEASE WRITE ANY COMMENTS YOU HAVE ON THE BACK OF THIS PAGE

Naar-King, Siegel, Smyth, & Simpson, (2000)

Author Index

Note: An *italicized page locator* indicates a complete bibliographic reference for a given author.

A

Abetz, L., 7
Abidin, R. R., *162*, 163, 164, *165*
Accardo, P. J., 91, *93*
Achenbach, T. M., *68, 71*, 72
ACTG 219 Team, 24, *25*
Addicoat, L., *43*
Albertsson-Wikland, K., 25, *26*
Alcock, D., *49*
Alexander, C. S., 169, 170, 171, *171*, 186, 187, *187*
Algina, J., 148, *150*
Allport, A., 133, *135*
Almond, P., *96, 98*
Alpert, B., 116, *118*
Altshuler, J. L., 58, *58*
Anderson, B. J., 28, *29, 31*
Andrellos, P. J., *17*
Aradine, C., *54*
Arant, C. B., 23, *26*
Archer, P., *103, 106*
Arick, J., *96, 98*
Armstrong, F. D., 2, *3*
Arndt, S. V., 76, *76*
Arnette, H., *82*
Arsenault, L., 24, *25*
Ashford, L. G., *106*
Asmussen, L., 23, *25*
Attkisson, C. C., 170, *171, 173, 177, 177*, 178, *179*

August, G., *68*
Auslander, W. F., 28, *29, 31*, 39, *40*
Austin, J. K., *124, 136, 137, 138*, 237–240, 263–265
Ayers, T., *123, 248*
Aylward, G., 90, 92, *93, 98, 100*

B

Bachanas, P., *46, 53, 58, 58*, 139, *140*
Baker, B., 115, *118*
Baker, R. R., 23, *26*
Bandura, A., 133, *135*
Barber, J. H., 24, *26*, 86, *87*
Barnes, H., 152, *153*
Bauman, L. J., 1, *3*
Baumeister, R. F., 134, *135*
Bekeny, P., *181*
Bell, G. L., 24, *26*
Bell, N., *100, 103*
Bell, R., *150*
Bellamy, C., 142, *142*
Bem, D., 133, *135*
Bennett, S. M., *44*
Benson, S. R., *35*
Bergner, M., 4, *4*, 5, *7*, 10
Bernhard, S., *35*
Bernstein, B., *56*
Bernzweig, J. A., *248*
Berry, C. C., xiv, *xv*

Bessette, J., 36, 37
Beyer, J., 53, 54
Biederman, J., 65
Bieri, D., 43
Biggs, D., 87, 87
Billings, A., 16, 16, 24, 25, 58, 59
Bishop, S., 82
Blackall, G. F., 58, 59, 183, 185
Blevedere, M., 39, 40
Blount, R., 42, 43, 45, 46, 53, 58, 58
Boggs, S., 24, 25, 148, 150
Bornstein, M. H., 58, 58
Boulton, T. J., 25, 25, 145, 145
Bowling, A., 2, 4
Bradlyn, A. S., 24, 25
Brady, N., 155
Braun, S., 22, 23
Breckler, S. J., 134, 135
Brenner, D. E., 35
Bresnick, B., 106
Bricker, D., 94, 96
Brooks, R., 186, 187
Brown, J. M., 115, 118
Brown, R. T., 39, 40
Bryne, K., 106
Buckingham, B., 39, 40
Bukowski, W. M., 147, 150
Burgess, E., 27, 29, 29
Burns, B. J., 79
Bursch, B., 145, 145
Bush, J. P., 138, 140
Bush, J. W., xiv, xv

C

Calan, M., 170, 171, 171
Calzone, K. A., 35
Cameron, M. E., 120, 120
Campbell, D. T., 148, 149
Campbell, H., 98
Caplan, D., 39, 40
Capute, A. J., 91, 93
Carnon, A. G., 169, 170, 171
Carter, B., 31, 77, 79
Carter, R., 37
Casari, E. F., 127, 127
Casey, P., 90, 93
Cassidy, L., 82
Castillo, C., 76, 76
Castro, C. M., 24, 26

Catanzaro, N. L., 22, 23
Cathers, T., 170, 171, 171
Causey, D., 79
Chambers, C. T., 44
Chambers, D., 98
Champion, G. D., 43
Chandler, M. J., 148, 150
Chaney, J. M., 149, 149
Chang, B., 106
Channell, S., 24, 26
Chapman, J., 46
Charles, J. M., 100, 103
Chen, T., 109
Christensen, M., 39, 40
Christie, M. J., 23, 25
Ciborowski, J., 36, 37
Clark, C., 24, 25
Cohen, L., 46
Cohen, M. E., 24, 26
Cole, E., 123
Collins, F. J., 169, 171
Combs, C., 116, 118
Cone, J. D., 148, 150
Conners, C. K., 72, 74
Copeland, D., 2, 3
Copeland, S. G., 257
Coryell, J., 17
Coster, W., 17, 18, 19
Cotter, M. W., 53
Cowell, J. M., 142
Cox, C. L., 142, 142, 143, 144, 145
Craig, K., 44, 48, 49
Cramer, J. A., 34, 138
Creer, T. L., 86, 87
Cronkite, R. C., 15
Crosby, R., 68
Cunningham, W., 37, 39, 39
Czajkowski, D. R., 28, 29, 35, 37
Czerwinski, A. M., 39, 40

D

Dady, I., 24, 26
D'Angelo, E., 36, 37
Danovsky, M., 56, 116, 118
Dashiff, C. J., 155, 155
Davies, A. R., 185, 186, 187, 187
Davies, W. H., 147, 150
DCCT Research Group, 24, 25
Deasy-Spinetta, P., 87, 87

Deci, E. L., 143, *144*
Denyes, M., *53, 54*
Derogatis, L. R., *165*
DeStefano, L., 147, *150*
Devinsky, O., *138*
Digaudio, K., 22, *23*
DiGirolamo, A. M., 149, *150*
Dishion, T. J., 260
Dodds, J., *103, 106*
Donabedian, A., 169, *171*
Donaldson, D., 116, *118*
Dowd, J. B., 169, *171*
Doyle, A., *65, 68*
Drotar, D., 1, 3, *3*, 27, 29, *29*, 31, *31*, 32, 33, *33, 39, 40*, 149, *150*
Dubow, E. F., 116, *118*
Duffy, C. M., 24, *25*
Duffy, K. N., 24, *25*
Duffy, L. C., 22, *23*
Dulberg, C., *49*
Dune, M., 87, *87*
Dunn, D. W., *137, 138*
Dunn, J., *46*
Dunn, S. M., 25, *25*, 145, *145*
Dworkin, P. H., 90, *93*

E

Eaves, R., *98*
Egan, M., 155, *156*
Eid, N., *31*
Eigen, H., *31*, 39, *40*
Eiser, C., 2, *3*
Eisert, D., 90, *93*, 169, *171, 172*, 178
Elbadri, A., 24, *26*
Elliott, C., *49, 52, 109*
Endler, N., 115, *118*
Engvall, J. C., *76, 77*
Ensminger, M., 4, *4*, 5, 6, *6, 7*
Epstein, J., *72, 74*
Erling, A., 25, *26*
Espelage, D. L., *31*
Eyberg, S., 148, *150*
Eyberg, S. M., 148, *150*

F

Faas, R. M., 18, *19*
Fagan, J., 23, *25*

Faraone, S. V., *65*
Farrand, L. L., *145*
Feeny, D. H., 24, *26*
Fehlings, D. L., 24, 25, *26*
Feldman, A. B., *17*
Field, T., 116, *118*
Fiese, B. H., 148, *150*
Fifield, B., 169, *171, 172*, 178
Figueroa, V., 147, *150*
Finlay, A. Y., 24, *26*
Finney, J. W., *15*
Firth, D., 24, *26*
Fish, J. T., *35*
Fisher, E., 39, *40*
Fisher, J. D., 133, *135–136*
Fisher, W. A., 133, *135–136*
Fiske, D. W., 148, *149*
Fitz, G. K., 23, *25*, 86, *87*
Fitzpatrick, J. R., 28, *29, 35*
Flannery, M. E., 39, *40*
Folkman, S., 115, *118*, 124, *126*, 129, *131*
Forrest, C. B., 6, *6, 7*
Fowler, M. G., 24, *25*
Fox, M. A., 39, *40*
Frank, N., *46*
Frank, R. G., 149, *149*
Frankenburg, W., 89, *93, 103, 106*
French, D., 23, *25*
Freund, A., 28, *29*
Frey, M., 27, *29*, 32, *33*, 39, *40*
Friedman, A. G., 2, *3*
Friedman-Bender, A., 24, *26*
Fritz, G., 32, 33, *33*

G

Garber, J., 58, *59*
Garrison, W. T., 87, *87*
Gavin, L., 32, 33, *33*, 39, *40*
Genevro, J. L., 58, *58*
Gerard, A. B., *160*
Gibney, L., *111*
Giesbrecht, K., *44*
Gil, K., 41, 42, *43*, 58, *59*
Gilbert, J., 145, *145*
Gilliam, J., *111*
Glascoe, F., 89, 90, 92, *93, 93, 103, 106*
Glasgow, R. E., 167, *167*
Goertzel, L., 141, *142*
Goertzel, T., 141, *142*

Goldenberg, D., *107, 109*
Goldstein, D. L., 149, *149*
Goldstein, S., 116, *118*
Goodman, J., 39, *40, 46*
Goodwin, D. A. J., 24, *25*
Gortmaker, S. L., 24, *25*
Gottlieb, J., 24, *25*, 58, *59*
Gragg, R., *56*
Graham-Pole, J., 24, *25*
Granger, C. V., 22, *23*
Grant, E. N., 23, *25*
Gravestock, F. M., 87, *87*
Greco, P., 39, *40*
Green, B. F., 4, *4*, 5, 6, *6, 7*
Greene, J. W., *9*, 10
Greene, P. G., *35*
Greenfield, T. K., *177*
Greer, M. K., *100*
Gresham Copeland, S., *131*
Grew, R. S., 145, *145*
Grey, M., 120, *120*
Griffin, W. A., *123*
Griffith, L. E., 24, *26*
Grunau, R. E., *49*
Grunau, R. V. E., *48*
Gudas, L. J., 36, *37*
Gustafson, K. E., 1, *4*
Guyatt, G. H., 24, *26*

H

Hackworth, S. R., 139, *140*
Haine, R. A., *123*
Haley, S. M., *17, 18, 19*
Halfon, N., 1, *4*
Haltiwanger, J. T., *17*
Hamilton, B. B., 22, *23*
Hampson, S., 145, *145*
Hanewald, G. J. F. P., 127, *127*
Hanson, C. L., 39, *40*
Hanson, V., *55*
Hargreaves, W. A., *173*, 177
Harper, M. B., 187, *187*
Harrell, L. M., 23, *26*
Harris, C. V., 1, *4*, 24, *25*
Harris, M., 32, *33*
Harrison, P. L., *109*
Harrison, R. J., *248*
Harter, S., *84, 86*, 143, 144, *145*
Hauenstein, E., 164, *165*
Hays, J., 142, *142*

Hedley, A. J., 169, 170, *171*
Heider, F., 134, *136*
Heimlich, T. E., *138*
Helders, P. J. M., 23, *23*
Hellriegel, D., 134, *136*
Henretta, J. C., 39, *39*
Hensey, O., 170, *171*
Hersh, S. P., 147, *150*
Herzberg, D. S., *82*
Higgins, M. J., 24, *26*
Hillier, V. F., 24, *26*
Hinds, P. S., 24, *26*
Hoare, P., 24, *25*
Hodge, M., 39, *40*
Hollingsworth, J. L., 39, *40*
Holmbeck, G. N., 39, *40, 138*
Holmes, T. H., 157, *158*
Holroyd, K. A., 128, *129*
Holsti, L., *49*
Hommeyer, J. S., 39, *40*
Horowitz, M. E., 2, *3*
Huber, C. J., 92, *93*
Huberty, T. J., *124, 136, 237–240, 263–265*
Humphrey, S., 89, *93*
Huntsman, E., *44*
Huster, G. A., *137, 138*
Huth, M. M., 120, *131*

I

IASP Task Force on Taxonomy, 41, *43*
Ievers, C., 31, 32, 33, *33*, 39, *40*
Ievers-Landis, C., *31*
Ingersoll, G. M., 24, *25*
Ireton, H., *100, 103*

J

Jacobsen, J., *31*
Jacobson, A. M., 87, *87*
Jay, S., *49, 52*
Jelalian, E., 149, *150*
Jellinek, M., *79, 82*
Jessop, D., 11, *11*, 12, *13*, 127, *127*
John, M., 145, *145*
Johnson, G., *46*
Johnson, K., *106*
Johnson, S., 28, *29*, 37, 38, 39, *39, 40*
Johnston, D., 4, *4*, 5
Jones, R. B., 169, 170, *171*

Jung, J., 28, *29*
Jung, K. C., *31*
Juniper, E. F., 24, *26*

K

Kalinyak, K., 147, *150*
Kamphaus, R. W., *65*
Kane, R., 186, *187*
Kang, M., *6*
Kaplan, R. M., xiv, *xv*
Karlberg, J., 25, *26*
Kashani, J. H., 149, *149*
Katikaneni, L. D., *100, 103*
Katz, E. R., 24, *26*
Kaugers, A. S., 27, 29, *29*
Kay, J., *49*
Kazak, A. E., 58, *59*, 147, 149, *150*, 183, *185*
Kazdin, A., 148, *150*
Keene, D. L., 24, *26*
Kelleher, K., 4, *4*, 5, 6, *7*
Kelley, M. A., 169, 170, 171, *171*, 186, *187*, *187*
Kelly, M., 39, *39,*
Ketellar, M., 23, *23*
Kieckhefer, G. M., *13*
Kim-Harris, S., 4, *4*, 5
King, D., 24, 25, *26*
King, G., 169, 170, 171, *171, 179, 181*
King, S., 169, 170, 171, *171, 179, 181*
Kinney, T., 41, 42, *43*, 58, *59*
Kinzer, C., 39, *40*
Kirpalani, H. M., 24, 25, *26*
Klein, R., 32, 33, *33*
Kline, S., 39, *40*
Klinnert, M., 39, *40*
Koeppl, G., *74*
Kolk, A. M., 127, *127*
Kolterman, O., 39, *40*
Koocher, G. P., 28, *29, 35, 36, 37*
Kotses, H., 86, *87*
Krahn, G. L., 169, *171, 172, 178*
Kraus, L., *65*
Kriege, G., *123*
Kronenberger, W. G., 77, *79*
Krug, D. A., *96, 98*
Kruus, L., 116, *118*
Kulkarni, R., 147, *150*
Kun, L. E., 2, *4*
Kundert, D., *111*
Kung, E., 39, *40*

Kunz, J. F., 147, *150*
Kurtin, P. S., *19, 21*
Kusek, J. W., *35*
Kwok, O.-M., *123*

L

LaForest, S., 22, *23*
LaGreca, A. M., 27, *29*, 39, *40*
Lambert, R. G., 39, *40*
Landgraf, J. M., *7*
Lansky, L. L., 24, *26*
Lansky, S. B., 24, *26*
Larsen, A., 152, *153*
Larsen, D. L., 173, 177
Lavee, Y., *151*
Lawrence, J., *49*
Lazarus, R. S., 115, *118*, 124, *126*, 129, *131*
Lee, J. Y., *35*
Lee, S., 24, *25*
Lehman, B. K., *65*
Leidy, N. J., 155, *156*
Lendering, W. R., 24, 25, *26*
Leonard, B. J., 145, *145*
Lesser, K., 90, *93*
Leventhal, J., 1, *3*
Levi, R., 27, 29, *29*
Lewis, C. C., *13, 174*, 181
Lewis-Jones, M. S., 24, *26*
Lilley, C., *49*
Lin, K., *123*
Lindgren, S., 74, 76, *76*, 77
Lindsley, C. B., *56*
Lipman, T., 120, *120*
List, M. A., 24, *26*
Little, M., *82*
Loveland-Cherry, C. J., 155, *156*
Ludlow, L. H., *17*
Lustig, J. L., *248*
Lyon, N. R., 22, *23*

M

Mace, L. D., 149, *149*
Macias, M., *100, 103*
MacMurray, S. B., *49*
Manimala, M. R., *46*
Mardell-Czudnowski, C., *107, 109*
Marero, D. G., 24, *25*
Marion, L. N., *142*

Martin, E. D., 89, 93
Mash, E. J., xiv, xv
Mattson, R. H., 34
Max, J. E., 76, 76
McCarthy, A. M., 76, 77
McCaul, K. D., 167, 167
McCubbin, H. I., 118–119, 124, 126, 152, 153, 156
McGrath, M. L., 140
McGrath, P., 49
McGrath, P. A., 41, 42, 43
McGrath, P. J., 46
McGuire, M., 39, 40
McKay, M., 170, 171
McKellop, J. M., 147, 150
McMahon, R. J., 139, 140
McQuaid, E., 32, 33, 33, 39, 40
Meek, J., 39, 40
Mehta, P., 123
Mele, C., 35
Mengeling, M. A., 76, 77
Meyer, M. P., 140
Miller, D., 149, 150
Miller, E. H., 142
Miller, J., 24, 25, 28, 29, 31, 58, 59
Miller, S., 116, 118
Miller, V., 24, 26
Mishoe, S. C., 23, 26
Montgomery, M., 103
Moos, B. S., 153
Moos, R., 24, 25, 58, 59
Moos, R. H., 15, 16, 16, 153
Moos, R. J., 156
Morales, A., 24, 26
Morris, N. M., 169, 170, 171, 171, 186, 187, 187
Morrone, A. S., 134, 136
Msall, M. E., 22, 23
Mulhern, R. K., 2, 3
Mullins, L. L., 149, 149
Munet-Vilaro, F., 155, 156
Murphy, J. M., 79, 82
Muxen, M., 152, 153
Myers, D. G., 134, 136

N

Naar-King, S., 27, 29, 32, 33, 169, 171, 173, 178, 183, 185, 293, 299
Nassau, J. H., 32, 33, 33

Newacheck, P. W., 1, 4
Newborg, J., 19, 19
Newcomb, M. D., 56
Nguyen, T. D., 170, 171, 173, 177, 178, 179
Nickel, R., 90, 93
Nobile, 27, 29, 29
Noll, R. B., 147, 150
Noojin, A. B., 158
Norris, K., 35
Northover, H., 24, 26
Nowicki, S., 134, 136

O

Oberlander, T., 49
Ochs, J., 2, 3
O'Connor, S., 32, 33, 33
O'Keefe, J., 115, 118
Oleske, J. M., 24, 25
Olson, D. H., 150, 151, 152, 153
Olson, L. M., 23, 25
Olvera, N., 142, 142
Opipari, L., 28, 29, 31
Orenstein, D., 39, 40
Ostrander, R., 68
Ottenbacher, K. H., 22, 23
Ouellette, V. L., 34
Overholser, J. C., 23, 25, 86, 87

P

Padgett-Jones, S., 123
Pagano, M., 82
Pantell, R. H., 13, 174, 181
Paquin, J. D., 24, 25
Parcel, G. S., 140, 141, 142, 277
Park, A., 181
Parker, J., 72, 74, 115, 118
Parker-Fisher, S., 24, 26
Parkin, P. C., 24, 25, 26
Pate, J., 46
Patterson, J. M., 118–119, 124, 124, 126, 156, 237–240
Penati, P., 58, 59, 183, 185
Penza-Clyve, S. M., 32, 33, 33
Perrin, E., 1, 3
Perrin, J., 65
Perry, S., 116, 118
Peterson, L., 149, 149

Peyrot, M., 167, *167*
Phipps, S., 24, *26*
Pichert, J. W., 39, *40*
Pierce, P. K., 169, *171*
Piers, E. V., *82*
Pike, R., *84*
Pino, C. J., *156*
Pintrich, P. R., 134, *136*
Pishevar, B. S., 39, *40*
Pless, F. B., 1, *3*
Polonsky, W. H., 87, *87*
Poole, S., 23, *26*
Portner, J., *150, 151*
Potter, L., *94, 96*
Power, T. G., 142, *142*
Powers, S., 45, *53*
Preher, M., 167, *167*
Prevey, M. L., *34*
Prinstein, M., 116, *118*
Program for Prevention Research, *121*

Q

Querido, J., 148, *150*
Quiggins, D. J., 24, *26*
Quigley, C. A., 25, *25*, 145, *145*
Quinn, K., *111*
Quittner, A. L., 24, *26*, 28, *29*, 31, 39, *40*,
    149, *150*

R

Rabbett, H., 24, *26*
Rahe, R. H., 157, *158*
Rapoff, M., *56*
Rappaport, L., 36, *37*
Rea, M., 39, *40*
Rebok, G., *6*
Reeve, R., *43*
Regli, M. J., 39, *40*
Regoli, M. H., *31*
Reid, D. T., 25, *26*
Remey, R., 142, *142*
Renwick, R. M., 25, *26*
Rescorla, L. A., 68, *71*
Rey, J., 148, *150*
Reynolds, C. R., *65*
Reynolds, L. A., *39*
Reynolds, R. V. C., 128, *129*

Rheinberg, J. D., 145
Rheinberger, J. D., *145*
Riekert, K. A., 27, 29, *29*
Riessman, C. K., *126*
Rifkin, L., *174*, 181
Riley, A., 4, *4*, 5, 6, *6*, 7
Ritchey, A. K., 24, *25*
Roberts, M. C., 139, *140*
Robertson, J., *6*
Robinson, E. A., 148, *150*
Rode, C. A., *21*
Roecker, C. E., 116, *118*
Rogers, B. T., 22, *23*
Roosa, M. W., *123*
Rose, D., *137*
Rosenbaum, P., 24, 25, *26*, 169, 170, 171,
    171, 179, 181
Rosenbloom, A., *37*
Rosenstock, I. M., 133, *136*
Routh, D. K., 92, *93*
Rubin, R. R., 167, *167*
Ruble, D. N., 58, *58*
Ruffle, T. M., *71*
Rupp, N. T., 23, *26*
Russell, M., 24, *25*
Ryan, M. E., 169, *171*
Ryan, N. M., *257*
Ryan, R. M., 143, *144*
Ryan, S. A., 4, *4*, 5, 6, *7*
Ryan-Wenger, N. A., 120, *121*
Ryan-Wenger, N. M., 129, *129, 131*, 257,
    260

S

Sameroff, A. J., 148, *150*
Sanders, M. R., 87, *87*
Sanders, S. H., 115, *118*
Sandler, I. N., *123, 248*
Santiago, J. V., 28, *29*, 31, 39, *40*
Saylor, C., *100, 103*
Scarr, S., 164, *165*
Schafer, L. C., 167, *167*
Scheyer, R. D., *34*
Schillinger, J., *46*
Schinkel, A., 39, *40*
Schipper, J. L., 127, *127*
Schlundt, D. G., 39, *40*
Schuhmann, E. M., 148, *150*
Schunk, D. H., 134, *136*

Schwankovsky, L., 145, *145*
Schwartz, C., 120, *121*
Schwartz, R., 120, *121*
Scrimgeour, A., 24, *26*, 86, *87*
Secord, E., 32, *33*
Seid, M., *19, 21*, 24, *26*
Shapiro, H., *106*
Sharrer, V. W., *257*, 260
Sherman, H., 116, *118*
Siegel, P. T., *173*, 178, *183, 185*, 293, 299
Silverstein, J., 28, *29, 37*, 39, *39*
Simonian, S. J., *181*
Simons, N., *156*
Simpson, P., *173, 183*, 293, 299
Sinks, L. F., 24, *26*
Sitarenios, G., *72, 74*
Skare, S., *68*
Skay, C. L., 145, *145*
Skinner, T., 145, *145*
Skyler, J. S., *39, 40*
Slawinowski, M. J., *156*
Slocum, J. W., Jr., 134, *136*
Smith, A., 42, *43, 46*
Smith, C. A., 58, *59*
Smith, D., *35*
Smyth, M., *173, 183, 185*, 293, 299
Snyder, M. K., *185*
Snyder, S. E., 86, *87*
Sowden, A., *23, 25*
Spetter, D., *39, 40*
Spieth, L. E., 1, *4*
Spilker, B., 1, *4*
Spirito, A., 115, 116, 117, *118, 128, 129, 129*
Squires, J., 90, *93, 94, 96*
Stabler, B., 145, *145*
Starfield, B., *4, 4*, 5, *6, 6, 7*, 11
Stark, L. J., 115, 116, *118*, 149, *150*
Stawczynski, H., 24, *25*
Stegner, B. L., 170, *171*, 178, *179*
Stein, R. E. K., 11, *11*, 12, *13, 126*
Stein, R. K., 127, *127*
Sternberg, R., 133, *136*
Straka, R. J., *35*
Strangler, S. R., 92, *93*
Strickland, B., *106*, 134, *136*
Strock, J., *19, 19*
Sturges, J., *45*
Suh, J. T., *35*
Sullivan, B., 87, *87*
Sullivan, T. N., *140*
Suter, J., *123*

Swan, S. C., *53*
Swanson, M., 90, *93*

T

Tambor, E., *6*
Tarnowski, K. J., *181*
Task Force on Pediatric Education, xiii, *xv*
Taylor, J. J., 25, *25*, 145, *145*
Taylor, W. R., 1, *4*
Tein, J., *123*
Tein, J.-Y., *123*
Terdal, L. G., xiv, *xv*
Testa, M. A., 24, *26*
Thomas, A. G., 24, *26*
Thomas, D., *77*
Thomas, J., 28, *29*
Thompson, K., *55*
Thompson, L., 25, *25*, 145, *145*
Thompson, R., 1, *4*, 41, 42, *43*, 58, *59*
Thurber, F. W., 120, *120*
Thwaites, R., 24, *26*
Tinsley, B. J., 3, *4*
Tobin, D. L., 86, *87*, 128, *129*
Tolbert, V. E., *39, 40*
Tomer, A., *39, 39*
Townsend, M., 24, *26*
Tsalikian, E., *76, 77*
Tsuang, M. T., *65*
Twohey, J. L., *123*
Tyc, V., 115, *118*

U

Underwood, L. E., 145, *145*
Uniform Data System for Medical
　Rehabilitation, *21*
U.S. Congress, 105th, 89, 91
Usherwood, T. P., 24, *26*, 86, *87*

V

Van Nie, A., 24, *25, 26*
Van Slyke, D. A., 58, *59*
Vannatta, K., 147, *150*
Varni, J., *19, 21*, 24, *26*, 42, *43*, 55, *56*
Vega-Lahr, N., 116, *118*
Ventureyra, E. C., 24, *26*

Verhulst, S. J., *100*
Vermeer, A., 23, *23*
Villarruel, A., *53, 54*
Vogel, K., 4, *4*, 5

W

Waibel, M. K., 58, *59*, 183, *185*
Walders, N., 27, 29, *29*
Waldron, S., 42, *43, 56*
Walker, L. S., *9*, 10, 58, *59*
Wallander, J. L., *158*
Walsh, M., *257*, 260
Wamboldt, F., 32, 33, *33*
Wampler, T. W., *248*
Wang, J., *109*
Wanstall, K., 87, *87*
Ware, J. E., *7*, *185*, 186, 187, *187*
Warner, J. E., 24, *25*
Waterhouse, D. M., *35*
Weiner, B., 133, 134, *136*
Weiss, K. B., 23, *25*
Welch, G. W., 87, *87*
West, A., 23, *25*
West, S. G., *123*
Westbrook, L. E., *138*
Weyer, J. L., *123*
Whitfield, M., *49*
Wiener, L. S., 147, *150*
Wigal, J. K., 86, *87*
Wiklund, I., 25, *26*
Wilczenski, F., 22, *23*
Wildrick, D., 24, *26*
Wilk, J., 155, *156*

Wilkening, B., *35*
Willan, A. R., 24, 25, *26*
Williams, C., 116, *118*
Williams, D., 41, 42, *43*, 58, *59*
Williams, R. W., 145, *145*
Williams, S. J., 170, *171*
Wilson, M., 152, *153*
Winder, J. A., 86, *87*
Wiren, L., 25, *26*
Wisian, N. B., 187, *187*
Wnek, L., 19, *19*
Wolchik, S., *123*
Wolf, M. H., *174*, 181
Woodman, R. W., 134, *136*
Woody, P., *49*
Woolf, A., 36, *37*
World Health Organization, 1, *4*
Wright, J. T., *35*
Wright, W. R., *185*
Wylie, H., 169, 170, *171*
Wypij, D., 36, *37*
Wysocki, T., 87, *87*

Y

Young-Hyman, D., 167, *167*
Youngblut, J. M., 155, *156*

Z

Zaboy, K., 24, *25*
Zeiger, R., 145, *145*
Ziegler, J. B., *43*